ALONE WITH OTHERS

Times of crisis expose how we experience social, physical, and emotional forms of distance. *Alone with Others* explores how these experiences overlap, shaping our coexistence. Departing from conventional debates that associate intimacy with affection and distance with alienation, Haustein introduces tact as a particular mode of feeling one's way and making space in the sphere of human interaction. Reconstructing tact's conceptual history from the late eighteenth century to the present, she then focuses on three specific periods of socio-political upheaval: the two World Wars, and 1968. In five reading encounters with Marcel Proust, Helmuth Plessner, Theodor Adorno, François Truffaut, and Roland Barthes, Haustein invites us to reconsider our own ways of engaging with other people, images, and texts, and to gauge the significance of tact today. **This title is part of the Flip it Open Programme and may also be available Open Access. Check our website Cambridge Core for details.**

KATJA HAUSTEIN teaches comparative literature at the University of Kent. She was a British Academy Research Fellow at Cambridge University, a Max Weber Fellow at the European University Institute in Florence, and the recipient of a Leverhulme Research Fellowship. She is the author of *Regarding Lost Time: Photography, Identity, and Affect in Proust, Benjamin, and Barthes* (2012).

ALONE WITH OTHERS

An Essay on Tact in Five Modernist Encounters

KATJA HAUSTEIN

University of Kent

CAMBRIDGE
UNIVERSITY PRESS

Shaftesbury Road, Cambridge CB2 8EA, United Kingdom

One Liberty Plaza, 20th Floor, New York, NY 10006, USA

477 Williamstown Road, Port Melbourne, VIC 3207, Australia

314–321, 3rd Floor, Plot 3, Splendor Forum, Jasola District Centre,
New Delhi – 110025, India

103 Penang Road, #05–06/07, Visioncrest Commercial, Singapore 238467

Cambridge University Press is part of Cambridge University Press & Assessment,
a department of the University of Cambridge.

We share the University's mission to contribute to society through the pursuit of
education, learning and research at the highest international levels of excellence.

www.cambridge.org
Information on this title: www.cambridge.org/9781009363280

DOI: 10.1017/9781009363259

First published 2023

A catalogue record for this publication is available from the British Library.

A Cataloging-in-Publication data record for this book is available from the Library of Congress.

ISBN 978-1-009-36328-0 Hardback

Für Antonin und Nicolaus

. . . I am deeply convinced that it is tactless to speak of tact (unfortunately, it is what I am doing).

Roland Barthes, 18 March 1978[1]

Contents

Preface

Times of crisis expose how we experience social, physical, and emotional forms of distance. This book is an invitation to explore how these experiences overlap, and how they shape our ways of living together. In contrast to much of what has recently been said about 'social distancing', I suggest that we not only look at the expansion or contraction of distance between people. Instead, I want to shed light on the idea of tact as a very specific way of making space and of feeling things out in the complex sphere of human interaction. Tact can be defined as an intuitive and creative mode of negotiating the appropriate distance between people. Thus, it becomes particularly significant in times of disruption, like ours, when established codes of sociability disintegrate and new modes of communication need to be found. Times of crisis give rise, I think, to the social practice of tact. In the chapters that follow, I look at this phenomenon from an intellectual–historical perspective and show how tact became a key concept in modern ethics and aesthetics. In a series of reading encounters with Marcel Proust, Helmuth Plessner, Theodor Adorno, François Truffaut, and Roland Barthes, I argue that all five authors react to a shared sense of crisis when exploring the distance we must maintain between ourselves and others if we are to (re)construct a society without estrangement, and a community without collision. I draw on the idea of tact as an ongoing negotiation between the demands of convention and the claims of the individual, to establish tact as a figure of difference and deviation. In so doing, I suggest that we look back at three specific periods of major social and political upheaval that characterized the twentieth century: the First World War, the Second World War and – different, but equally significant in terms of the radical rupture of traditional ways of living together – the period of social revolution in 1968 and beyond. This will allow us, I hope, to reconsider our own ways of engaging with other people, images, and texts, and to contemplate the significance of tact in our time.

Abbreviations

Works by Theodor Adorno

M *Minima Moralia: Reflexionen aus dem beschädigten Leben*, in *Gesammelte Schriften*, ed. by Rolf Tiedemann in collaboration with Gretel Adorno, Susan Buck-Morss, and Klaus Schultz, 20 vols. (Frankfurt: Suhrkamp, 2003), vol. IV.

... and in Translation

MM *Minima Moralia: Reflections from Damaged Life*, trans. by E. F. N. Jephcott (London: Verso, 2005).

Works by Roland Barthes

CVE *Comment vivre ensemble: Simulations romanesques de quelques espaces quotidiens: Notes de cours et de séminaires au Collège de France (1976–1977)*, ed. by Claude Coste (Paris: Seuil/Imec, 2002).

CC *La Chambre claire: Note sur la photographie* (Paris: Gallimard/Seuil, 1980).

PR *La Préparation du Roman I et II: Notes de cours et de séminaires au Collège de France 1978–79 et 1979–80*, ed. by Natalie Léger (Paris: Seuil/Imec, 2003).

DA *Le Discours amoureux: Séminaire à l'École pratique des hautes études 1974–1976*, ed. by Claude Coste (Paris: Seuil, 2007).

N *Le Neutre: Notes de cours au Collège de France (1977–78)*, ed. by Thomas Clerc (Paris: Seuil/Imec, 2002).

OC *Œuvres complètes*, ed. by Éric Marty, 5 vols. (Paris: Seuil, 2002).

A *Roland Barthes Album: Inédits, correspondances et varia*, ed. by Éric Marty with the help of Claude Coste (Paris: Seuil, 2015).

JD *Journal de deuil*, ed. by Nathalie Léger (Paris: Seuil/Imec, 2009).

... and in Translation

LDF *A Lover's Discourse: Fragments*, trans. by Richard Howard (New York: Hill and Wang, 1978).

CL *Camera Lucida: Reflections on Photography*, trans. by Richard Howard (London: Vintage, 1993).

HLT *How to Live Together: Novellistic Simulations of Some Everyday Spaces: Notes for a Lecture Course and Seminar at the Collège de France (1976–1977)*, ed. by Claude Coste, trans. by Kate Briggs (New York: Columbia University Press, 2013).

MD *Mourning Diary*, ed. by Nathalie Léger, trans. and with an afterword by Richard Howard (New York: Hill and Wang, 2009).

TN *The Neutral: Lecture Course at the Collège de France (1977–78)*, ed. by Thomas Clerc, trans. by Rosalind E. Krauss and Denis Hollier (New York: Columbia University Press, 2005).

Works by Helmuth Plessner

G *Grenzen der Gemeinschaft: Eine Kritik des sozialen Radikalismus* (Frankfurt: Suhrkamp, 2002).

... and in Translation

L *The Limits of Community: A Critique of Social Radicalism*, trans. by Andrew Wallace (Amherst, NY: Humanity Books, 1999).

Works by Marcel Proust

RTP *À la recherche du temps perdu*, ed. by Jean-Yves Tadié , 4 vols. (Paris: Gallimard, 1987–9).

F *Les Soixante-quinze feuillets et autre manuscrits inédits*, ed. by Nathalie Mauriac Dyer, preface by Jean-Yves Tadié (Paris: Gallimard, 2021).

... and in Translation

SLT *In Search of Lost Time*, ed. by Christopher Prendergast, trans. by Carol Clark, Peter Collier, Lydia Davies, James Grieve, Ian Patterson, John Sturrock, and Mark Treharne, 6 vols. (London: Penguin, 2002–3).

Works by François Truffaut

BV *Baisers volés* (Munich: Concorde Home Entertainment, 2005).

AD *Les Aventures d'Antoine Doinel* (Paris: Mercure de France, 1970).

Introduction

Alle Kultur und Kunst, welche die Menschheit zieret, die schönste gesellschaftliche Ordnung, sind Früchte der Ungeselligkeit . . .

All the culture and art which adorn mankind and the finest social order man creates are fruits of his unsociability . . .

Immanuel Kant, 1784[1]

What Is Tact?

There is a signature scene in François Truffaut's 1968 film *Baisers volés* (*Stolen Kisses*) that exemplifies the social practice of tact. In the course of the film, the protagonist Antoine Doinel, a young bachelor and Truffaut's alter ego, finds temporary employment with a detective agency. One of his jobs is to work as a shop assistant in a shoe store to find out why everyone detests its owner, M. Tabard. As things proceed, Antoine is increasingly entranced by M. Tabard's wife, the beautiful Fabienne. One day, Antoine is asked to come up to the Tabard's apartment where he joins the couple for lunch. When M. Tabard temporarily leaves, Fabienne serves coffee. We see them sitting opposite each other, stirring spoons, sipping their hot drinks. To break the silence, Fabienne gets up to put on some music. Turning to Antoine she asks: '*Vous aimez la musique, Antoine?*' (Do you like music, Antoine?') To which he replies: '*Oui, Monsieur!*' They look alarmed. The music roars. Antoine drops his cup onto the tray on the table. Black coffee spills like blood at a crime scene. The quick succession of close-ups emphasizes the overwhelming sense of embarrassment until Antoine rushes to his feet, dashes to the next exit, chases down the winding stairs, and disappears from our sight. Much later, Antoine returns to his home, where he finds a gift by his door. It is from Fabienne. Attached is a note containing the following little story:

> *Quand j'étais au collège, mon professeur expliquait la différence entre le tact et la politesse. Un monsieur, en visite, pousse par erreur la porte d'une salle de bains et*

I

découvre une dame absolument nue; il recule aussitôt, referme la porte et dit: 'Oh pardon, Madame!' Ça c'est la politesse! Le même monsieur, poussant la même porte, découvrant la même dame absolument nue et lui disant: 'Oh pardon, Monsieur!' Cela, c'est le tact.

When I was at school, my teacher explained the difference between tact and politeness. A gentleman caller accidentally opens a bathroom door and sees a naked lady. He quickly withdraws and, closing the door, he says: 'Pardon, Madame!' This is politeness. Should the same gentleman open the same door, discover the same naked lady and withdraw by saying: 'Pardon, Monsieur!' – that would be tact. (BV 1:05 and 1:12)[2]

The social practice of tact, Fabienne's story suggests, is linked to the mental ability to empathize. The gentleman must be able to imagine what it may feel like to be in the position of the naked lady in the bathroom to find a way to ease her – and possibly also his own – feeling of distress. Empathy can be defined as an affective and cognitive process that helps us to get a sense of what it may be like to be another person.[3] It supports us in forming a concern for, and a connection with, other people. Empathy, writes Richard Wollheim, is based on a kind of 'twofold attention'. We feel, or imagine, what it may be like to be in another person's place while simultaneously retaining an awareness of not being in their place.[4] This makes empathy a potentially valuable guide to suitable forms of responding, an 'informer', as Heinz Kohut notes, 'of appropriate action'.[5] But there is a critical edge to empathy. For empathy does not only involve a general recognition of the existence of a world of experience beyond our own. By taking an 'other-oriented perspective' to 'replicate the target's experience', as Amy Coplan writes, the practice of being empathetic entails a potential threat of intrusion. The etymology of the term hints at this: 'empathy' as *empátheia* comes from '*en*' = 'in, at' and '*pathos*' = 'passion, suffering'. The German term '*Einfühlung*' (in-feeling; feeling into) further accentuates what Coplan specifies as the process of understanding the other person 'from the "inside"'.[6] Empathy suggests more than just a sense of proximity. It implies the idea of being able to climb into and out of each other's minds. ('*J'ai compris votre fuite, Antoine*', Fabienne will add to her story, 'À demain' (I know why you fled, Antoine. See you tomorrow.)) Herein lies an important distinction between empathy and tact. Although the ability to empathize may provide a route to tactful behaviour, tact, unlike empathy, does not aim to facilitate nearness. On the contrary, its goal is to acknowledge difference and to generate distance ('*Pardon, Monsieur!*').

The word tact stems from the Latin *tactus*, which means 'touch', 'tactility', 'feeling', 'influence'. From the late fifteenth century, the word '*Takt*' was also used in German as a musical term to signify 'beat', 'bar', 'meter', or 'pulse'. These etymological connotations underline the spatial and temporal dimensions of the term. They emphasize the aspects of distance, duration, rhythm, and speed. Being tactful towards one another implies the shared negotiation of the right balance between approach and detachment, assonance and dissonance, coincidence and deferral. The image of dance or game formations that emerges here is further accentuated by the suggestive assonance between 'tact' and Greek *tachus*, meaning 'quick' or 'sudden', as well as *taxis*, meaning 'arrangement' or 'order', 'status', and 'position'.[7] Despite the etymological connection with 'touch' and 'contact', tact, unlike empathy, is often associated with discretion and the respect for the space of the other person. Tact, we might say with Jacques Derrida, who plays with these etymological implications of the term, 'is the name for the aporia of a touching that does not touch, "a contact without touch"'.[8]

Fabienne's story thematizes this. The tactful behaviour of the gentleman is based on the pretence of not noticing what caused the embarrassment. The aim is to preserve and to respect the intimate sphere of the other person, and in this way restore their dignity. Being tactful is here defined by what one does not say (Lat. *tacere*: 'to be silent', 'to conceal') and yet it presupposes mutual awareness of the unspoken thing (i.e., the fact that the gentleman has seen the lady naked). This should not necessarily be confused with repression, denial, or lying. If anything, it could be understood in the sense of a certain form of role-play which, in order to function, needs to be recognized, and adopted, by all individuals involved. Tact, writes Niklas Luhmann, is characterized by the obvious, but jointly unacknowledged discrepancy between 'reality' and 'fiction'. Tactful behaviour, he explains, consists in '*das Offenlassen der Entscheidung, von der jeder weiß, daß sie entschieden ist, die geistreiche Indirektheit, die schöngesagte Falschheit, die die Richtigkeit des Gegenteils erraten läßt*' (the (apparent) leaving of a decision open even where everybody knows that it has been decided quite before that, that witty indirectness and elegant half-truth which of course allows us to sense just how right its opposite is).[9] Tact, Luhmann argues, is based on the expectation of expectations. More specifically, tactful behaviour does not simply consist in the fulfilment of the other's expectations. Instead, it can be defined as a 'behaviour with which A presents himself as the one whom B needs as a partner, to be able to be the one that he would like to present in A's eyes'.[10] (In the case of Fabienne's story this means that the gentleman presents himself as a stranger whom the lady can look straight in the eye as if her nakedness had never been exposed to his gaze in an intimate situation.) The goal is to overcome or avoid embarrassment, to mend a face-to-face relationship that is temporarily damaged, or broken, and to restore what Erving Goffman calls the 'normal state' between the interlocutors.[11] This cannot be achieved simply by means of politeness. Politeness, as Fabienne's story suggests, is based on convention, a set of tools, a code (of etiquette). Tact, by contrast, is an individual's variation of that code. It is a spontaneous and situational deviation from the present norm – although, like any variation, tact presupposes (and implicitly accepts) the existence of this norm in the act of transcending it. Otherwise, it could not be understood. Tact, writes Adorno, is a 'determination of differences' based on 'conscious deviations' (M 40/MM 37). Tact, we could say, is situated in between the conventional demands of social roles and their actual execution. It organizes the relations between the social persona (Lat. *persona* = 'mask') and the intimate self.[12] In direct contrast to the general mission of Antoine's detective agency to expose '*les affaires du cœur*' (the matters of the heart), the goal of tactful behaviour is not the revelation, but the protection of the intimate lives of others.

Politeness can be described as a skill that may be acquired with the help of a manual. Tact, by contrast, is a form of behaviour that is difficult to learn or teach by way of instructions.[13] It can best be obtained through first-hand experience, by being part of a group of people who know how to interact tactfully. Tact, Jean-Paul Sartre notes, 'takes on its whole meaning only in a strictly defined community with common ideas, mores, and customs'.[14] This is why tact is frequently defined as a marker of social distinction and associated with class, privilege, and power.[15] Tact is seemingly effortless. It must be lived, like taste or grace, for tact, as David Caron rightly emphasizes, depends on the individual's high degree of awareness, sensitivity, and attention.[16] Tact means to be able to understand a situation intuitively. It oscillates between reason and unreason.[17] Tact is, to use Theobald Ziegler's words – and this is one of the things which Fabienne's husband, the widely detested M. Tabard, fails to comprehend – '*die Treffsicherheit des Gefühls*' (the accuracy of feeling).[18]

I have dwelt on the example of Fabienne's parable about the gentleman and the naked lady in the bathroom (to which, in fact, we shall return in Chapter 4) because it dramatizes one aspect of tact in particular that I want to explore in this book. Tact, Truffaut shows us here, is based on a dialectical relationship between nearness and distance, identification and separation. Its purpose is to determine the appropriate distance between people, both literally and metaphorically. The crucial diagnosis Truffaut makes with the help of this story is, and Slavoj Žižek points to this in a different context, that the key challenge for the modern subject is not, as one might suspect, the disappearance of intimate space, with our most personal secrets 'open to public probing'. The key challenge is, by contrast, the disappearance of public space, where distance and disguise may serve to protect our privacy and our dignity.[19] Following on from this idea, Truffaut's parable promotes a mode of physical and social distancing based on a reversal of conventional notions of proximity and distance. In Fabienne's story, and, as we shall see, in Truffaut's work more generally, nearness is not linked to warmth and affection. On the contrary, nearness is frequently experienced as potentially harmful and threatening, while keeping your distance does not lead to alienation but is associated with benevolence, protection, and care. This seemingly paradoxical figure of thought (that resonates with the social and psychological side-effects of the distancing regulations put in place at the time of my writing this book) not only occurs in Truffaut's œuvre. It is also at the core of the theories of tact proposed by the four other authors whose works we shall encounter in the course of this book: Marcel Proust (1871–1922), Helmuth Plessner (1892–1985), Theodor Adorno (1903–1969) and, closest in age to Truffaut (1932–84), Roland Barthes (1915–80).[20]

Material and Method

At first glance, this combination of authors may seem an unlikely group for comparison. To begin with, both Plessner and Adorno returned to Germany from exile in 1949. They knew each other well and became temporary colleagues at the University in Frankfurt am Main. But they were also rivals who essentially stood for two competing and mutually exclusive schools of thought: the critical theory of society (Adorno) and the philosophical anthropology of modernity (Plessner). This did not prevent Plessner from actively engaging with Adorno's work, while references to Plessner are notoriously absent from Adorno's writing. If the relationship between Adorno and Plessner was complicated and occasionally toxic, it is difficult to find any traces at all of a connection between Adorno, Barthes, and Truffaut – except, perhaps, via Proust, for whom they shared a life-long passion.[21] But although Proust represented a constant source of inspiration and, especially in the case of Adorno and Barthes, identification, their joint admiration was paired with a shared reluctance to ever systematically engage with his work. Despite its omnipresence in their writing, both Adorno and Barthes composed no more than a few essays and lectures on *À la recherche du temps perdu*. In the same vein, Truffaut, reportedly an avid reader of the novel, and an intimate connoisseur of

Proust's correspondence, was appalled when invited to produce a film adaptation of the second part of the novel's first volume, *Un Amour de Swann*. '*Seul un charcutier*', Truffaut replied, '*accepterait de mettre en scène le salon Verdurin*' (Only a butcher would be prepared to film the Verdurin salon).[22]

For all the potential significance of this intellectual affinity between Adorno, Barthes, and Truffaut, and although their periods of international prominence partially overlapped, Adorno and Barthes never publicly acknowledged each other's existence, nor did they actively engage with Truffaut (or vice versa).[23] And yet, the works that serve as the core material for this book – Plessner's fervently written socio-political essay *Grenzen der Gemeinschaft: Eine Kritik des sozialen Radikalismus* (*The Limits of Community: A Critique of Social Radicalism*) (1924), Proust's monumental novel *À la recheche du temps perdu* (1909–1922), Adorno's 'chapbook of philosophy', *Minima Moralia* (1951), Truffaut's film *Baisers volés* (1968), and Barthes' lecture courses at the Collège de France, *Comment vivre ensemble* (*How to Live Together*) (1976–7) and *Le Neutre* (*The Neutral*) (1977–8) – share a number of communalities that are, I believe, crucial when thinking about the theory and history of tact.

All five works in question were produced in times of immense social and political upheaval and, in the case of Plessner and Adorno, ensuing fascism and war. Proust wrote *À la recherche du temps perdu* between 1909 and his death in 1922 and most parts of the novel are famously set in the Belle Époque (ca. 1884–1914). In his novel, Proust describes this period as a continuous process of a kaleidoscopic reshuffling, revealing the ways in which the established hierarchies that marked French society at the time were disintegrating while traditional social norms and conventions were transforming. This development was, as the fourth volume, *Le Temps retrouvé*, illustrates, catalysed by the outbreak of the First World War, an event that helped extinguish a social class the demise of which is so mercilessly portrayed in Proust's novel. Plessner wrote *Grenzen der Gemeinschaft* in 1923. The book was conceived as a direct response to the politically and socially unstable situation in Germany between the wars, and articulates a passionate warning against the rise of social and political radicalism from the right and the left. Adorno, Plessner's junior by eleven years, composed *Minima Moralia* during the 1940s in exile in the United States. Contemplating the effects of fascism on German society, he explored how the smallest occurrences in everyday life may reflect the most catastrophic crimes in human history. Truffaut's film *Stolen Kisses*, in turn, was produced in Paris during the months leading up to the street protests of May 1968. In contrast to Barthes, who preferred to stay clear of any direct political engagement, Truffaut got involved in the movement precisely at the time when the filming of *Stolen Kisses* was about to begin. But like Barthes, who conceptualized and convened his lecture courses, *Comment vivre ensemble* and *Le Neutre*, in the post-revolutionary Paris of the 1970s, in his film Truffaut, too, experimented with new forms of individuality and sociability in response to the student revolution.

The initial observation guiding my reading encounters with Proust, Plessner, Adorno, Truffaut, and Barthes, is that the works I look at – the differences in historical and intellectual context notwithstanding – react to a shared sense of crisis when responding to the following questions: what distance must I maintain between myself and others if we are to (re)construct a society without alienation, and a community without collision? How can we associate this distance with a form of individual freedom that may imply solitude, but not isolation?[24] Rowing against the intellectual and political currents of their times, all five authors develop answers that are decidedly anti-communal. They prioritize the individual over the collective and, in so doing, contribute to an ethics of indirectness.[25] Thus, they reveal how tact, as a very specific mode of distance regulation, becomes particularly significant in times of fundamental social and political upheaval, when established codes of human cohabitation disintegrate and new modes of communication have to be found. Within this context tact, understood with Adorno as the ongoing negotiation between the changing demands of convention and the claims of the individual, turns into a figure of personal difference, distance, and divergence. This interpretation allows us to think of tact as the aesthetic side of the ethical.[26] Tact, we could say with the second part of Fabienne's parable in mind, is based on the principle of the 'as if' ('*Pardon, Monsieur!*'). It therefore subsumes both social behaviour and the theory and practice of intellectual and creative production. Defined in this manner as a mode of individual deviation from (however disintegrating) forms of normative codification, tact can not only serve to describe the art of finding an intuitive and appropriate response to a particular situation (Plessner), it can also help to explore new ways of writing (Proust) and to invent alternative modes of interpretation (Adorno, Barthes, Truffaut).

Over the last two decades, various forms of social and emotional distance have become a much-discussed topic. Amanda Anderson's *The Powers of Distance: Cosmopolitanism and the Cultivation of Detachment*, Eva Illouz' *Cold Intimacies: The Making of Emotional Capitalism*, Richard Sennett's *Together: The Rituals, Pleasures and Politics of Cooperation*, and, more recently, Corina Stan's *The Art of Distances: Ethical Thinking in Twentieth-Century Literature* are only a few of the many important contributions to the interdisciplinary debate. In contrast, research on tact and, more specifically, on the relation between ethical, anthropological, and aesthetic tact, is scarce. To my knowledge, David Russell's book on *Tact: Aesthetic Liberalism and the Essay Form in Nineteenth-Century Britain* and David Caron's *The Nearness of Others* are the only significant exceptions. Russell presents a brilliantly elegant account of tact in the British context, providing a psychoanalytical frame to work with. Caron offers a personal, social, and philosophical exploration of tact and touch in the age of HIV that is equally stimulating. In my book, I hope to complement what they have achieved by offering an account of tact that sheds light on the continental European side of the debate. My historical starting point is the late eighteenth century, which, in the shadow of the French Revolution, demarcates a fundamental paradigm shift from 'tact' primarily understood as a sense of feeling or touching to 'tact' as a form of social interaction. Reconstructing some of the key characteristics of the debate, I then focus on three distinct periods of social and political upheaval that have shaped the twentieth-century history of Europe: The First World War, the Second World War, and the period of social revolution in 1968 and after.

Despite the historical orientation of this book, it was not my ambition to write a history of actual tact. As may have become discernible from the opening pages of this introduction, my aim is not to reconstruct the largely undocumented reality of tactful behaviour, its enduring as well as its variable practices, its changes in refinement and prevalence, its shifting agents, objects, settings, motivations, and consequences.[27] Nor is it my goal to reconstruct notions of tact on the basis of conduct books and their reception (not because this would not be worthwhile, but because these would be very different projects). I am interested, by contrast, in the conceptual history of tact as it emerges in the late eighteenth century, and in reconstructing key facets of the rise (and occasional fall) of the concept in modern times.

The concept of tact is situated at the interface of social and anthropological theory, conceptual history, ethics, and aesthetics. I see this as an opportunity to develop an interdisciplinary approach to the history of the word by mobilizing a set of different methods that combine classic philosophical, social, and anthropological theory with seminal contributions to affect studies and modern and contemporary literary hermeneutics. In so doing, my aim is to offer an account of some of the most significant theories of tact in the twentieth century, carefully situating them within the wider cross-disciplinary debates that reach back to their eighteenth-century foundations. My hope is that, through the medium of these theories of tact, fragments of the largely unveiled history of the word may become more easily accessible. My arrangement of the material, although broadly chronological, is not intended to imply a linear development. I do not think there is progress, nor decline, in the course of the history of modern tact. What is remarkable, however, is the lasting significance and influence of certain theories of tact, and of unchanging criteria that characterize prominent definitions of the term from the eighteenth century to the present day, although this does not mean that these theories have not frequently been challenged, disputed, or outrun, as I will show in the chapters that follow. Many of the writers, scholars, and artists I discuss have not been systematically treated as theorists of tact before.[28] Bringing them together in this book offers an opportunity to discover new constellations of ideas and to open unexpected avenues of thought that are significant both in the view of the theory and history of the concept tact, and in terms of reversing existing assumptions concerning the individual authors and their works considered.

The Book's Content

Classic theories of human interaction tend to depict tact as a marker of social distinction (Sartre, Bourdieu), and a tool for the cementation of bourgeois power (Foucault). By contrast, in the individual chapters that constitute this book, I wish to contribute to a different account of tact that not only considers tact's discriminating effects but also gives room to its equalizing dynamic and democratic potential. Unlike empathy, tact is not based on the assumption that we feel what the other person feels or know what they know. Instead, tact offers a way to explore openly the space that expands between people. Tact is linked to uncertainty. It throws us into the unknown. It defies definite answers, classifications, and judgements. This is why, on the receiving end, we may find tactful behaviour on occasion quite difficult to deal with. At the same time, tact is based on an appreciation of the singularity of the other person. This involves a willingness to meet the other person on their own terms. It can serve as an antidote to a rhetoric based on the categories of identification and exclusion, a rhetoric that provides quick answers and easy solutions. It can be used as a means of safeguarding against any form of domination. As an indirect mode of communication, tact offers a particular kind of reciprocal protection. It can be described as a potentially infinite process, based on the careful approximation of different horizons of people, images, and texts. In the chapters that follow I set out both to confirm and to challenge these descriptions of tact, to consider and cross some of their potential limitations, while also solidifying some of their more durable components. Chapters 2 to 5 in this book focus on the encounter with the works of one or two authors. Chapter 1 serves as a frame to their findings, reconstructing key aspects of the conceptual-historical context and ranging across the last 250 years.

In Chapter 1, 'Tact's History', I reconstruct the conceptual history of modern tact as a social, ethical, and aesthetic category. My historical starting point is Voltaire's 1769 description of tact, one of the first definitions that indicate a fundamental paradigm shift from 'tact' as a sense of feeling or touching to 'tact' as a social practice. In the chapter, I go on to demonstrate how Voltaire's definition marked the beginning of the career of a word that would evolve into a highly significant concept in nineteenth- and twentieth-century pedagogical, philosophical, and literary discourse. I discuss tact's conceptual history within the context of the demise of the *ancien régime* and the rise of the bourgeois subject as an autonomous figure, reflecting on a variety of different historical and philosophical explanations (Elias, Adorno, Foucault). I reconstruct how and why, around 1800, tact turns into a key philosophical term, depicting an intuitive form of empirical judgement (Kant). I show how, in the second half of the nineteenth century, tact, understood as a spontaneous and individual deviation from normative structures, came to occupy a key position in the methodological dispute between the humanities and the natural sciences (Helmholtz). I conclude the chapter by reflecting on how psychological tact went on to become a key category in modern and contemporary hermeneutics, uniting the otherwise rather antagonistic work of scholars including Adorno, Hans-Georg Gadamer, Barthes and, more recently, Rita Felski, and Marielle Macé. The purpose of this chapter is twofold: it can be read as a conceptual-historical introduction to the case studies that follow, and as an essay on the history of the word tact that stands on its own.

Chapter 2, 'Proxemics', is dedicated to Proust's *À la recherche du temps perdu*. The novel portrays the Belle Époque as an age marked by growing social and political anxieties bubbling underneath its seemingly glamorous surface. The Dreyfus affair (1894–1906), the first and the second Morocco crisis (1904–06 and 1911) and, in the later volumes, the outbreak of the First World War, are recurring conversation topics in the Proustian salons. The novel describes how existing hierarchies are falling apart and established social norms and conventions disappearing. It reveals how we may associate this disintegration with crisis and decay, while we can also interpret it as an opportunity for liberation, opening up greater space for individual action. In this chapter I show how it is within this context that tact, as a concept that negotiates between the general norms and individual deviation, becomes a key figure in Proust's work. I start out by considering the novel's long-lost earliest drafts, *Les Soixante-quinze feuillets*, published posthumously in 2021, to then focus on a close reading of the manifold facets of tact offered on occasion of a series of face-to-face encounters between Marcel, the narrator, and Andrée, one of the 'young girls in flower'. In so doing, I address the following themes: if tact can, with Proust, be described as a particular kind of choreography that allows us to determine the appropriate distance between characters, in what ways does social tact relate to what Edward T. Hall calls the 'silent language' of proxemics? Tact, Proust's novel suggests, can be interpreted as a social leveller, an egalitarian force, indicating a balance of power between individuals and groups. At the same time, the novel also implies that tact can be seen as a marker of social distinction. Tactful behaviour can create a power imbalance between the person who exercises tact (the tactor) and the person who appears to be flustered and weak (the tactee). This conflict gives rise to a number of questions. For example: is tact a moral or an amoral category? More specifically, can we say that a tactful person – in this case, Andrée – is also a good person? If tact is based on a potential discrepancy between what is said and what remains unsaid, where do we draw the line between tact, hypocrisy, and lying? And how do we deal with the uncertainty of interpretation as it begins to turn into one of the Proustian narrator's most tantalizing concerns? By drawing on a variety of different theories of tact already introduced in the opening sections of this book, I contemplate in this chapter to what extent Proust's tact may be described as a paradoxical category that suggests autonomy while also exerting control, and that classifies while simultaneously undoing the classifications it appears to impose.

Chapter 3, 'Alienation', offers a comparative study of the two antagonistic thinkers Adorno and Plessner. Critics have long depicted Plessner as an advocate of 'immunity' (Esposito) and 'cool conduct' (Lethen). And like Plessner's texts, Adorno's writing, too, is not exactly known for its lightness of touch, its openness, its improvisation, or a deliberate lack of direction – qualities, in short, that characterize the dynamics of tact. And yet, the two texts that serve as the main material for this chapter – Plessner's uncompromising and occasionally aggressive essay on *The Limits of Community* and Adorno's at times opaque yet equally provocative *Minima Moralia* – make for a surprisingly revealing combination. Both texts were written at different historical turning points of the twentieth century. Plessner introduces tact as an antidote to the rising populism and radicalism of the interwar years. Adorno, in turn, sketches a dialectical theory of tact as a concept that also contributes to the collapse of the humaneness it initially helped to preserve. Situating both texts within their wider intellectual context, I reveal in this chapter how, although starting out from conflicting theoretical assumptions, both Plessner and Adorno arrive at unexpectedly similar conclusions. Both scholars fundamentally disagree on a series of key concepts that shape their theories of tact: alienation, to start with, is for Adorno a temporary state of human existence that we need to overcome. For Plessner, by contrast, alienation is what makes us human in the first place. Alienation is what sets us apart from animals and plants. Moreover, both scholars make a distinction between our private selves and the social personae, the metaphorical masks we put on in public. But while for Adorno these masks are a sign and symptom of objectification, for Plessner they provide an essential means of protection. And yet, despite these and other differences, Plessner and Adorno share a suspicion of certain forms of intimacy and touch, and a preference for individual difference over communal identification. By offering a comparative analysis of their writing, I argue that Plessner's and Adorno's theories of tact contribute to variations of an ethic of indirectness that seeks to resist any possible strategies of incorporation. On a hermeneutic level (Adorno), these theories allow us to develop a new mode of non-violent contemplation. On a social level (Plessner), they find their literal realization in times of a pandemic, when keeping your distance and wearing a mask does not necessarily have to be interpreted as a dystopic sign of isolation but can also be seen as an expression of cooperation (not fusion), of responsibility, and care.

Chapter 4, 'Individuation', brings us back to the example of tact with which the book began: the story about the gentleman and the naked lady in the bathroom told by the character Fabienne in Truffaut's film *Baisers volés*. In this chapter I revisit my initial interpretation of the story to locate it within the context of the entire film and the director's political engagement that coincided with its making. The aim of the chapter is thus to reread Truffaut's film in the light of the historical crisis from which it arose. *Stolen Kisses* was produced in the months running up to one of the most violent conflicts post-war France had ever seen: the street protests in Paris of May 1968. The film premiered in the autumn that followed. In contrast to his contemporary Roland Barthes, who left France in the immediate aftermath of these events, Truffaut got caught up in 'une double vie de cinéaste et de militant' (a double existence as a film maker and a militant)[29] precisely at the time when the filming of *Stolen Kisses* was about to begin. By mapping a series of signature scenes of the film against selected material from earlier versions of the script, director's notes, letters, and interviews, the chapter reads the film against the grain of its general reception as a light-hearted romantic comedy that was, in Truffaut's own words, about '*rien du tout!*'.[30] Positioning the film within a network of intertextual relations, the chapter distils a conception of tact from the film that is based on a dialectical relationship between nearness and distance, identification and separation. Mapping the film against its political background, I show in this chapter how, while sympathetic to the revolutionary cause, *Baisers volés* occupied a bystander position in relation to the political parties involved in the conflict. Against politicized ideologies of fusional collectivity – a symbiotic form of existence in which we experience ourselves as one with others – Truffaut experiments with new forms of individuality, freedom, and communication. In striking assonance with key aspects of Plessner's theory of tact, Truffaut shows how tactful behaviour can become a means to facilitate ways to come close to one another without meeting, and drift apart again without damaging one another through indifference. Using the protagonist Antoine's romantic entanglement with the two female lead characters, Fabienne and Christine, as an example, I highlight the ways in which the film erects barriers against the potential onslaughts of frankness, intimacy, and empathetic incorporation, simultaneously confirming and undermining modern conceptions of tact as a touchless form of sociability. Carefully unpacking the paradoxical dynamics of tact in *Baisers volés*, I argue that – counter to the widespread expectation that when relations are close they are warm, and when they are warm they are beneficial to all individuals involved – Truffaut advocates the idea of an impassioned distance. Intimacies, Truffaut shows us, do not necessarily bring us closer together. On the contrary, inasmuch as they may infringe upon the singularity and dignity of the individual person, they can have a deeply alienating effect.

In the concluding chapter, '*Approchement*', I turn to the later work of Roland Barthes. The aim of this chapter is to engage with Barthes' conception of tact, and to use my interpretation to draw this book's findings to a close. As a reader of Hegel, Marx, and Brecht, Barthes shared with Plessner and Adorno a concern for the formation of totalitarian forms of knowledge and power. In contrast to the two German authors, however, for Barthes the formative experience that influenced much of his later work was not fascism, occupation, and war, but what he called, in line with Truffaut, 'la rupture de mai 1968'.[31] In this chapter I engage with Barthes' conception of tact by situating it within a philosophical landscape that expands from the West (Kant, Rousseau, Nietzsche) to the East (Okakura, Suzuki). In so doing, I reconstruct the manner in which Barthes explores the connection between human sociability and intellectual productivity in view of its hermeneutic potential. I argue that the 'non-method' Barthes develops as an alternative practice of critical inquiry, based on the principles of digression and deviation, bears striking resemblance to the idea of hermeneutical tact suggested earlier by Adorno. Barthes and Adorno chime with each other in thinking that intellectual practice should be marked by a Kantian sense of resistance that differs from the flow of familiar speech. Critical thinking, they argue, must not obey any sense of belonging or contact. Instead, it should be driven by a sensitivity to the particular and a non-dogmatism that avoids rather than establishes the shortest connection between two points. The result consists in a form of critical judgement that defies the pressure of identification. Instead, it approaches the object of its desire by way of a plurality of digressions. In this chapter I demonstrate that Barthes' theory of tact, although unfashionable in the 1970s, is crucial to ongoing debates that challenge the 'hermeneutic of suspicion' (Gadamer, Ricœur) and transgress the 'limits of critique' (Felski). At the same time, I question, however, whether the intuitive and essentially democratic idea of a tactful hermeneutics, which goes all the way back to Kant, fully translates into the theories of tact proposed by Barthes, Adorno, and Gadamer. Tact, they jointly contend, cannot be taught. Unlike politeness, it must be lived. The elitism this idea implies, and its implicit vicinity to the Romantic idea of the genius, give rise to the suspicion that, while aiming to suspend any class-oriented conceptions of tact, in the end, this may be precisely what their theories of tact help reproduce. The question of the extent to which Barthes succeeds in resolving this key antagonism of tact that runs through the entirety of this book is the object of the concluding part of this chapter.

I wrote much of this book during a time when we seemed to have lost our balance. What had earlier been considered an act of politeness (coming close, shaking hands, kissing cheeks) had turned into a potential threat, while keeping your distance (staying 2.0 metres apart, covering your face) was described as 'the only expression of care' (Angela Merkel).[32] We had reached a point in history when in most parts of the world Plessner's metaphorical call for 'the right to wear masks' (or not to) had, temporarily at least, become real. It is beyond the scope of this book to take the debate on tact into the present. But from the chapters that follow, it should become apparent that in my reading encounters with five key figures of twentieth-century literature, film, and thought I make the case against a dystopic vision of future societies where isolated individuals float aimlessly like debris in space. Instead, I mobilize the concept of tact to argue that interpersonal distance is at the heart of any well-working society. Cultivated as the art of making space when we fear colliding, and of bridging gaps when we drift too far away from each other, tact is a mode of being alone with others that exists not to destroy but to protect our societal ways of living together.

CHAPTER I

Tact's History

The *Oxford English Dictionary* traces the word tact back to early thirteenth-century Middle English. Borrowed from the Latin *tactus*, the participial stem of *tangere*, the word *tactpe* was widely used to depict the sense of touching or feeling.[1] In French, 'tact' first gained prominence in the fourteenth century. The *Littré* quotes a passage from Henri de Ferrières' *Livre du roi Modus et de la reine Ratio*, which uses the word to address the extraordinary tactile abilities of spiders – and, in some very rare cases, humans – who can feel the touching hand even before it reaches the surface of their skin.[2] From French, the word was adapted into German where, from the late fifteenth century onwards, it also acquired a musical connotation. Next to rhythm and meter, German 'Takt' provides the ordering structure in music, as in measure or bar, serving as a frame for the notation of rhythms. In fact, the three most important German dictionaries of the long eighteenth century, Zedler's *Universal-Lexicon* (1731–54), Brockhaus' *Conversations-Lexikon* (1807), and Adelung's *Grammatisch-kritisches Wörterbuch der hochdeutschen Mundart* (1811) list musical tact as their sole definition of the word, drawing on the semantic proximity of musical tact and physical touch to explain the word's origin and signification. The *Zedler* in particular emphasizes this etymological connection. Here we read that, derived from the Latin *tangendo*, the word originally referred to the tap of the foot and, later, the correct stroke or motion of the hand in beating the time that choir and orchestra must follow. Associated with regularity and harmony, 'Takt' is also used in the context of dance, poetry (pedes), and horse riding.[3]

Over the course of the nineteenth century, a new semantic field associated with the word tact rapidly gained in significance in the German, English, and French context. Tact was no longer primarily associated with physical touch or musical beat but underwent a metaphorical turn. Now tact came to signify a particular mode of social interaction. The entry on 'Tact' in the *Brockhaus* edition of 1911 illustrates this: by the end of the long nineteenth century, a certain refined and particularly sensitive type of sociability, '*Feingefühl, Feinheit und Sicherheit des Benehmens*' (sensitivity, delicacy, and confidence of conduct) had become tact's primary definition, pushing the word's musical and physical connotations to the second and third places on the register.[4]

Tact's Sociability

If the conceptual history of tact as tactility reaches back to the High Middle Ages, the notion of tact as a metaphor describing a particular form of sociable interaction is essentially modern. Its earliest traces date back to the second half of the eighteenth century and coincide with the era shaped by the French Revolution. Marked by fundamental social and political change, this period also saw significant transformations in language, crystalizing on the shift in meaning of key socio-political and philosophical terms. The time period spanning from 1750 to 1850 was a transition period that has not only been associated with the beginning of modernity but also with modern ways of thinking in Europe.[5] The figurative usage of tact, meaning a particular way of dealing with other people, as well as with artworks, objects, and texts, is a result of and a response to this period, as it mediates between the Enlightenment and the age of sensibility that followed.

The *Oxford English Dictionary* credits Voltaire (1769) as one of the first to describe tact as a form of social practice. 'Tact', we read, is 'a ready and delicate sense of what is fitting and proper in dealing with others, so as to avoid giving offence or win good will; skill or judgement in dealing with men or negotiating difficult or delicate situations; the faculty of saying or doing the right thing at the right time.'[6] This definition illustrates the fundamental shift in register from a definition of 'tact' primarily understood as a sense of feeling or touching, tapping or beating – a definition still offered by the 1765 entry on 'tact' in Denis Diderot and Jean le Rond d'Alembert's *Encyclopédie*[7] – to the interpretation of tact as an art of social interaction. The new usage of the word was quickly adapted into English. Dugald Stewart was among those who remarked upon 'the use made in the French tongue of the word tact, to denote that delicate sense of propriety which enables a man to feel his way in the difficult intercourse of polished society'.[8] Stewart explained the need for tact in the context of the French Revolution, where disorientation was the order of the day and new forms of recognition and judgement had to be developed, no longer relying on general codification, but based on individual forms of subjective perception.

Tact, he observed, becomes particularly important in times of crisis, when established social hierarchies collapse, and norms and conventions crumble. In line with Stewart, one of his students, Sidney Smith, highlighted the new and swiftly increasing use of tact as a metaphor specifically applied to depict a form of social interaction. In one of his lectures convened in London between 1804 and 1806 Smith observed that people had formerly used tact's etymological neighbour, the word 'taste', as a metaphor to describe a person's sensibility. Now, however, 'we have begun ... to use the word *tact*; we say of such a man that he has good tact in manners, that he has a fine tact exactly as we would say he has a good taste'.[9]

In German, too, the word 'Tact' or 'Takt' gained in prominence around 1800. The entry on tact in Jacob and Wilhelm Grimms' *Deutsches Wörterbuch* (1890) quotes two poets, Friedrich von Matthisson (1761–1831), referring to 'aesthetic tact', and Johann Gottfried Seume (1763–1810), using the concept of 'fine tact' (*feiner Takt*) to depict a particular sense of what is right and proper. The entry also lists Immanuel Kant who, in his *Anthropologie in pragmatischer Hinsicht* (1796/7), associates tact with 'taste' and applies the term as 'logical tact' in the sense of an ethical and aesthetic judgement that, operating a priori without scientific principles, is based on the '*im Dunkeln des Gemüts liegenden Bestimmungsgründe des Urteils*' (determining grounds of judgement that lie in the obscurity of the mind).[10] Before long, tact as a social and aesthetic category had lost its novelty and established its firm place in the German, French, and English vernaculars as well as in philosophical and aesthetic discourse. In the German context, the works of Johann Wolfgang Goethe, also extensively referenced in Grimms' *Wörterbuch*, offer a particularly rich example. Goethe's widespread use of the term reflects its increasing popularity and significance and illustrates the variety of different semantic models attached to the concept during the first three decades of the nineteenth century. A brief look at a few passages from his work will help us trace the transition from literal to figurative tact or, more specifically, from a word depicting modes of touch and the beating of time to a term describing a particular form of social and aesthetic perceptivity.

Goethe's Tact

One of the earliest references to the word tact in Goethe's writing can be found in the novel *Die Wahlverwandtschaften* (*Elective Affinities*) (1809). The passage uses tact in the sense of a psychological sensitivity, especially associated with women. '*Für solche Verhältnisse*', Goethe's narrator observes, in this case meaning the advantages of one potential husband over another, '*ist den Weibern ein besonderer Takt angeboren und sie haben Ursache so wie Gelegenheit ihm auszubilden*' (Women have a particularly fine feeling, inborn in them, for these distinctions, and have reason, as well as the opportunity, to develop it).[11] During the two decades that follow, we find the word tact used in manifold ways, sounding out the term's wide range of possible meanings.[12] Tact is applied figuratively in reference to forms of sociability,[13] and as a capacity for aesthetic judgement (or rather, the absence thereof, in the case of the Germans).[14] It is employed as a criterion for philological sensitivity,[15] in association with a scholar's special gift for empirical judgement in the natural sciences,[16] in reference to a regular movement and its interruption[17] and, as late as 1833, in its original and literal sense as an umbrella term for the lower senses of the body: '*Das Gesicht ist der edelste Sinn*', Goethe writes in his *Sprüche in Prosa*, '*die andern vier belehren uns nur durch die Organe des Tacts, wir hören, wir fühlen, riechen, und betasten alles durch Berührung*' (The face is the finest of the senses, the other four inform us merely with the help of the organs of tact; we hear, we feel, smell, and touch everything through contact).[18] The semantic model of tact that best illustrates the shift in register undergone by the word in German in the first half of the nineteenth century is, however, the musical one. A brief look at two different passages from Goethe's work serves to illustrate this point.

The first example stems from Goethe's *Italienische Reise* (*Italian Journey*), an account based on the travel diaries written between 1786 and 1788, composed retrospectively between 1813 and 1817. The entry of particular interest to us takes us back to 3 October 1786. Goethe recalls walking through the labyrinthine alleys in Venice, 'map in hand', trying to find the Church of the Mendicanti with the aim to attend a concert by its highly acclaimed conservatory. The women's choir performs an oratorio, standing behind the church's grating. Goethe recalls that the church was fully attended, the music infinitely beautiful, the voices glorious. Indeed, the whole aesthetic experience would have been perfect,

> *wenn nicht der vermaledeite Kapellmeister den Takt mit einer Rolle Noten, wider das Gitter, und so unverschämt geklappt hätte, als habe er mit Schuljungen zu tun, die er eben unterrichtete; und die Mädchen hatten das Stück oft wiederholt, sein Klatschen war ganz unnötig und zerstörte allen Eindruck, nicht anders als wenn einer, um uns eine schöne Statue begreiflich zu machen, ihr Scharlachläppchen auf die Gelenke klebte. Der fremde Schall hebt alle Harmonie auf. Das ist nun ein Musiker und er hört es nicht, oder er will vielmehr, daß man seine Gegenwart durch eine Unschicklichkeit vernehmen soll, da es besser wäre, er ließe seinen Wert an der Vollkommenheit der Ausführung erraten.*

if the damned conductor had not beaten time against the screen with
a rolled sheet of music as insolently as if he were teaching schoolboys. The
girls had so often rehearsed the piece that his vehement slapping was
unnecessary as if, in order to make us appreciate a beautiful statue, someone
were to stick little patches of red cloth on the joints. This man was
a musician, yet he did not, apparently, hear the discordant sound he was
making which ruined the harmony of the whole. Maybe he wanted to
attract our attention to himself by this extraordinary behaviour; he would
have convinced us better of his merits by giving a perfect performance.[19]

On the face of things, the Maestro di Capello does nothing more than
conduct the musicians in recognition of the concept of musical tact we saw
earlier described by Zedler's *Universal-Lexicon* as the 'correct motion of the
hand which chorus and orchestra must follow'.[20] In the mind of Goethe's
narrator, however, this concept of tact seems dramatically outdated. By
blindly following the prescribed rhythm, the Maestro does not advance the
musical performance, but in effect offends the musicians and, by extension,
his listener. The lack of sensitivity prevents the Maestro from intuitively, and
appropriately, responding to the singularity of the communicative situation.
Instead of shifting the emphasis from imposing the 'correct' beat of time to
guiding the singers by trusting one's own interpretation of the notation, the
unhappy Maestro is openly dominating the scene. In so doing, he not only
destroys any possibility of musical harmony, he also commits an offence to
propriety (*Unschicklichkeit*). His rudeness (*Unverschämtheit*) originates from
his attempt to force the correct rhythm onto his fellow musicians while not
paying any attention to the quality of their performance, and from emphasizing his own presence rather than communicating it indirectly through the
resulting music. The Maestro's insistence on following the regulatory system
of the notation, rather than relying on his own interpretation and the skills
and talent of the other performers, reveals him as a person who is musically
insensitive and socially inept. Inasmuch as the notion of tact applied by the
Maestro does not arise from the musical content itself but from the empty
order of time, his claim to domination, his attempt to discipline the musicians and to terrorize them by the beat of his hand into obedience, proves
ultimately ineffective.[21] By insisting on his power, the Maestro loses this
power, revealing himself as an outsider to the performance (*der fremde
Schall*). In the eyes and ears of the narrator he appears as someone who is
out of tune with his place and time. Just like Goethe's anonymous person
who, in the same passage, takes the idea of 'grasping' (*begreifen*) the aesthetic
value of a statue literally by sticking little patches of red cloth onto its joints,
the Maestro, too, fails to translate sensuality into sensitivity, literal beat into

figurative tact. In so doing, he demonstrates his incapacity to sublimate physical proximity into the spiritual distance, and mechanical accuracy into a form of individual and intuitive deviation that is necessary for beauty to evolve. Goethe's parable of the concert in Venice could be a revolutionary one.[22] Curiously, however, Goethe notes in hindsight that, against his own expectations, the Italian audience of the year 1786 seemed accustomed to the Maestro's demeanour and did not appear to mind his nonsensical obedience to the prescribed metric regularity.[23]

Goethe's recollection of the concert in Venice in his *Italian Journey* resonates with the description of another concert that features in the novel *Die Wahlverwandtschaften*. This time, the scene is set in the salon of a country house somewhere in Germany. It is evening. The married couple Charlotte and Eduard and their two guests, Lieutenant Otto and Ottilie, Charlotte's beautiful orphaned niece, are present. A romantic affection has secretly grown between Eduard and Ottilie, and the impression evoked by Eduard playing the flute and Ottilie accompanying him on the piano brings this to light. Comparing Ottilie's performance to that of Charlotte, the narrator observes:

> *Die Zuhörenden waren aufmerksam und überrascht, wie vollkommen Ottilie das Musikstück für sich selbst eingelernt hatte, aber noch mehr überrascht, wie sie es der Spielart Eduards anzupassen wußte. 'Anzupassen wußte' ist nicht der rechte Ausdruck: denn wenn es von Charlottens Geschicklichkeit und freiem Willen abhing, ihrem bald zögernden, bald voreilenden Gatten zuliebe, hier anzuhalten, dort mitzugehen, so schien Ottilie, welche die Sonate von jenen einigemal spielen gehört, sie nur in dem Sinne eingelernt zu haben, wie jener sie begleitete. Sie hatte seine Mängel so zu den ihrigen gemacht, daß daraus wieder eine Art von lebendigem Ganzen entsprang, das sich zwar nicht taktgemäß bewegte, aber doch höchst angenehm und gefällig lautete. Der Komponist selbst hätte seine Freude daran gehabt, sein Werk auf eine so liebevolle Weise entstellt zu sehen.*

Those listening noticed and were amazed how completely Ottilie had learned the piece for herself, but what amazed them even more was how she managed to accommodate it to Eduard's manner of playing. 'Managed to accommodate' is not the right expression; for whereas Charlotte skilfully, and of her own free will, held back to suit her husband when he hesitated and kept up with him when he raced ahead, it seemed that Ottilie, who had heard them play the sonatas on a number of occasions, had only learned them in the way that belonged to the man she was accompanying. She had made his faults so much her own that in the end something whole and alive came out of them that did not keep up proper time [*nicht taktgemäß*], it is true, but was extremely agreeable and pleasing to listen to nevertheless. The composer himself would have been delighted to see his work distorted in such a loving way.[24]

In contrast to Charlotte's deliberate and controlled assimilation of her own playing to Eduard's idiosyncratic interpretation of the rhythm prescribed, Ottilie adjusts her interpretation of the piece to Eduard's seemingly arbitrary delaying and hastening of time by intuitively recognizing these shortcomings (*Mängel*) to make them her own. The outcome does not abide by the correct beat of the notation. But, precisely because Eduard's and Ottilie's joint interpretation is '*nicht taktgemäß*', it is harmonious. With both musicians jointly deviating from the metric regularity, they emerge as two unique individuals who are in tune with each other. The result is a 'loving distortion' of the piece that, in stark contrast to the concert in Venice described above, is 'extremely pleasant' and 'agreeable' to the ears of the audience. To be tactful is not to mechanically follow regulated structures. Tact is what deviates from the score and, in so doing, makes room for a spontaneous, situational, and intuitive interpretation that results in a harmony of minds. This harmony is fragile and mobile inasmuch as it exists outside the rule of convention. It is also potentially disruptive. In deviating from the rule, both Eduard and Ottilie acknowledge that the rule is still objectively in place. However, by witnessing Ottilie perceptively responding to Eduard's subjective deviation rather than to the objective meter prescribed, we get a sense of individual empowerment that may begin to threaten the objectivity of the rule itself. The audience, consisting of Charlotte and the Lieutenant, sense as much. Their response points to the uncertainty that, while being deviated from, the nature of the rule might be changing too. More radically still, the individual deviation may no longer be perceived in relation to an objective norm at all. Instead, subjectivity may begin to posit itself as normative objectivity.[25] This is a concern Adorno will raise in his observations on the dialectic of tact.[26] But the crisis associated with Eduard's and Ottilie's tact is limited in its long-term effects. By the end of the novel, the rule is shaken but not overthrown. The marriage bond between Eduard and Charlotte is not dissolved, and Ottilie starves herself to death without anyone noticing in time to come to her rescue – a most tactful form, it seems to me, of self-effacement.

Tact's Distance

Tact belongs to the wider semantic field of civility and manners. And yet, it cannot simply be described as a way of positioning oneself within the social hierarchies created by a refinement of conduct. In contrast to politeness, tact, defined by Reginald Baliol Brett as a 'fine instinct in the management of men',[27] an individual and spontaneous response to a particularly sensitive situation, broke with the predominance of aristocratic etiquette and existing normative codifications. Within the context of an attempt to reduce the combative aspects of social interaction, tact depended less on a placement of people in categories of class and status, but involved the consideration and accommodation of the particular needs of others. This is not to say that tact always worked as a social leveller. Because the concept of tact presupposed a high level of refinement and self-formation (*Bildung*), we shall see that tact had its limitations as a democratic social practice and an equalizing force. But since the late eighteenth century, the notion of tact nevertheless involved an appreciation for the singularity of the individual and attention towards otherness. In that sense, the rise of tact coincided with the rise of the idea of bestowing each bourgeois subject their right to freedom and autonomy.

Within this context, a particular tension emerged that became one of the long-term thrusts of tact's history: although originally arising from the notion of physical proximity (touch), in the newly emerged semantic field of the nineteenth century, tact became closely linked to the idea of social distantiation. The steep uptake of the word tact as a metaphor for a particular mode of 'feeling one's way' in an increasingly unstable social terrain (Stewart)[28] took off precisely at a time when urbanization, industrialization, and population growth began to have an unprecedented effect on human relations. As with its older neighbouring concepts 'civility', '*honnêteté*', '*délicatesse*', 'politeness', 'good breeding', 'etiquette', and '*guter Ton*', social tact was born in the open, unstructured social space of towns and cities.[29] As an individual and intuitive variation of codified polite behaviour, tact helped one negotiate one's way in the lengthening chains of social and economic interdependence in the world outside the court.[30] In areas where strangers lived alongside one another in conditions of physical proximity and emotional distance, tact was seen as a strategy of making space where things got too tight and bridging gaps where people tended to drift too far away from one another. Albrecht Koschorke's notion of a 'social separation energy' (*soziale Trennungsenergie*) helps to further illuminate this point.[31] Drawing on Norbert Elias' theory of the civilizing process, Koschorke identifies a series of 'distancing thrusts' (*Distanzierungsschübe*) that distinguish modern from early modern societies in Europe. The social and moral change this entailed was marked by an increasing need for isolation and privacy, and a heightened demand for discretion concerning all things physical that came to mark the code of conduct of the middle classes in the second half of the eighteenth century. The growing expansion and differentiation of the networks of social interdependency meant that affects and emotions had to overcome ever-growing distances via ever-extending chains of communication.[32] As a consequence, the affects and passions that adapted to the new modes of social intercourse took on an increasingly ephemeral and imaginary character. This process of spiritualization (*Vergeistigung*), Koschorke argues, was not caused by a change in moral premises, but by a change in the new structures of communication. The lived experience of social distancing coincided with a growing need for a written culture of nearness, of which the literature of sensibility was one possible expression.[33] The shift in meaning of the concept of tact mirrors this process of sublimation. Sensuality turned into sensibility, physical proximity was translated into an encounter of minds, and touch became tact.

The change in register of the word tact from external touch to internal ways of 'feeling one's way in uncertain times', as Stewart had it, and tact's subsequent career as a form of psychological sensitivity and aesthetic judgement, can be further unpacked by what Ernst Cassirer described as 'the emancipation of sensibility' in eighteenth-century psychology, ethics, and aesthetics. The Cartesian doctrine, Cassirer observes, according to which the passions were supposed to be nothing but 'perturbations of the soul', was gradually supplanted. Now they were seen as 'vital impulses', the real motivational forces which stimulate the mind as a whole and keep it in operation.[34] As a consequence, human sensibility – one's feelings, perceptions, and unconscious desires – gained significance compared to one's intellect. This led to a rise in appreciation of the so-called lower faculties of cognition, the exterior senses, in particular the senses taste and touch that, as earlier exemplified by Goethe, had long been disqualified vis-à-vis the sense of sight and the 'interior senses' of subjective imagination and intuition. As Herder famously exclaimed in free adaptation of Descartes' phrasing: '*Ich fühle mich! Ich bin!*' (I feel myself! I am!)[35] The rise of the concept of tact reflects this emancipation in two ways. Its ongoing literal use as external touch shows that sensual perception became a valid criterion within the context of social and aesthetic judgement and appreciation. Its figurative use illustrates the growing significance of subjective, interior feeling(s).[36] The first was based on the notion of physical proximity; the second and more important one, I would argue, was built on the idea of a sublimation of that physical proximity into a figure of imagined, internalized, and disembodied distance. To flesh out this rather abstract idea, I suggest that we look at another example.

Diderot's and Herder's Tact

The unresolved tension between proximity and distance that shapes modern conceptions of tact is best described with the help of the two different responses offered by Denis Diderot and Johann Gottfried Herder to a question put forward by the Irish scientist and politician William Molyneux and addressed by John Locke in his *Essay Concerning Human Understanding* (1690). 'Molyneux's Problem', which preoccupied most key figures of eighteenth-century thought across Europe, was whether a man who was born blind and has learnt to distinguish and name a globe and a cube would be able to distinguish and name these objects simply by sight, once he had been enabled to see. Diderot used the question to turn upside down the existing hierarchy of the senses and establish 'tact', meaning touch, as a key category of modern aesthetics. '*L'exemple de cet illustre aveugle*' he observed, '*prouve que le tact peut devenir plus délicat que la vue lorsqu'il est perfectionné par l'exercice*' (This celebrated blind man proves that touch, when improved by exercise, may become more precise than sight).[37] Herder followed suit when contemplating the notion of touch as '*Gefühl*' (feeling) within the context of a wider theory of art and the senses. In *Plastik* (1778), Herder begins by turning Molyneux's example on its head. Imagine, he suggests, a seeing person who blinds his eyes to regain himself as a feeling person. This allows Herder to establish touch, not sight, as the original organ of the experience of bodies and bodily form. In Herder's thought experiment the hand is associated with immediacy, proximity, originality, and nature, while the eye is linked to distance, artificiality, and alienation. In line with Diderot, Herder proves himself a sensualist when arguing that we do not perceive a statue with the help of sight but through touch, so as to distinguish it from a flat picture and recognize it as a three-dimensional body. But – and here comes the important part for us – Herder's touch has a peculiar quality. It solely takes place in the imagination. Unlike Goethe's anonymous person who commits an offence by sticking little patches of red cloth on the joints of a statue, Herder's blind observer does not touch the statue. Instead, he turns, with the help of his imagination, his interior eye into his hand. He 'observes' the statue *as if* he were touching it. The result is the capacity to feel at a distance, non-sensually, and imaginatively.[38] This idea, which Goethe would have approved of, is mirrored in the semantic transformation of the concept of tact. Tact appears as an imaginative form of touch that does not take place in the proximity of but at a distance to the object of one's attention. As a 'blind' form of touch, tact takes place by circumventing our eyesight and with it our intellect or reason. The tension between proximity and distance, between exterior sense and interior sensibility, between intuition and ratio, still characterizes the concept of tact today, informing different ways of theorizing tact. Derrida's notion of tact as 'contact without touch', mentioned earlier, and Adorno's idea of tact as a 'distanced nearness', to be discussed in the chapters that follow, are only two of the more recent examples.

Tact's Genius

Modern tact, we have come to establish, arises from the increasing appreciation and sublimation of touch. It can be defined as an alternative form of social and aesthetic perception that is based on individual intuition. We saw that Kant develops this idea in his *Anthropologie in pragmatischer Hinsicht* when introducing the concept of 'logical tact'. Based on an intimate alliance between psychology and aesthetics, the concept describes an intuitive mode of ethical and aesthetic judgement that operates a priori without scientific principles.[39] This does not mean that Kant's tact exists regardless of any general principles or norms. In fact, Kant was quick to dismiss any ill-justified and speculative uses of the term as '*mystische[n] Takt, ein[en] Übersprung (salto mortale) von Begriffen zum Undenkbaren*' (mystical tact, an overleap (*salto mortale*) from concepts to the unthinkable).[40] As with its neighbouring concept, taste (*Geschmack*), Kant's tact is a capacity that grows out of the ongoing negotiation between one's own intuitive judgement and the judgement of others, whereby the latter should not be misunderstood as an empirical generality, a consistent unanimity of other people's views. Instead, we should conceive of it as the consensus of an ideal community. The idea is one of harmony (*Zusammenstimmung*), not conformity (*Übereinstimmung*)[41] Tact is a particular sensitivity for what may or may not be appropriate in a specific (social or scientific) situation. Tact negotiates between existing rules and principles and the observer's spontaneous instinct and imagination. Tact is a situational deviation from existing regulatory patterns, categories, or norms. Drawing on this key aspect of Kant's conception, 'tact', Adorno will write in the 1940s, is a 'determination of differences'. It consists in 'conscious deviations' (M 40/MM 37). We shall return to this idea.[42]

The rise of tact as an intuitive form of aesthetic perception based on the idea of individual deviation is closely associated with the aesthetic of genius that preoccupied eighteenth-century debates. Established as a counter movement to the classicist concept of general rules for poetry (*Regelpoetik*), this aesthetic was to be applied to the creation of art and its appreciation. It centred on the idea that the artist, liberated from the constraints of cultural tradition, refers to nature in a subjective and immediate way, not with the aim to emulate nature, but seeking to recreate it and, by doing so, bring it to perfection. '*Genie*', observed Kant in his *Kritik der Urteilskraft* (1790), '*ist die angeborne Gemütslage (ingenium), durch welche die Natur der Kunst die Regel gibt*' (Genius is the inborn predisposition of the mind (*ingenium*) through which nature gives the rule to art).[43] But although the genius may be superior to all general rules, s/he cannot completely ignore their existence. On the contrary, if we follow Kant's argument, there is no fine art that does not to some degree comply with the existing rules to pass before judgement.[44] All fine art is therefore the product of a negotiation between the originality of the genius and the more mechanical aspects of convention. Unlike brilliance or intellect, the workings of genius cannot be explained. (This is why Kant associates genius with the arts alone, and not with the sciences.[45] According to this definition, Newton or Einstein may have been brilliant, but they were no geniuses.) The ingenious thought is one that departs from the ordinary and leads to a new and surprising view of things. But it cannot exist without the ordinary. Inasmuch as ingenious art does not simply apply general convention but expands, transforms, and rectifies it, it becomes an achievement of tact. 'Genius', writes Cassirer, discussing the relation between genius and taste, is 'the gift of receptivity; fine tact'.[46] Ingenious creativity, Adorno will later argue, pushing the boundaries of Kant's definition to add the philosopher's own name to a list of geniuses that also includes figures such as Goethe and Beethoven, is essentially tactful precisely because it negotiates between the general rules and the author's individual autonomy. Ingenious art and thought exist to explore the space opening up between general norm and subjective deviation. Their precondition is, with Adorno, the '*in sich gebrochene und doch noch gegenwärtige Konvention*' (convention no longer intact yet still present) (M 39/MM 36).

The geniality of aesthetic creativity, Kant writes, requires an equally ingenious notion of judgement.[47] Winfried Menninghaus addresses this point when discussing tact's etymological neighbour, taste, as part of his study on disgust. The liberation from general rules for poetry, with the help of a logic whereby we judge the particular on purely subjective grounds, is a key moment in the evolution of modern aesthetics as an independent discipline, and for the conception of art as an autonomous system. When works of art are supposed to stand out by way of their originality, and in conscious deviation from existing conventions, as Adorno might add, then, we can conclude, 'a faculty of judgement is likewise required that, without presupposing any fixed criteria, is capable of doing justice to the singular achievements of genius'.[48] Such a capacity for judgement is almost as tactful and unpredictable as the process of artistic creation itself. It moves away from a 'spirit of correctness' to a 'spirit of sensitivity', as Cassirer observes. In contrast to a mathematical mode of thinking, which is aimed at the consolidation, stabilization, and fixation of concepts, tactful thinking expresses a certain lightness and a flexibility of thought. Intuitively recognizing the finest nuances and quickest shifts in meaning, tactful perception is not geared to establish any direct connection between two points but guided by a different ideal marked by imprecision and indirection. Tactful thinking is a mode of non-linear, unfinished contemplation.[49] Lodged within the 'great depth of the individual mind', as Kant observed, tactful thinking breaks away from the predominance of existing hierarchies and normative codifications. It makes sense, therefore, to associate the rise of tact with the rise of the figure of the autonomous subject.[50]

On the one hand aesthetic tact, we could say, is egalitarian. Like Kant's taste, it is a common sense that can be shared by all and that, as such, is at the heart of all cultural activity.[51] On the other hand tact, as 'fine tact', arguably presupposes an elevated level of refinement and education. Fine tact cannot arise from spontaneous, subjective inspiration alone. It must relate to convention and be shaped by formation *(Bildung)*, or else it may remain the result of a mere coincidence, an arbitrary and unintelligible fluke (see, again, Kant). In the nineteenth century, this association of fine tact with social elevation and formation allowed for tact to be appropriated by the rising bourgeoisie. As an aesthetic and social category, fine tact, like good taste, became an ideal of the educated middle class. At a time when the aristocracy had increasingly forfeited its economic wealth and political power, tact, like taste, had the potential to overthrow the existing hierarchies based on birthright and norms. But despite its democratic promise, tact also led to a new form of social distinction. In contrast to the case of 'good taste', the opposite of 'fine tact' is not 'bad tact' but 'no tact'. And so, as a category, tact helped separate people who had it from those who, allegedly, did not. (The former referred to members of the mostly urban educated upper middle class, the latter was frequently associated with workers, country people, so-called parvenus or snobs, and Jews.)[52] As a category of social distinction, 'fine tact', like 'good taste', thus became an essential criterion for the newly formed elite, the 'polite society' *(gute Gesellschaft; bonne société)*, whose members recognized and legitimized themselves no longer primarily by birth and rank but on the basis of the communality of their social and aesthetic judgements.[53] But tact, as an infinitely refined sense of discrimination of the particular, did not only function to distinguish those who belong from those who did not. It also allowed for a number of nuanced distinctions within the class of the 'cultivated'. We shall see in Proust's novel how the late nineteenth-century nobility sought to compensate for their economic and political decline and to hold on to their powers by making refined distinctions that would help keep them separate from everybody else – a dynamic, as Menninghaus observes, that draws on aspects of Luhmann's system theory, which is of particular significance in social systems with weakened authorities and complex hierarchies.[54] Inasmuch as tact has the capacity to create a momentary equilibrium between individuals beyond the boundaries of existing hierarchies and conventions, it can be seen as a driver for the formation and transformation of group identities, allowing, as Proust's novel shows only too well, for the ongoing dynamic of pushing and shifting the boundaries of acceptability and membership in certain social groups and circles. How fine tact – as a capacity for social and aesthetic judgement – became not only a category that helped distinguish the members of an educated elite from everybody else but was also turned into a key concept of modern hermeneutics is the object of the following and concluding sections of this chapter.

Helmholtz's and Gadamer's Tact

In 1862 Hermann von Helmholtz gave a lecture on the occasion of the inauguration of the vice chancellor's office at Heidelberg University that would be of lasting significance for the rise of modern hermeneutics. In this lecture, entitled '*Über das Verhältniss der Naturwissenschaften zur Gesammtheit der Wissenschaften*' (The Relation of the Natural Sciences to Science in General), Helmholtz addressed the methodological dispute that marked the relationship between the natural and the human sciences throughout the nineteenth century and beyond. What, if anything, he asked, distinguishes the thought processes at work in the human sciences from those that mark the natural sciences? At first, the answer the professor of physiology provided seemed ambivalent. The humanities may be morally superior to the natural sciences insofar as they are not primarily concerned with indifferent matter and its practical consequences, but with the precious formation of the human mind.[55] At the same time, however, the humanities can only define themselves negatively, mimicking the natural-scientific methodological ideal of induction. To solve this epistemological problem, Helmholtz goes on to introduce a distinction that is not methodological but psychological. It has to do with the disposition of the scientific mind. In the case of the natural scientist induction is based on conscious conclusion. By contrast, for a philologist (or indeed any other humanist), induction is guided by artistic

intuition. The natural sciences can translate their logical inductions into
general rules and laws. The human sciences, by contrast, are predominantly
concerned with judgements that are not the result of the slow and indefatig-
able work of rational conclusion, but take shape in the form of sudden
inspirations (*schnelle Geistesblitze*). These sudden inspirations, Helmholtz
concludes, presuppose the scientist's capacity for a particular type of aesthetic
sensibility. He calls this capacity a certain kind of '*psychologischer Takt*'.[56]

In resonance with Kant's conception of logical tact, and the Kantian
theory of the power of judgement to which it contributes, Helmholtz's
tact is not guided by any recognizable rule or principle but arises from
spontaneous and intuitive perception. The tactful philologist, endowed
with a congenial form of artistic sensitivity paired with a heightened level
of social and aesthetic awareness, compassion, and refinement, does not
critically analyse but 'feels out' the potential meaning of a text by
responding instinctively to its manifold nuances and indirect allusions.
Like Kant's power of judgement, Helmholtz's philological tact is
a capacity that cannot deliberately be acquired or enforced. And yet it
does not arise from personal talent alone. It requires the ongoing existence
of a spiritual culture that is based on the humanist ideal of self-formation
paired with a romantic belief in individuality and individual creativity. In
the form of an individual variation, Helmholtz's tact resists normativity
and classification. And yet, it must relate to norms and principles if it
wants to be understood. Tact helps Helmholtz's humanist to negotiate in
the open space between general principle and individual inclination, and
to form a judgement that is appropriate in relation to the object of
interpretation.

In his baselines of a philosophical hermeneutic, *Wahrheit und Methode*
(*Truth and Method*) (1960), Hans-Georg Gadamer revisits Helmholtz's
observations on philological tact to develop them on two different levels.
On the one hand Gadamer articulates an ontology to which modern
philosophical hermeneutics should be committed. On the other, he
describes an ideal form of ethical behaviour which every humanist should
uphold.[57] Unlike Helmholtz, Gadamer is not only concerned with the
epistemological differences between the natural and the human sciences.
Gadamer's interest is much more comprehensive. He wants to know how
human understanding is possible, and how it works. Within this context,
Gadamer suggests that understanding is not a separate activity, functioning
in distinction to, or in competition with, life. On the contrary, understanding is an essential part of the practice of everyday life and one of the
daily means by which we shape our existence. It is a way of being in an

ethical relation with the world, with ourselves, and with other people. Understanding stands, and Gadamer draws on a formulation by Heidegger here, for the basic motivation of our existence (*Grundbewegtheit des Daseins*).[58] It is within this context that Gadamer asks what the conditions of knowledge are that, in turn, facilitate science. To answer this question, he turns to Helmholtz's introduction of tact. Tact, Gadamer argues, pushing the boundaries of Helmholtz's earlier definition of the concept, is not just a mode of artistic intuition or psychological insight. Nor is it merely a spiritual disposition particularly conducive to human-scientific thought. For Gadamer, tact is a mode of being that points us to the way in which human scientific inquiry may overcome the epistemological constraints so powerfully imposed by the natural sciences.[59] It flourishes within the context of a spiritual culture shaped by the humanist ideal of formation. Formation does not simply mean an acquisition of knowledge here. Understood with Hegel as a process marked by distantiation and alienation, Gadamer's use of the term '*Bildung*' refers to an engagement with reality that is based on the human capacity for abstraction and generalization. It signifies our ability to elevate ourselves from a natural to a spiritual being and, in so doing, to assume an ex-centric position in relation to ourselves. '*Bildung*', in the Hegelian sense, means to be able to shift focus from the particular onto the general, in relation to which the particular can then be measured.[60] It means to be able to recognize oneself in the other. '*Im Fremden das eigene erkennen, in ihm heimisch werden*', Gadamer writes, paraphrasing Hegel, is '*die Grundbewegung des Geistes, dessen Sein nur Rückkehr zu sich selbst aus dem Anderssein ist*' (to recognize one's own in the alien, to become at home in it, is the basic movement of spirit, whose being consists only in returning to itself from what is other).[61] The essence of formation is consequently not the alienation itself, but the homecoming that presupposes this alienation. For Gadamer, perfect formation (*voll-endete Bildung*) is the ideal of the human sciences and the element in which the humanist moves. Perfect formation (of body and spirit) describes a state of maturity that transcends any notion of development, allowing for what Gadamer describes, in implicit allusion to Kleist's marionette, as the 'harmonious movement of all one's limbs'.[62] It is precisely in this sense, Gadamer concludes, once more returning to Helmholtz's notion of tact, that the human sciences presuppose a scientific mind that is already formed (*gebildet*). And it is for this reason that the humanist is endowed with what Gadamer defines as the appropriate tact, in his words, '*den rechten unerlernbaren und unnachahmlichen Takt ..., der die Urteilsbildung und die Erkenntnisweise der Geisteswissenschaften wie ein Element trägt*' (the right, unlearnable and inimitable tact that envelops the human sciences' form of judgement and mode of knowledge as if it were the element in which they move).[63]

Gadamer's deduction of tact from the Hegelian concept of '*Bildung*' as distantiation highlights a conceptual tension that has marked the word tact from its very beginnings. Like Kant's logical tact, Gadamer's tact, too, is an intuitive sense that enables us to make distinctions and form judgements 'for which we cannot give a reason'.[64] However, in distinction to Kant's notion of the term, Gadamer's tact, as '*der rechte Takt*' (the correct tact)[65] is not a sense common to all. As a 'rare distinction' (*seltene Auszeichnung*) that allows members of the educated class to stand out from the crowd,[66] appropriate or fine tact, like good taste, is also a social virtue, shaped by the delicate process of balancing one's own judgements with those (real or possible) of the other members of the same formatively homogenous group. It implies, as Sartre writes in words that are almost identical with Gadamer's formulation, 'that the doer of the act has adopted a certain conception of the world, one that is traditional, ritual, and synthetic, one *for which he can give no reason*'.[67] But the aspect of tact as a form of class appropriation, which Sartre exposes, is counter-balanced by Gadamer's notion of tact as shaped by a resistance to any form of convention or classification. A look at the following passage, in which Gadamer describes tact as an individual and intuitive deviation from the norm, and a particular mode of social distantiation, helps to illuminate this point.

> *Wir verstehen unter Takt eine bestimmte Empfindlichkeit und Empfindungsfähigkeit für Situationen und das Verhalten in ihnen, für die wir kein Wissen aus allgemeinen Prinzipien besitzten. Daher gehört Unausdrücklichkeit und Unausdrückbarkeit dem Takt wesentlich zu. Man kann etwas taktvoll sagen. Aber das wird immer heißen, daß man etwas taktvoll übergeht und ungesagt läßt, und taktlos ist, das auszusprechen, was man nur übergehen kann. Übergehen heißt aber nicht: von etwas wegsehen, sondern es so im Auge haben, daß man nicht daran stößt, sondern daran vorbei kommt. Daher verhilft Takt dazu, Abstand zu halten, er vermeidet das Anstößige, das Zunahetreten und die Verletzung der Intimsphäre der Person.*

(By 'tact' we understand a special sensitivity and sensitiveness to situations and how to behave in them, for which knowledge from general principles does not suffice. Hence an essential part of tact is that it is tacit and unformulable. One can say something tactfully; but that will always mean that one passes over something tactfully and leaves it unsaid, and it is tactless to express what one can only pass over. But to pass over something does not mean to avert one's gaze from it but to keep an eye on it in such a way that, rather than knock into it, one slips by it. Thus, tact helps to preserve distance. It avoids the offensive, the intrusive, the violation of the intimate sphere of the person.)[68]

The social tact Gadamer describes in this passage is not identical with the hermeneutic tact at work in the humanities. And yet they not only share the element of unconscious intuition, they are also both defined, simultaneously, as a mode of being and of cognition.[69] Gadamer's hermeneutic tact, like his social tact, is defined as a perceptual situation based on a particular kind of choreography. Distinct from any purely theoretical form of knowledge, it consists in a mode of action that involves us as individuals. Described as a delicate movement in space, rather than one of abstract critical analysis, it follows a choreography that exists to replace intimacy by distance, directness by deviation, and potential collision by intuitive circumvention or omission. In resonance with what Edward T. Hall called the 'silent language' of proxemics, Gadamer's hermeneutic tact allows us to define the process of understanding as a form of conduct that involves our minds and our bodies. It implies a dynamic way of interacting spatially with other people, artworks, and texts. It describes understanding as a process during which we negotiate the effects of physical and emotional distance and proximity, a form of distance regulation whereby we try not to come too close to the subject of our attention nor stay too far away from it either. Instead of identifying with another person, an artwork, or a text, incorporating it, reading it against the grain, operating on it, digging into it or tearing it apart to expose its hidden meanings, causes, and conditions, we stand back in respect of its otherness, attentive towards its singularity, giving space to allow meaning to evolve.

It may be tempting to dismiss Gadamer's 'gentleman's concept of hermeneutics' (Habermas) for its alleged methodological imprecision and the bourgeois elitism it implies.[70] This elitism undoubtedly exists, and the chapters that follow will grapple with its implications. But the epistemological potential and, I would argue, the timeliness of Gadamer placing tact at the heart of hermeneutic inquiry, lies elsewhere. Gadamer's introduction of tact as the element in which the human sciences move contributes to a hermeneutic that does not define the act of reading as an act of decoding, of classification, or of appropriation. Instead, and in agreement with the other celebrated hermeneutical philosopher, Paul Ricœur, Gadamer's tactful reading appears as an act of respect, and of faith (based on a willingness to listen) rather than one of suspicion (aimed at demystification), of making rather than unmaking.[71]

Understood as a daily means of our life, reading appears as an act based on the realization that the other (person, object, text) cannot be classified or deduced according to general rules or laws. Instead, reading is based on the individual and spontaneous act of deviation from the general rules and laws in response to a concrete and particular situation. This is an idea that implies a sense of empowerment for self and other, reader and artwork alike. The emphasis does not lie on empathic identification (*Einfühlung*) (something that Helmholtz had suggested), but on a joint exploration of space that aims to create and maintain a balance between self and other, reader and text. This balance is mobile, fragile, and under constant negotiation, inasmuch as it is located in a place beyond (albeit not entirely detached from) the sphere of general principles. Therefore, more helpful than the interpretation of tact as a tool of privilege and power is, I would suggest, a consideration of the significance of the Greek ethic of measure, introduced by the Pythagoreans, Plato, and Aristotle. Gadamer briefly refers to this ethic, focusing on Aristotle's notion of *mesotes* developed in *The Nicomachean Ethics*, meaning the middle way or middle ground.[72] Within the context of Gadamer's argument, Aristotle's *mesotes* can be understood as a situation and an ethical possibility for action.[73] As a particularly perceptive, intermediate mode of communication, it allows us to appreciate the individuality and the singularity of the other. Subjective, resisting conflict, and with it the dynamic of power and appropriation, this concept of the middle ground offers a key to Gadamer's ethic and hermeneutic of tact, and to the theory of tact more generally.[74]

Tact's Topicality

The idea that reading is not just a cognitive activity but, in the words of Rita Felski, an 'embodied mode of attentiveness that involves us in acts of sensing, perceiving, feeling, registering, and engaging'[75] has, in recent years, experienced a remarkable revival, notably in French and US American critical theory. Eve Kosofsky Sedgwick's notion of 'reparative reading', Felski's own concept of 'post-critical reading'[76] (according to which critique not only appears as 'a matter of method but of a certain sensibility', something she suggests be called a 'critical mood'[77]), and Marielle Macé's '*façons de lire*' as '*manières d'être*' (ways of reading as modes of being) are only some of the most stimulating contributions to an ongoing debate, the goal of which is to challenge the hermeneutics of suspicion (Ricœur) and to reconsider the premises of critique.[78] Explicitly or implicitly, the source of all these contributions lies in

Gadamer's baselines of a philosophical hermeneutic, liberated from their streak of bourgeois elitism and cleared of their lingering reputation of being unscientific. Macé's endeavour to 'reintegrate reading into life' is a particularly good example here.[79] Offering an alternative to semiotic and narratological models of textual analysis which tend to describe the activity of reading as a hermetically sealed procedure, reading, Macé suggests, should not be defined as a form of decoding dissociated from everyday life but as 'a certain kind of conduct by a subject of experience, both body and consciousness'.[80] In fact, Macé maintains – and here lies one of the main thrusts of the ongoing hermeneutic revival – the act of reading should be understood as based on a particular type of choreography that describes a dynamic and open form of interaction. This choreography grows out of a tension between keeping one's distance and exploring the possibilities of contact between ourselves and other people, artworks, objects, and texts. It exists to facilitate a certain kind of reading encounter that, as Felski observes, avoids 'the original sin of appropriation'.[81]

In 1985 Gadamer wrote an essay in which he responded to Ricœur's critique of a hermeneutics of suspicion. Reconstructing the history of philosophical hermeneutics, Gadamer referred to Friedrich Schleiermacher to emphasize, once more, the central place he assigned to hermeneutics in viewing human experience. Schleiermacher, Gadamer explained, was among the first to establish the problem of hermeneutics as the primary aspect of social experience – not only, he specified, when pertaining to the scholarly interpretation of texts but also for understanding, and for respecting, one might add, 'the mystery of the inwardness of the other person'.[82] This distant feeling for individuality, combined with an awareness of the limits of what it is we can know, was at the heart of a significantly new approach to the realization of the concreteness and the singularity of the other. It is the source, I would argue, for a model of reading born out of the spirit of tact.

Tact, as this brief conceptual history of the term has shown, negotiates between proximity and distance, general norms and individual deviation, ratio and affect. Tact helps explore the unknown space that opens up between the self and the other, between readers and texts. The aim is not to 'help illuminate' what the other person has to offer, nor to find the 'real meaning' of a text or an object,[83] but to establish meaning itself as a fragile, precarious, and mobile concept, something that is negotiable, and held in a balance between the interpreting subject and the object of their attention. The idea is not one of empathic incorporation or identification, but of establishing an appropriate distance. Modern tact, we could say, corresponds to an imagined form of touch, a light touch, not a grip. As an ethical and aesthetic category, it is based on a dialectical tension. Adorno called it a 'distanced nearness'; Plessner later described it as a kind of *'unmerklicher Vorfühlung … unter sorgfältiger Innehaltung der Distanz'* (imperceptible intuition (lit.: 'feeling out') under careful obedience to distance) (G 110/L 166) and Barthes explored it as *'une distance amoureuse'*.[84] The chapters that follow are here to illuminate this peculiar space as it manifests itself in the form of five reading encounters.

CHAPTER 2

Proxemics (Proust)

... aucun être ne veut livrer son âme.

... no being wants to expose their soul.

Marcel Proust, 1923[1]

Marcel Proust's novel, *À la recherche du temps perdu*, famously portrays the Belle Époque (ca. 1884–1914) – a period widely associated with prosperity, technological advance, and a widespread belief in the value of progress – as an age that was also marked by growing social and political anxieties bubbling under the seemingly glamourous surface. The Dreyfus affair (1894–1906), triggering a wave of anti-Semitism, and causing a polarization of French society into passionate defenders on the one side and fierce opponents on the other, casts its long shadow in *La Recherche*.[2] The rise of the nationalist and revanchist movements within the context of the first and second Morocco crisis (1905 and 1911) are reflected in the changing character descriptions and, like the Dreyfus affair, they serve as frequent conversation topics in the Proustian salons. Large parts of the final volume, in turn, and indeed of Proust's correspondence at the time, are preoccupied with the outbreak of the First World War and its reverberations through Paris society.[3] Negotiating the decline of the aristocracy, represented by the salon Guermantes, and the rise of the educated bourgeoisie, embodied by the salon Verdurin, Proust's novel describes a time period marked by a continuous process of social reshuffling, meticulously exposing the ways in which existing hierarchies are dissolving, and established social norms and conventions falling apart. The novel reveals how we may associate this dissolution with crisis and decay, while we can also interpret it as an opportunity for liberation, making room for individual action.[4] In the first of my series of reading encounters with five major European authors, I wish to show how it is within this context that tact, as a concept that negotiates between general norms and individual deviation, becomes a key figure in

Proust's work.[5] Considering *La Recherche* in light of its earliest drafts,
I suggest that we read the novel as an exercise in the manifold practices of
tact. Tact, we said in the previous chapter, is based on a particular form of
proxemics. It can be described as a mode of distance regulation that involves
our minds and bodies alike. The aim of tactful behaviour is to not come too
close to the object of one's attention nor to drift too far away from it. In what
follows, I argue that, in *La Recherche*, this search for the appropriate distance
not only occurs between the characters that populate Proust's pages; it also
marks the relation these characters have with objects, artworks, or texts.
I explore the ways in which the characters in Proust's work negotiate the
ideal distance between each other and the various objects of their attention,
and reconstruct the choreographies of physical, social, and aesthetic distancing this process involves. In so doing, I engage with the opportunities and
limitations posed by tactful forms of communication and interpretation,
their potentially paradoxical nature, the ethical implications this may have,
and the existential feeling of uncertainty, of being alone, that sometimes
occurs when we try to be with others.

Missing Pieces

My writing of this chapter coincided with what many Proust readers
considered a literary sensation: the publication of *Les Soixante-quinze
feuillets* (2021), the (in reality seventy-six) handwritten pages that constitute
the earliest version of the seven volumes later published as *À la recherche du
temps perdu*. First mentioned in Bernard de Fallois' preface to his 1954
edition of *Contre Sainte-Beuve*, the 'seventy-five folios' had become
legendary in Proust scholarship, especially when they failed to emerge
from the manuscripts purchased by the Bibliothèque Nationale in 1962
from Proust's niece Suzy Mante-Proust. Considered lost, they were only
rediscovered in 2018, in a folder labelled 'Dossier 3', tucked away somewhere in the archives of the late Fallois.[6] Written in the Autumn of 1908,
three years after the death of Proust's mother, Jeanne Clémence Weil, *Les
Soixante-quinze feuillets* offer the last missing pieces in the puzzle to *La
Recherche* as it evolved between 1908 and 1922, the year of Proust's death. In
the *Feuillets*, Proust not only abandoned the distanced 'he' of the *Jean
Santeuil* fragment (1899) to shift to the more intimate 'I'; he also openly
uses his own first name, Marcel. And so the series of disconnected drafts
that emerge resemble a confession or an autobiography much more than
the auto-fictional novel they were to become. Despite the discrepancy in
perspective and tone, the *Feuillets* already contain most of the leitmotifs

that will give the future novel its structure: the mother's goodnight kiss, the family walks by way of two different sides (the '*deux côtés*'), a group of young girls seen from afar on the beach, a contemplation of aristocratic names, the visit to Venice. Above all, however, the 'seventy-five folios' struck me as being filled with an all-pervading sense of isolation. Whether we witness the grandmother arriving at the hotel by the sea or the narrator contemplating the inexplicable otherness of the girls on the beach, the notion that '*par ici je ne connaissais personne*' (F 54) is one of the sketches' most recurrent motifs.[7] Mostly set away from the density of social life in the capital – a rural setting (Auteuil), a hotel by the sea (Querqueville), on the beach itself, or in a foreign city (Venice) – the sketches contemplate the experience of estrangement, of physical and social distance that is frequently motivated, and justified, by the idea of social and moral 'distinction' (F 38).[8] But this sense of distinction that the narrator and the other characters who inhabit these pages so frequently address stands in sharp contrast to the immediacy with which they are portrayed. Not only are their real identities and names openly exposed: the mother, in the novel simply referred to as '*ma mère*' or '*maman*', is Jeanne; the grandmother Adèle (later '*grand-mère*' or Bathilde); the uncle Louis (later Adolphe, leaving some of his character traits to the semi-fictional Charles Swann); and the younger brother, later erased from the novel, is here still very present as the strong-headed Robert. Even more remarkable is the narrator's lack of tact vis-à-vis these characters, including those who, like the grandmother, in *La Recherche*, will be worshiped and adored. In the *Feuillets* we learn, for example, about the grandmother's untidy appearance ('*elle avait horriblement crotté sa jupe prune*' (she had terribly soiled her prune-colored skirt) (F 26, 32).[9] We read about her rugged character and unconventional demeanour. We are surprised by the disclosure of her social insecurity that manifests itself in her fear '*d'être dédaignée de ceux à qui elle souhaitait de plaire*' (of being disdained by those whom she wished to please) (F 74), which triggers the uncle's frequent outbreaks of mockery and anger ('*Ma parole elle est folle*' (My word, she is crazy) (F 39), and makes the fellow hotel guests raise their eyebrows in condescending bemusement at this '*client peu chic*' (F 73). We are told of a nightmare featuring the mother flustered and splattered with mud (F 41). Details about the amorous escapades of the uncle, in the novel mostly assigned to Swann, are openly exposed (F 79). The round-faced brother, dressed to be photographed, is snobbishly portrayed with a ridiculous hairdo, curled '*comme aux enfants de concierge*' (like the concierge's children) (F 45), and the red colour of the fuchsias is described as ugly, naughty, and nasty, just like the

'*vilain rouge*' (hideous red) of the gardener's daughter's cheeks (F 55).
Throughout, the manuscript exposes character traits and gives away secrets
which the novel will be careful to misplace or conceal.[10] '*Un livre*', Proust
will famously write in *Le Temps retrouvé*, summarizing one of the leading
principles of his novel, '*est un grand cimetière où sur la plupart des tombes on
ne peut plus lire les noms effacés*' (A book is a great cemetery where the names
have been effaced from most of the tombs and are no longer legible (RTP
IV 482/SLT VI 212). (RTP IV 482). The *Feuillets* not only caricature this
idea in the example of the grandmother who, for reasons of '*prudence*',
composes her letters with such great caution that they end up being
perfectly illegible to everyone, including herself (F 28); they also dramatically undermine it by telling us directly, ruthlessly, shamelessly, what in the
novel we will only learn by way of shifts, distortions, deviations, digressions, or not at all. How does one deal with things one does not want or is
not supposed to talk about? How does one say something in an appropriate
manner? And how does one then in turn interpret the enigma that, as in the
case of the grandmother's letters, may seem all that remains of a message
when delivered with tact? This will be one of the novel's key concerns. In
the *Feuillets*, it is still in the making.[11]

Writing and Reading Tactfully

Although the *Feuillets* already contain most of the thematic seeds that will
grow into complex narratives filling the volumes of *La Recherche*, they do not
yet formulate the main psychological and aesthetic principles that will later
give shape to the novel. Memory, for example, is mentioned in the *Feuillets*.
But it is not yet discernible as the psycho-philosophical concept that, in the
shape of the celebrated '*mémoire involontaire*', will add substance to Proust's
poetics. Triggered by the involuntary sensation of immediate physical
contact (taste, touch, smell, or sound), the concept significantly contributes
to the novel's unresolved tension between the idea of contact and fusion on
the one side, unlocking pleasure or pain, and Proust's writing practice on the
other, which relies, by contrast, on the principles of deviation, indirection,
and (potentially infinite) digression. We could call this a tension between
proximity and distance or, more specifically, between touch and tact.

   In his *Theory of the Novel*, written in 1914–15, a time when Proust had
just published the first volume of *La Recherche* and was contemplating how
to proceed, Georg Lukács made an important observation. Thinking about
what may distinguish the novel from other literary genres, he argues that
one important difference lies in the fact that the novel arises from a special

relation between ethics and form. In most literary genres, Lukács maintains, ethics precedes form. This is different in the case of the novel, however, where ethics features as a form-giving element, providing the literary work with its genre-defining characteristics.[12] At the time he was writing, Lukács had not yet encountered the work of Proust.[13] But his emphasis on the programmatic openness, the incompleteness and indecisiveness of novelistic writing resonates with the style of Proust's '*écriture*'. The novel, Lukács contends, borrowing from Hegel, is defined by a permanent state of becoming.[14] Its aesthetic features – and this is the crucial point within our context – are determined by the concept of tact. As an open art form, Lukács writes,

> *schreibt also [der Roman] eine noch strengere und unfehlbarere künstlerische Gesetzlichkeit vor, als die 'geschlossenen Formen', und diese Gesetze sind desto bindender, je mehr sie ihrem Wesen nach undefinierbar und unformulierbar sind: es sind Gesetze des Taktes. Takt und Geschmack, an und für sich untergeordnete Kategorien, die durchaus der bloßen Lebenssphäre angehören und selbst einer wesentlichen ethischen Welt gegenüber belanglos sind, gewinnen hier eine große und konstitutive Bedeutung: bloß durch sie ist die Subjektivität von Anfang und Abschluß der Romantotalität imstande, sich im Gleichgewicht zu halten, sich als episch normative Objektivität zu setzen und so die Abstraktheit, die Gefahr dieser Form, zu überwinden.*

> the novel ... prescribes still stricter, still more inviolable artistic laws for itself than do the 'closed' art forms, and these laws are the more binding, the more indefinable and unformulable they are in their very essence: they are the laws of tact. Tact and taste, in themselves subordinate categories which belong wholly to the sphere of mere life and are irrelevant to an essential ethical world, here acquire great constitutive significance: only through them is subjectivity, at the beginning of the novel's totality and at its end, capable of maintaining itself in equilibrium, as positing itself as normative objectivity and thus of surmounting abstraction, the inherent danger of the novel form.[15]

Lukács' idea that a theory of the novel should grow out of the concept of tact as an ethical sensitivity to form can help unlock Proust's experiment in style, especially when its digressive, and potentially infinite, dynamic fully unfolds in *Albertine disparue* and *La Prisonnière*, the two middle volumes that Proust wrote last. But, as indicated in the introduction, this is not what this chapter is primarily about. For more than thinking about the ways in which tact may influence the development of a particular style of writing, I am interested in how tact may shape the ways of reading that, within the context of Proust's writing, are essentially linked to modes of being.[16] A return to two scenes in the *Feuillets* serves to unpack this idea. In the first example, Marcel sits down, '*à vingt ans de distance*', to reconstruct the potential meaning of his grandmother's illegible letters (F 30). In the second, he meets one of the young girls from the beach for the first time. Pleased at first to receive her friendly greeting, he is quick to question the sincerity of her communication the minute they part ('*J'étais pourtant bien sûr qu'elle avait ri et avait eu l'air impoli tout à l'heure*' (I was quite sure that she had laughed and seemed rude earlier) (F 90). Although both scenes describe two different kinds of reading encounters, one with a text, the other one with a real person, they address the hermeneutical challenge posed by indirect forms of communication, and they share a similar concern. In the first case Marcel must acknowledge that, despite all his painstaking effort, he will never be able to reconstruct the full meaning of the letters written by a person he loves. In the second, he is left with a nagging doubt as to the true significance of an utterance by a girl he desires. In what follows, I shall look at a series of different facets of tact that contribute to the existential feeling of uncertainty this creates.

A Rare Form of Distinction

Tact can be described as egalitarian. Like Kant's taste, it can be defined as a sense that is common to all and that, as such, resides in the heart of all cultural activity. At the same time, however, 'fine tact', understood as a particularly sensitive form of social and aesthetic judgement, can be associated with social elevation and formation. We saw in Chapter 1: Tact's History, how tact, as a particular form of ethical and aesthetic judgement, offered a gradual liberation from fading modes of social codification based on birthright and aristocratic norms, while it also allowed for new and refined forms of social distinction within the class of the 'cultivated'.[17] In a well-known passage from *Journées de Lecture* (1905), Proust addresses this point in association with a portrayal of his great-aunt. When thinking about novels or poetry, Proust recalls, she would always refer to the judgement of other, presumably more competent, people. But when it came to the things the rules and principles of which had been taught to her by her own mother, cooking, playing the piano, and entertaining, she was certain to have a precise idea of perfection and could always detect the degree to which other people would come close to it or not.

> *Pour les trois choses, d'ailleurs, la perfection était presque la même: c'était une sorte de simplicité dans les moyens, de sobriété et de charme. Elle repoussait avec horreur qu'on mît des épices dans les plats qui n'en exigent pas absolument, qu'on jouât avec affectation et abus de pédales, qu'en 'recevant' on sortît d'un naturel*

parfait et parlât de soi avec exagération. Dès la première bouchée, aux premières notes, sur un simple billet, elle avait la prétention de savoir si elle avait affaire à une bonne cuisinière, à un vrai musicien, à une femme bien élevée. 'Elle peut avoir beaucoup plus de doigts que moi, mais elle manque de goût en jouant avec tant d'emphase cet andante si simple'. 'Ce peut être une femme très brillante et remplie de qualités, mais c'est un manque de tact de parler de soi en cette circonstance'. 'Ce peut être une cuisinière très savante, mais elle ne sait pas faire le bifteck aux pommes.' Le bifteck aux pommes! morceau de concours idéal, difficile par sa simplicité même, sorte de 'Sonate pathétique' de la cuisine, équivalent gastronomique de ce qu'est dans la vie sociale la dame qui vient vous demander des renseignements sur un domestique et qui, dans un acte si simple, peut à tel point faire preuve, ou manquer, de tact et d'éducation.

For those three things, moreover, perfection was almost the same: it was a kind of simplicity in the means, a kind of sobriety and charm. She rejected with horror the idea that one would put spices in dishes that did not absolutely require them, that one would play the pedals with affectation and excess, that when receiving one would depart from perfect naturalness and speak of oneself with exaggeration. At the first mouthful, at the first notes, at receiving a simple message, she would claim to know whether she had to do with a good cook, a true musician, a well-bred woman. 'She may have quicker fingers than I have, but she lacks taste, playing with so much emphasis this andante that is so simple.' 'She may be brilliant and full of qualities, but it is a lack of tact to speak of oneself in that way.' 'It may be that she is a very learned cook, but she cannot fix a beefsteak with potatoes.' Beefsteak with potatoes! Ideal competition piece, difficult in its very simplicity, a kind of '*Sonate Pathétique*' of cookery, gastronomical equivalent of what in social life is the visit of a lady who comes to ask you for information about a servant and who in so simple an act can so markedly show proof of, or lack, tact and good manners.[18]

Tact, this passage tells us, is not a skill. It cannot be measured by way of proficiency. Instead, it is defined as a particular talent that exceeds a person's abilities and qualifications. Tact refers to an additional form of refinement that grows out of an intuitive sense for propriety, simplicity, and naturalness. Tact is a way of knowing how to do things 'the right way'. As a sense of measurement that exceeds education, tact cannot be studied but can only be obtained through first-hand experience. In order to learn how to be tactful, one needs to be surrounded by other people (in this case, the great-aunt's mother) who have internalized, and can therefore also recognize, this particular practice. Tact thus turns into a sign of superiority and a marker of social distinction. Like Bourdieu's taste (and when defining the concept Bourdieu refers to Proust's great-aunt as an example), tact classifies, and it classifies the classifier.[19] Within this context, tact can serve as a mode of policing, sanctioning certain ways of expression and censoring others. Foucault highlights the restrictive side of its economy when pointing to the disciplining aspects of tact and discretion.[20] But tact, as a refined sense for discriminating the particular, not only serves to separate those who have it (and therefore belong) from those who do not. Although tact relates to convention and is shaped by formation, it is essentially driven by individual variation. It is, as Adorno argues in a passage already familiar to us, a determination of differences that consists in conscious deviations (M 40). In *La Recherche*, the narrator's characterization of Swann helps to explore this point.

In the first volume of the novel, *Du Côté de chez Swann*, we meet Swann as the epitome of fine tact and good taste (RTP I, 16, 287, 320, 322, 332). Highlighting, in the second volume, the particular ways in which Swann excels in the game of social life, Marcel, the narrator, recalls that Swann's secure sense of propriety and elegant appearance was paired with a '*spontanéité dans les manières et ces initiatives personnelles, même en matière d'habillement*' unique to his character:

> *C'est ainsi que le salut que m'avait fait, sans me reconnaître, le vieux clubman n'était pas le salut froid et raide de l'homme du monde purement formaliste, mais un salut tout rempli d'une amabilité réelle, d'une grâce véritable, comme en avait la duchesse de Guermantes par exemple ... par opposition aux saluts plus mécaniques, habituels aux dames du faubourg Saint-Germain. C'est ainsi encore que son chapeau, que, selon une habitude que tendait à disparaître, il posa par terre à côté de lui, était double de cuir vert, ce qui ne se faisait pas d'habitude mais parce que c'était (à ce qu'il disait) beaucoup moins salissant, en réalité parce que c'était fort seyant.* (RTP II 867)

> And so the greeting the old clubman had given me without recognizing me was not the cold, stiff greeting of a man of the world merely going through the motions, but a greeting full of real friendliness, of genuine charm, similar to those, say, of the Duchesse de Guermantes ... in contrast to the more automatic greetings practised by the ladies of the Faubourg Saint-Germain. Similarly the hat he placed on the floor beside him, in conformity with a custom that was beginning to disappear, was lined, unconventionally, in green leather because (as he would have us believe) it showed the dirt far less, but in fact because it was extremely chic (SLT III 579).

Swann's tact is a rare form of distinction that does not simply comply with normative forms of convention, nor does it grow out of individual inspiration alone. Instead, Swann's tact is based on a tension between existing codes and their creative individual variation. We could call it, to borrow from Rudolph von Jhering, '*ein Erfindungsvermögen in Sachen des Anstandes*' (an inventiveness in all matters concerning civility and decorum).[21] Swann's tact manifests itself in the form of an exaltation. It is an excessive form, as it were, of politeness. For Swann's tact does more than simply facilitate, or guarantee, the uninterrupted flow of conversation, 'the smooth transmission and reception by which encounters are sustained'.[22] As an individual deviation from normative modes of behaviour, Swann's tact exists to transcend what Plessner will call the '*öde Salonlöwentum, jenen wie geschmiert gehenden Formalismus von Tadellosigkeit und Unterhaltung, mit dem die Menschen des kleinsten Formates Leute gleichen Schlages zu bluffen pflegen*' (desolate kind of social interaction, a formalism – going like clockwork – of slickness and conversation with which persons of the smallest stature seek to bluff persons of the same kind) (G 107/L 163). By pairing good breeding with fine tact, Swann shows that he is more than an '*homme du monde*' – a quality that, according to Proust's narrator, is not a signature of a person's intellectual stature but, on the contrary, an impediment to the creativity of his mind (RTP IV 319). Swann's tact is shaped by the delicate process of balancing his own individual social and aesthetic judgements with those of the other members of the formatively homogenous group to which he, temporarily at least, belongs. His tactful behaviour implies, as we saw Sartre observe, 'that the doer of the act has adopted a certain conception of the world, one that is traditional, ritual, and synthetic, one *for which he can give no reason*'.[23] 'It also suggests', Sartre continues, 'a particular sense of psychological ensembles, it is in no sense critical, and we might add that it takes on its whole meaning only in a strictly defined community with common ideas, mores, and customs'.[24] Tact may allow us to include those people who allegedly have it, and can recognise and understand it, and exclude those who do not. And yet, by creating a (temporary) equilibrium between himself as the tactor and Marcel as the tactee – an equilibrium that exists outside, albeit not entirely detached from, conventional forms of polite interaction – Swann's tact also carries a sense of empowerment, of the self and of the other. It involves an attention towards the singularity of the other person, suggesting a glimpse of equality. As an individual deviation, Swann's tact offers a gradual liberation from existing, yet disintegrating, forms of social codification. Although not revolutionary (Swann's tact does not exist to overthrow the norms and conventions in place) it can be seen as a mobilizing force, a driver of the formation and transformation of group identities, a trigger for the ongoing dynamic of pushing and shifting the boundaries of acceptability and belonging that keeps the Proustian kaleidoscope of sociability turning.[25]

In *La Recherche*, tact as a particular form of ethical and aesthetic judgement works both ways. On the one hand, it serves as a means to erect social boundaries, effecting and cementing social cohesion within an existing social community while excluding others. On the other hand, by deviating from traditional norms and conventions, and by reaching across social distinctions, tact can also help to mobilize and rearrange existing systems of power and domination. Therein lies tact's paradoxical structure. In a free adaptation of Bourdieu's principle mentioned earlier: tact classifies, and it classifies the classifier. But in so doing, it also simultaneously helps to undo these classifications. The association with individual autarchy and freedom this implies is paired with a sense of insecurity. This insecurity does not only pertain to one's (potentially unstable) social position, but also extends to the essential ambivalence of the tactful communication itself. In the mind of Marcel, the authenticity of Swann's 'grace' is by no means guaranteed. While during the encounter itself Swann's personal warmth and affection seemed perfectly real to Marcel, he only learns in hindsight that Swann had not yet recognized him at that particular moment of their encounter. Tact, we said earlier, is not so much linked to what one says but to what one does not say. Tact is essentially associated with the 'as if'. As such, it consists in a particular art of handling that requires a particular way of reading. Some of the choreographies this involves are explored in the sections that follow.

Too Close – Too Far Away

The characters in the world of Proust's novel are constantly negotiating their positions in relation to each other. In a seemingly endless series of different game or dance formations they either get too close to each other – so that the contours of their counterpart dissolve into individual grains, as in the famous scene in *À l'ombre des jeunes filles en fleur* where the narrator tries to kiss his lover, Albertine (RTP II 659) – or they drift too far away from each other, as in the equally well-known scene in *Du Côté de chez Swann* where the narrator's aunts, Céline and Flora, try to thank Swann for contributing a case of Asti to the garden party. Unfortunately, their joint efforts are so excessively indirect, and formulated with such great tact ('*délicatement*' (RTP I 34)) that it becomes impossible for Swann, or indeed any other person present at the table, to make out their meaning (RTP I 25, 34). Unlike Arthur Schopenhauer's notoriously freezing porcupines, who finally manage to settle on a form of well-tempered distance, protecting each other from both injury and isolation,[26] Proust's characters find it difficult to establish an appropriate physical or social distance between each other. Their frequent efforts that fill the pages of *La Recherche* thus read like a series of carefully choreographed yet frequently failing experiments in the 'silent language' of proxemics.[27] Two particular scenes that come to mind involve Marcel and M. de Charlus, and Marcel and Albertine. The first scene is taken from *À l'ombre des jeunes filles en fleur*. It tells of the first of a series of face-to-face interactions between Marcel and M. de Charlus, who is only at a later point in the novel identified as the uncle of Marcel's friend, Robert de Saint-Loup. Set in front of the Casino in Balbec, the scene examines the ways we position ourselves in a public space, and how this may reflect on our social and emotional relation to each other. The narrator recalls:

> *Le lendemain matin du jour où Robert m'avait ainsi parlé de son oncle tout en l'attendant, vainement du reste, comme je passais seul devant le casino en rentrant à l'hôtel, j'eus la sensation d'être regardé par quelqu'un qui n'était pas loin de moi. Je tournai la tête et j'aperçus un homme d'une quarantaine d'années, très grand et assez gros, avec des moustaches très noires, et qui, tout en frappant nerveusement son pantalon avec une badine, fixait sur moi des yeux dilatés par l'attention. Par moments, ils étaient percés en tous sens par des regards d'une extrême activité comme en ont seuls devant une personne qu'ils ne connaissent pas des hommes à qui, pour un motif quelconque, elle inspire des pensées qui ne viendraient pas à tout autre – par exemple des fous ou des espions. Il lança sur moi une suprême œillade à la fois hardie, prudente, rapide et profonde, comme un dernier coup que l'on tire au moment de prendre la fuite, et après avoir regardé tout autour de lui, prenant soudain un air distrait et hautain, par un brusque revirement de toute sa personne il se tourna vers une affiche dans la lecture de laquelle il s'absorba, en fredonnant un air et en arrangeant la rose mousseuse qui pendait à sa boutonnière.* (RTP II 110–11)

On the morning following the day when Robert told me these things about this expected uncle, who had eventually failed to materialize, I was walking back to the hotel room when, right in front of the Casino, I had a sudden feeling of being looked at by someone at quite close quarters. I glanced round and saw a very tall, rather stout man of about forty, with a jet-black moustache, who stood there nervously flicking a cane against the leg of his trousers and staring at me with eyes dilated by the strain of attention. At times they seemed shot through with intense darting glances of a sort which, when directed towards a total stranger, can only ever be seen from a man whose mind is visited by thoughts that would never occur to anyone else, a madman, say, or a spy. He flashed a final look at me, like the parting shot from one who turns to run, daring, cautious, swift and searching; then, having gazed all about, with a sudden air of idle haughtiness, his whole body made a quick side-turn, and he began a close study of a poster, humming the while and rearranging the moss rose in his buttonhole. (SLT II 332)

From reading this passage it is clear that M. de Charlus' demeanour does not comply with the established norms and conventions regulating the spatial interaction between individuals in public at the time of Proust's writing. The rapid alternation between close fixation and roaming distraction which

Charlus' eye movement performs interfere with what would generally have
been perceived as an appropriate mode of distance regulation between two
individuals who, unknown to each other, are occupying different positions
in a public space. Exposing himself in the role of both hunter and prey,
constantly switching from attack modus into flight modus and back,
Charlus' unusually tactile practice of looking is enhanced by his general
kinaesthetic behaviour. The nervous beating of the cane against the leg of his
trousers in particular appears as a substitutional action for wanting to
approach and touch the object of his attention, as he will later do, repeatedly
and inappropriately, preferably by grabbing the narrator by his chin, or
gently feeling his muscles (RTP II 851 and III 304). Goffman observes that
working relations in public rely on 'civil inattention' as a benign form of
disengagement. (We dead-eye each other on the tube and ignore our
neighbours on the bus.) This serves as a mode of reciprocal protection and
compensates for the discrepancy that arises from the simultaneity of physical
proximity and emotional distance.[28] But if, again with Goffman, the main
point of 'normal' behaviour in public is to *not* do or say anything that
suggests you are insane,[29] then this is precisely what Charlus is struggling to
achieve, the 'singularity of his expression' making him seem in the eyes of
Marcel at times a spy or a thief, at times a fool, a lunatic perhaps, '*un aliéné*'
(II 111–12).[30] By focusing on Charlus' deviating body language, the scene
thus indicates what, together with the narrator, we will only learn as the
novel proceeds, namely that the Baron's unsettled position in space is, at
least partially, linked to his precarious standing as a homosexual aristocrat in
turn-of-the-century France. At the same time, however, the scene is para-
digmatic for a more general question that affects most if not all of the
characters in *La Recherche*. It is one of the guiding questions throughout
this book: how can we approach one another without colliding, and how do
we depart from each other without ending in isolation? A brief look at a well-
known series of scenes in *La Prisonnière*, centring on the motif of Marcel
watching Albertine sleeping, helps to unpack this point further.

At first, the scenes seem to describe the fulfilment of what Charlus so
desperately desired but feared to achieve: the realization of physical and
emotional intimacy between two people. A closer look at the encounter
between Marcel and Albertine reveals, however, that physical proximity does
not always coincide with affective intimacy. Contemplating Albertine's
sleeping body, Marcel observes:

> *Sa figure avait perdu toute expression de ruse ou de vulgarité, et entre elle et
> moi . . . il semblait y avoir un abandon entier, un indissoluble attachement . . .
> Son sommeil n'était qu'une sorte d'effacement du reste de la vie, qu'un silence*

uni sur lequel prenaient de temps à autre leur vol des paroles familières de tendresse. En les rapprochant les unes des autres, on eût composé la conversation sans alliage, l'intimité secrète d'un pur amour. (RTP III 621–2)

Her face had lost any expression of deviousness and vulgarity, and . . . each of us seemed entirely given up to the other, indissolubly joined. . . . Her slumber was a kind of blotting out of the rest of life, a level silence from which familiar words of affection would sometimes take flight. By piecing these words together, one could have composed the perfect conversation, the secret intimacy of pure, unalloyed love. (SLT V 101–2)

In this passage the narrator imagines an encounter between the two lovers who, having shed their social personae, are able to merge on a most intimate level. As the scene unfolds, however, Marcel's desire for immediate contact with Albertine is revealed as illusionary. Carefully separating Marcel's observations from his own expectations, we realize that his conjured ideal of pure love is quick to disintegrate into a series of images marked by estrangement, desired control, and possession. In resonance with Freud's metaphor of the amoeba, a defenceless 'little fragment of living substance which is suspended in the middle of an external world charged with the most powerful entries',[31] Albertine's body undergoes a partial death. Enveloped by a shell of statuesque beauty, Albertine's physical surface turns into a screen onto which the narrator is able to project his personal fantasies of romantic attachment (RTP III, 78–9, 887–8). When later 'embarking' on Albertine's sleep, Marcel's desire to penetrate and possess Albertine's body and mind is further undermined by the movement of her eyeballs and the murmurs during which the name 'Andrée', her suspected lover, escapes her lips (RTP III 621). While Marcel and Albertine's bodies are pressed together, their minds are wide apart. In the same way that Albertine becomes the victim of the narrator's solitary satisfaction, Marcel turns into an imaginary (and female) lover for Albertine. The expectation of immediate physical and emotional contact turns into an experience of affective difference and mental isolation. This failed encounter suggests that the cherished fantasy of pure and unalloyed love can only ever be realized in the form of a simulation.[32] We shall see how Adorno will formulate the seemingly para-doxical idea that it is not intimacy (*Nähe*) but strangeness (*Fremdheit*) that may help us overcome the state of alienation (*Entfremdung*) (M 105/MM 94). It seems to me that in scenes such as the above Proust's novel makes a similar claim. And it is precisely at this point that tact – understood with Gadamer as a way of passing over the object of one's attention, not in the sense of looking away but of keeping the object in sight so as to avoid indecency and collision – comes into play.[33] In Proust's novel, tact is described as a particular form of distance regulation, of accepting difference, and of giving space. The outcome consists in a series of exercises that explore the opportunities, but also the limitations, the benign as well as the potentially harmful and traumatic aspects this notion involves.

Exercises in Tact

A lesser-known passage in *À l'ombre des jeunes filles en fleur* once more addresses the same tension between intimacy and distance we already saw at play in the encounters considered above. This time, the narrator ponders over the complex nature of his relation to Albertine. The scene opens with Marcel's (rather tactless!) effort to sing Albertine's praises in front of Andrée, hoping that the latter might communicate some of his compliments to her friend. Although visibly displeased, Andrée manages not to articulate any of her irritation. This behaviour in turn provokes the narrator, for the first time in the novel, to engage in a detailed contemplation of what he calls '*l'ensemble de ces qualités qui s'appelle le tact*' (these qualities that, taken together, are what is known as tact) (RTP II 277/SLT II 500[34]). He begins by considering the potential differences in character between the object of his desire, Albertine, and Andrée:

> *Andrée avait pourtant bien plus qu'elle [Albertine] l'intelligence des choses du cœur, le raffinement dans la gentillesse; trouver le regard, le mot, l'action qui pouvaient le plus ingénieusement faire plaisir, taire une réflexion qui risquait de peiner, faire le sacrifice (et en ayant l'air que ne fût pas un sacrifice) d'une heure de jeu, voire d'une matinée, d'une garden-party, pour rester auprès d'un ami ou d'une amie triste et lui montrer ainsi qu'elle préférait sa simple société à des plaisirs frivoles, telles étaient ses délicatesses coutumières.* (RTP II 275–6)

> Andrée was vastly more perceptive [than Albertine] in things of the heart, more gifted with considerateness, to be nice to others with a carefully chosen word or a thoughtful glance, to keep to herself a remark which might hurt somebody's feelings, to sacrifice (while making it appear that it was no sacrifice) an hour of possible play-time, even an outing to a matinée or a garden-party, for a friend who was feeling sad, so as to show him or her that she preferred such simple moments to indulging in frivolous pastimes, these were everyday acts of kindness for Andrée. (SLT II 499)

Tact, the narrator suggests, is related to empathy as a person's ability to form an emotional and cognitive awareness of the mental state of another person. But the capacity to acknowledge the existence of a world of perception outside one's own is not sufficient in itself to produce a basis for tact. Empathy, we said in the introduction to this book, creates a connection between individuals.[35] And yet, it is a form of bonding that is not necessarily associated with any specific emotion, such as compassion, or affection. In contradiction to a widespread understanding of the term, empathy is not always a benign sentiment. Empathy may also be motivated by, and used in, the service of hostile or destructive aims. Empathy, we could say, following Heinz Kohut's argument, is neither good nor bad. It is an amoral category.[36] Tact, by contrast, is based on the establishment of a concern for the other person. Tact, Proust's narrator suggests in the passage quoted above, grows out of the fragile negotiation between reason (intelligence) and emotion (*cœur*). Seemingly intuitive, it manifests itself as an art of handling that requires a certain level of refinement. This refinement cannot be reduced to a code of etiquette. And yet, it would not exist without the code it simultaneously confirms and undoes.

Tact, the narrator's observations on Andrée's conduct confirm, is motivated by the effort to protect another individual from any form of discomfort, to put their interests above one's own, and, if necessary, to remain silent about any potential forms of displeasure this may cause oneself. Tact, writes Goffman, is the capacity to avoid causing oneself and others embarrassment.[37] It consists in the joint effort not to destroy the images (the personae) that both the narrator, here in the role of the tactee, and Andrée, in the role of the tactor, have been careful to create for themselves. The goal is to protect their intimate selves and, in order to do so, to not interrupt the smooth transmission and reception by which the 'normal encounter' between the two participants in this face-to-face interaction is sustained.

Tact, the passage also shows, is based on the joint awareness of a discrepancy between reality and fiction. Andrée knows that Marcel knows and vice versa. And yet this must not be openly acknowledged. Tact, Proust's passage confirms, is not so much linked to what one says but to what one does not say.[38] The '*raffinement*' of Andrée's tact does not only consist in the non-verbalization of her own desires; it is complemented by her discretion concerning any other information, the conversations between friends, for example, that may cause harm to the mental and affective state of the narrator. It is a concern that extends to wanting to protect the narrator from the potential consequences of his own indiscretions, and the possible damage they may inflict (on himself): '*bien plus, si c'était moi-même qui le racontais*', the narrator continues to observe, '*elle faisait semblant de ne pas le croire ou en donnait une explication qui rendît le propos inoffensif*' (if I myself told her of some such thing, she would pretend to disbelieve it, or else she explained it away as meaning something quite innocuous) (RTP II 277/SLT II 500). These, the narrator concludes in the aforementioned passage, are the qualities that, taken together, form the concept of tact. They are to be found, he explains, in

> *l'apanage des gens qui, si nous allons sur le terrain, nous félicitent et ajoutent qu'il n'y avait pas lieu de le faire, pour augmenter encore à nos yeux le courage dont nous avons fait preuve, sans y avoir été contraint. Ils sont l'opposé des gens qui dans la même circonstance disent: 'Cela a dû bien vous ennuyer de vous battre, mais d'un autre côté vous ne pouviez pas avaler un tel affront, vous ne pouviez faire autrement.* (RTP II 277)

> the man who compliments you in having fought a duel, then adds that there was no need for you to take up the insult, thereby magnifying in your own eyes the courage you showed without being obliged to. Such a man is the opposite of those people who greet the same event with the words, 'What a bore it must have been to fight a duel! Although of course you couldn't let him get away with such an insult – you really had no choice.' (SLT II 500–1).

Not to be tactful is to comply with the code of honour that still reverberates in the '*bonne société*' of the fin-de siècle.[39] Not to be tactful is to disregard the potential sentiments involved for the individual concerned. To be tactful, in turn, is to shift focus away from existing codes of conduct and to find an individual response suitable within the context of the specific face-to-face interaction between the individuals involved. Tact, Proust's narrator tells us here, is specifically required in situations when we can no longer rely on general rules or widely acknowledged principles (such as, in this case, the outdated concept of honour). It requires a high level of openness towards situational circumstances combined with a flexibility as to the manifold (and potentially unpredictable) ways of response. Tact, to return to Gadamer's aforementioned definition of the concept, helps to establish a benevolent distance between the interlocutors. Drawing on the spatial implications of the terminology, we remember reading in *Truth and Method*, that tact '*vermeidet das Anstößige, das Zunahetreten und die Verletzung der Intimsphäre der Person*' (avoids the offensive, the intrusive, the violation of the intimate sphere of the person).[40]

The choreography of physical and social distantiation evoked by Gadamer's description of tactful behaviour, and the association he establishes between tact, touch, and proxemics, helps to illuminate more carefully the reasons why Andrée seemingly succeeds in what M. de Charlus' awkward manoeuvres in space failed to achieve. During her face-to-face encounter with Marcel, Andrée manages to carefully bypass any information that might cause collision. In contrast to Charlus, she seems to be able to create, and to safeguard, a shared space between herself and her counterpart, Marcel, that allows for individual movement. In this way, she appears to bring about a form of bonding that is not based on the idea of intimacy and intrusion, but that respects the existing boundaries between the two individuals involved. By restoring and maintaining distance, Andrée offers the narrator the opportunity to protect his private sphere, and allows for the possibility for him, as well as for herself, to keep face.

Tact Between Autonomy and Control

But (and there is always a 'but' in Proust), as the narrator's contemplations proceed, the uncertainty created by Andrée's tactful behaviour is experienced by Marcel as increasingly problematic. If tact is a form of role-play that is not so much based on what one says but on what one does not say, then how can we, on the receiving end, endure the uncertainty this entails? How can we, in the role of the tactee, tell whether it is our shared interests and not just their own which the tactor pursues? In other words, where should we draw the line between discretion and insincerity, tact and manipulation? How can we trust a person who exercises tact in the first place?

I suggested above that empathy should be considered an amoral category, while tact is motivated by a benign concern for the other person. As we read on, however, Proust's narrator begins to complicate this assumption. He notes that to openly communicate a potentially distressing piece of information to a flustered individual may indicate indifference, or even Schadenfreude. This also implies an (at least temporary) inability or unwillingness to empathize – whereby empathy is defined as the capacity to enter, and to momentarily inhabit, somebody else's mind; '*Ils ne se mettent guère dans notre peau au moment où ils nous parlent*' (they are deficient in fellow-feeling [lit. they do not quite climb into our skin], at least at the moment when they are speaking to us) (RTP II 277/SLT II 501).[41] To withhold any such information, in turn, may indicate a sense of tact. But, the narrator goes on to inquire, how can we distinguish between tact as a benevolent mode of silence and tact as a finely crafted form of deceit that may be based, he adds, on '*une forte dose de dissimulation*' (RTP II 277)? Hardly noticeable at first, but increasingly visible as the narrator's contemplations on the nature of tact unfold, the emphasis shifts from Andrée's tact as a potentially laudable and virtuous character trait to considering it a wilful strategy that may not only be based on a concern for the mental state of the other person but may also, and perhaps even primarily, be motivated by a pursuit of her own goals. In the case of Andrée these may consist, at this particular point in the novel, in outmanoeuvring

Albertine as the apparent competitor for Marcel's affection. Proust enters the grey zone between tact and tactics here, as his narrator begins to explore, and indeed to question, the boundary between these two concepts which, as we shall see, someone like Plessner will so carefully re-erect.

Tact, I argued earlier, can be interpreted as a sign and symptom of the liberation and empowerment of the modern subject. Inasmuch as tact is seen to reach out to the other person, even, and especially when, this reaching out entails the crossing of social barriers, tact can be said to be a democratic social practice and an equalizing force.[42] Tact, we said, has the capacity to create, or to restore, a power balance between individuals that exists beyond the boundaries of existing hierarchies, norms, and conventions. Tact, if we follow Georg Simmel, is a form of sociability that, by bracketing off both the socially constructed and the most intimate attributes of ourselves, allows for a frictionless co-operation between equals.[43] But tact, Proust reminds us as the dialogue between Marcel and Andrée unfolds, may also be simultaneously seen to create, and conceal, a power gap between the interlocutors involved. Marcel wants to know something that Andrée apparently knows. He appears increasingly anxious and flustered, displaying a state of mind that is, in Goffman's words, 'considered evidence of weakness, inferiority, low status, moral guilt, and other unenviable attributes'. Andrée seemingly wishes to restore 'the smooth transmission and reception by which encounters are sustained'.[44] In assuming the role of the tactor, however, she also wields the power to manipulate her counterpart and to guide him in the direction that might suit her own interests rather than his (at least this is what the narrator suspects). The shift in Proust's character arrangement challenges Simmel's assumption that tact may be distinguished from tactics in that it is not strategic, target-oriented, or egoistic.[45] It also throws into relief a facet of tact the implications of which we have yet to consider. We could call this the twin structure of tactful communication that arises from the potential conflict on the side of the tactor, in our case Andrée, between wanting to allow for autonomy while seeking control.[46]

Tact's Morality

The conflict between freedom and domination unveiled by the tactful encounter between Marcel and Andrée has moral implications. Empathy, we said earlier, is an amoral category. But what about tact? If we follow Marcel's suspicion that Andrée's tact may simulate autonomy while effecting manipulation, does this still allow us to define the principle of tact, as Roland

Barthes later suggests, as a 'form of Sovereign Good'?[47] Proust's narrator addresses this question when proposing to make a distinction between two different types of goodness whereby the first refers to a widely expected feature of the role we play in society and the second means a natural disposition. Considering Andrée's '*délicatesses coutumières*', Marcel observes:

> *quand on la [Andrée] connaissait un peu plus on aurait dit qu'il en était d'elle comme de ces héroïques poltrons qui ne veulent avoir peur, et de qui la bravoure est particulièrement méritoire, on aurait dit qu'au fond de sa nature, il n'y avait rien de cette bonté qu'elle manifestait à tout moment par distinction morale, par sensibilité, par noble volonté de se montrer bonne amie.* (RTP II 276)

> when you came to know her a little better, she put you in mind of one of those people whose poltroonery, through their reluctance to be afraid, can rise to heroism of a particularly meritorious kind: it seemed as though in her heart of hearts there was no trace of the constant kindness which, out of moral nobility, responsiveness to others and a magnanimous desire to appear the devoted friend, so marked her conduct. (SLT II 499)

A tactful person, Proust tells us here, may not necessarily be a good person, while the absence of tact does not necessarily indicate a lack of goodness. On the contrary, goodness is not associated with the person who seems capable of articulating a wide-ranging register of moral noblesse and delicacy (Andrée) but with the person who the narrator, at this point in the novel at least, deems incapable of any such expression (Albertine) (RTP II 276).[48]

The distinction between morality and civility Proust introduces here chimes with a similar distinction made by Kant when addressing the concept of moral appearance (*moralischer Schein*).[49] Thinking about the anthropological theory of didactics, Kant observes that the more civilized a person, the more of an actor they become. '*Die Menschen*', Kant writes, '*sind insgesamt, je zivilisierter, desto mehr Schauspieler: sie nehmen den Schein der Zuneigung, der Achtung vor anderen, der Sittsamkeit, der Uneigennützigkeit an*' (On the whole, the more civilized human beings are, the more they are actors. They adopt the illusion of affection, of respect for others, of modesty, and of unselfishness).[50] Curiously perhaps, within the context of Kant's argument, this mode of role-play is not considered false or deceptive. On the contrary, it is morally sanctioned inasmuch as all persons involved in the face-to-face interaction are aware of and in agreement with the fact that the civility expressed does not correspond to any heartfelt sentiment ('*eben nicht herzlich gemeint sei*').[51] For Kant, this role-playing has a didactic effect: '*Denn dadurch, daß Menschen diese Rolle spielen, werden zuletzt die Tugenden, deren Schein sie eine geraume Zeit hindurch nur gekünstelt haben, nach und nach wohl wirklich erweckt, und gehen in die Gesinnung über*' (For when human beings play these roles, eventually the virtues, whose illusion they have merely affected for a considerable length of time, will gradually really be aroused and merge into the disposition).[52] Although Proust initially seems to agree with Kant's distinction between moral appearance (decorum) and moral being (disposition), the conclusions drawn by the narrator are much less optimistic. According to Kant's model, moral appearance is a civilizing force and the element of deceit it necessarily contains is morally sanctioned by this fact. In Proust's scenario, however, the narrator makes a point of stating that in the case of Andrée, the expression of '*noble volonté*' practically never translates into benevolent action ('*elle ne fit jamais usage*' (RTP II 276)). Although, or perhaps even because, Andrée is capable of expressions of goodness, she is not good-natured. The Kantian idea that civility creates morality does not apply in the particular case made by Proust. The gap between appearance and being cannot be bridged. On the contrary, for the narrator, the (real or assumed) discrepancy between what is being articulated on the surface of the tactful communication and what may be hidden underneath is met with rising levels of anxiety. If a person's intentions are good, the fact that their tactful behaviour may contain a strong element of deceit is not in itself objectionable, he observes. But we cannot assume that there is a categorical correlation between natural goodness and its tactful expression. Or at least, as is the case with Andrée, we can never be '*absolument sûr*' (RTP II 277).

Tact's Paradox

The existential uncertainty which Andrée's tactful '*Spiel mit Verstellungen*' (play with pretences)[53] causes in the mind of the narrator is not only associated with the alleged discrepancy between Andrée's moral decorum and her moral disposition. It is further enhanced by the potential '*Herablassung*' (condescendence)[54] her communication entails, and hence with the power imbalance between the tactor and the tactee we began to explore earlier. In his essay, 'Takt und Zensur im Erziehungssystem' (1996), Niklas Luhmann develops a theory of tact that helps to further unpack this point. Luhmann, like Kant, is interested in the relation between civility and didactics. But, as the title suggests, Luhmann's theory does not explore the impact of civility on morality. Instead, Luhmann is interested in the tension between causality and freedom that characterizes the relationship between teacher and student. At the heart of the pedagogical strategy to tackle this tension, Luhmann argues, lies 'tactful communication'. It is essentially defined as a 'paradoxical communication' inasmuch as it is based on a conflict between freedom (*Freiheit*) and effectiveness (*Wirksamkeit*): '*In der Sache geht es um den Versuch, Einfluß zu nehmen, ohne die freie Selbstbestimmung des anderen offensichtlich in Frage zu stellen*' (The matter in hand is the attempt to influence someone without openly jeopardizing their free self-determination).[55] In Luhmann's arrangement, both the tactor and the tactee are aware of this ambivalence. But, within the context of the communication system in place, this ambivalence must not be addressed or, more specifically, it must not become part of the surface structure of the communication.[56] During the tactful encounter, the tactor '*kommuniziert erkennbar paradox und erzeugt, als Reaktion auf paradoxe Kommunikation, den Verdacht auf nichtmitteilbare Hintergedanken*' (communicates in an openly paradoxical way, thereby causing as a reaction a suspicion of undisclosed background considerations).[57] Such a communication is based on a twin structure inasmuch as it simultaneously communicates two different messages that either contradict one another or are in fact mutually exclusive. Although originating from a different starting position, Luhmann's analysis of the tactful interaction between teacher and student can help explain the dynamic unfolding between Andrée and Marcel. On one level, Andrée's tactful behaviour towards Marcel can be interpreted as benevolent, protective of his flustered state of mind, bypassing potential obstacles, avoiding collision, allowing for space to manoeuvre. At the same time, however, it could be interpreted in less virtuous ways (and this is indeed what Marcel does). It could be understood as strategic, and motivated by egoistic rather than altruistic concerns. However, none of this is openly addressed. For Proust, as for Luhmann, one key effect of the tactful communication is '*eine im System selbst erzeugte Ungewißheit*' (an uncertainty caused within the system itself).[58] This built-in uncertainty is not always without problems. Within the context of Luhmann's teacher-student relation, exams and grades, as formally unambiguous (and therefore neither tactful nor tactless) communications, can help reduce the scope of tactful communication and ease its detrimental effects.[59] But while, according to Luhmann, they are a vital component of education in that they stabilize the relation between teacher and student, such precise points of orientation, he observes, are absent from the sphere of private relations. Tact, Luhmann concludes, is a form of '*wohlmeinend-hinterhältige[r] Kommunikation*' (well-meaning and yet perfidious communication).[60] Its effects can go both ways:

> *Sie kann als taktvoll, sozial sensitiv, schonend, pädagogisch überlegt und hilfreich gelobt werden. In der Wirklichkeit hat sie jedoch unvorhersehbare Folgen. Im Familienleben oder in sonstigen Intimbeziehungen befürchtet man 'double-bind' und pathologische Entwicklungen.*

It can be praised as tactful, socially sensitive, gentle, pedagogically consider-
ate and helpful. But in reality it can have unforeseen consequences. In family
life and other forms of intimate relations one fears a 'double-bind' and
pathological developments.[61]

Within the context of the tactful encounters both Proust and Luhmann are
interested in, the absence of any reliable *'points de repère'* is a problem
inherent in the communication system that, in the case of Proust's narrator, leads to a state of existential uncertainty, giving rise to the anxiety and
jealousy that drives much of the writing in *La Prisonnière* and *Albertine
disparue*. Just like the interlocutors involved in Luhmann's tactful communication, Proust's characters operate *'im Horizonte* selbsterzeugter
Ungewißheit' (in the horizon of a self-generated uncertainty). This may
have positive or negative, creative or destructive repercussions, or none at
all.[62] In the case of Marcel and Andrée, at least, we can observe that
Marcel's interrogations of Andrée intensify over the years and reach their
climax after the death of Albertine. And yet the uncertainty remains. The
following passage, taken from *Le Temps retrouvé*, brings this into relief once
more. Resuming the contemplations which he began in volume II on the
relation between moral decorum and moral disposition in the case of
Andrée's character, the narrator observes:

> *Car elle [Andrée] n'était pas foncièrement mauvaise, et si sa nature non
> apparente, un peu profonde, n'était pas la gentillesse qu'on croyait d'abord
> d'après ses délicates attentions, mais plutôt l'envie et l'orgueil, sa troisième
> nature, plus profonde encore, la vraie, mais pas entièrement réalisée, tendait
> vers la bonté et l'amour du prochain.* (RTP IV 183)

> For she was not basically wicked, and if, below the surface, her slightly
> deeper, rather surprising nature did not confirm the kindness that her first
> delicate attentions had led people to suppose but rather envy and pride, yet,
> at an even deeper level, her third degree, that is, her true nature, even if never
> quite fully realized, tended towards goodness and love of her neighbour.
> (SLT V 568)

One should not rush into thinking that the narrator's (rather late!) discovery of a 'third nature' in the unfathomable depths of Andrée's character
might serve the purpose of mitigating the pessimist anthropology Proust's
writing generally exerts. Instead, I would read the conclusions he draws as
the product of the narrator's ongoing search for the right meaning.[63]
A futile attempt, as we shall learn. For in the case of Andrée, as in the
case of Albertine, any message discerned from her communication will
only ever be one of the *'mille versions'* (RTP III 840) possible. To Marcel,

Andrée's tactful communication remains, to paraphrase Luhmann, unambiguously ambiguous.[64] For Luhmann as for Proust, nothing can help resolve the paradoxical nature of tact.

Conclusion

This brings us back to a question raised earlier in relation to Proust's *Soixante-quinze feuillets*: How does one say something in an appropriate manner, and how does one then, in turn, interpret the potential enigma that, as in the case of the grandmother's illegible letters mentioned in the *Feuillets*, or indeed Andrée's unambiguously ambiguous communication described in *La Recherche*, may be all that remains of a message when delivered with tact? How can we regulate the distance that constitutes any reading encounter, be it with other people, with texts, or indeed, as on the occasion below, with a great work of art? In the introduction to his translation of John Ruskin's *Bible of Amiens* (1904) Proust makes a few observations that I believe are crucial within this context. Considering Ruskin's recommendations as to how one should act when approaching the Cathedral of Amiens, Proust quotes the following passage:

> *Mais vous devez être impatients d'entrer dans la cathédrale. Mettez d'abord un sou dans la boîte de chacun des mendiants qui se tiennent là. Ce n'est pas votre affaire de savoir s'ils devraient ou non être là ou s'ils méritent d'avoir le sou. Sachez seulement si vous-mêmes méritez d'en avoir un à donner et donnez-le joliment et non comme s'il vous brûlait les doigts.*

> But you will be impatient to go into the church. Put a sou in every beggar's box who asks it there – it is none of your business whether they should be there or not, nor whether they deserve to have the sou – be sure only that you yourself deserve to have it to give; and give it prettily, and not as if it burnt your fingers.[65]

Ruskin's advice prepares us for the idea that an encounter with a work of art should not be considered one of pure critical analysis distinct from everyday life. When setting out to appreciate the singularity of an artwork, in this case the south portal of the Cathedral of Amiens, we engage in an ethical relation with others, with ourselves, and with the object of our attention. The aesthetic encounter we are about to experience is described as a mode of action that involves us as individuals, and as morally and ethically responsible beings. For works of art, Ruskin tells us here, are to be approached like human personalities. Regardless of their social and cultural origin or historical ranking, they have what Peter Szondi calls in adaptation of a formulation by Paul Valéry, a monarchical character.[66] They want to be treated with respect, and with tact.[67]

It was with Ruskin's itinerary in hand that Proust visited Amiens. He recalls how, the moment he caught sight of the cathedral's south portal, he saw the beggars Ruskin had written about. Following the instructions, Proust gives them alms. '*Puis*', he writes, '*étant trop près du portail pour en voir l'ensemble, je revins sur mes pas, et arrivé à la distance qui me parut convenable, alors seulement je regardai*' (Then, being too close to the portal to see its general effect, I retraced my steps, and having arrived at the distance I thought proper, only then did I look).[68] The aesthetic experience Proust then goes on to describe does not resemble a rational act of decipherment but a form of ethical and aesthetic conduct that involves both his body and mind. It is a slow and delicate movement in space that exists to establish the appropriate distance between the onlooker and the object of his attention. Observing how the sun 'visits' the saints framing the portal, Proust notices how its beams give '*aux épaules de celui-ci un manteau de chaleur, au front de celui-là une auréole de lumière*' (to the shoulders of one a mantle of warmth, to the face of another a halo of light). Eventually settling on the Virgin herself, he notes that '*c'était à sa caresse momentanée qu'elle semblait adresser son sourire séculaire*' (it was to its momentary caress that she seemed to direct her centuries-old smile).[69] Under the observer's attentive gaze the work of art comes to life, and looks back. Within this context, seeing takes on a haptic quality. Mediated by the beams of the sun, Proust looks at the saints *as if* he was to touch them. Thus, the act of looking appears as a mode of feeling, albeit a feeling at a distance, an imaginary touch that, like Herder's tact, does not take place in the physical and affective proximity of but at a distance from the object of one's attention.[70] The appreciation of beauty, Proust tells us here, arises from a particular tension between nearness and distance. It is based on a special form of distance regulation whereby we try not to come too close to the object of our attention nor drift too far away from it. Instead of identifying with another person, an artwork, a text, grasping it, incorporating it, reading it against the grain, operating on it, digging into it or tearing it apart to expose its hidden meanings, causes and conditions, we stand back in respect of its otherness, attentive towards its singularity, giving space to allow for meaning to evolve.[71] This is not always easy. It requires a sense of balance that cannot always be achieved. We saw this in Marcel's tactful encounter with Andrée in *La Recherche*. We see it again in the final paragraph of the *Soixante-quinze feuillets*. Once more Proust describes a visit to a church. And again, he has a guide by Ruskin under his arm. This time, however, it is not the Cathedral of Amiens he is about to approach but the Basilica of San Marco in Venice. And whereas the encounter with the former was marked by a sense of mutual respect and recognition, the latter appears to trigger an ethical and aesthetic shock that culminates in a strong sense of estrangement:

> *j'arrive à Saint-Marc qui me paraît aussi différent d'une église que Venise d'une ville. La personnalité de l'église constituée, délimitée, saisissable en hauteur est étendue en largeur, s'élevant très peu au-dessus du sol, et le Dieu que nous savons notre//Dieu mais qui apparaît presque comme un bouffon pacha d'Orient est si peu élevé au-dessus de nous qu'il nous faut faire refluer les vagues de marbre qui viennent s'écrêter de chaque côté de lui et suivre ailleurs la personnalité de l'édifice. . . . Et dans l'église quand tout au fond nous apercevrons Notre Seigneur l'air efféminé, oriental et bizarre, son geste transformé en une prétention de gras syriote suspect, nous sentirons combien les signes des mêmes dispositions morales changent et combien nous aurions de la peine à reconnaître chez des êtres de race autre les équivalents des choses que nous appelons distinction, bonté, courage, simplicité, finesse, tact, noblesse et qui ont dans ceux de notre sang leurs signes quelquefois imités, quelquefois trompeurs mais esthétiquement certains.* (F 108–9).

I arrive at San Marco, which seems to me as different from a church as Venice is from a city. The personality of the church, delimited and comprehensible in height, is extended in width, rising very little above the ground, and the God we know is our // God but who virtually appears as a buffoonish, Oriental pasha, is so low above us, that we must push back the waves of marble breaking on either side of him, and follow the personality of the building . . . And in the church, at the very back, we see Our Lord looking effeminate, Oriental, and bizarre, his gesture transformed into the pretension of a fat, suspicious Syriot, and we feel how the signs of the same moral dispositions change, and how much we would have difficulty in recognizing in beings of another race the equivalents of those things we call distinction, goodness, courage, simplicity, finesse, tact, nobility, which have in those of our blood their own signs, sometimes imitated, sometimes deceptive, but aesthetically certain.

The description of the portrait of Christ as an Oriental, bizarre, and effeminate fool appears to reflect a fundamental incapacity to comprehend the Byzantine splendour of the Basilica. Its chauvinist and nationalist tone seem to contribute to a form of judgement that contrasts dramatically with that which Ruskin recommends.[72] But the ambivalence of the lines that follow makes it difficult to decide whether the passage is as depreciative and exclusive as it first seems, or if it pleads for the recognition of a shared sense of virtue underneath the seemingly alienating surface. Taking into account that Proust declared elsewhere that he did not belong to those who thought San Marco '*une monstrosité babare*', we might consider a more benevolent reading and suggest that Proust's apparent lack of understanding for an aesthetic that is so different from the cathedrals of Northern Europe, triggers a reflection about judging different people and cultures on the basis of familiar ethical and aesthetic canons.[73] It contemplates the limitations of a definition of tact as a social virtue exclusive to those who belong to certain socially and culturally homogenous groups and circles in power. It hints at the paradoxical structure of tact as a mode of ethical and aesthetic judgement that works as a classifier while also helping to undo the classifications it tends to impose. Tact, I have tried to show in this chapter, can go both ways. It can suggest tolerance and individual freedom while also exerting effectiveness and domination. It can convey harmony while also causing uncertainty, anxiety, and distress. And it can be interpreted as a sign of identification and exclusion, while also promoting an appreciation for singularity and difference. The next chapter, focusing on the two theories of tact proposed by the antagonistic pair of Helmuth Plessner and Theodor Adorno, will further help to explore the ethical and political implications this entails.

CHAPTER 3

Alienation (Plessner – Adorno)

Die Entfremdung erweist sich an den Menschen gerade daran, daß die Distanzen fortfallen.

Alienation shows itself precisely in the elimination of distance between people.

Theodor Adorno, 1951[1]

Takt ist der ewig wache Respekt vor der anderen Seele und damit die erste und letzte Tugend des menschlichen Herzens.

Tact is the eternally alert respect before the other soul; that is why it is the first and the last virtue of the human heart.

Helmuth Plessner, 1924[2]

Helmuth Plessner (1892–1985) and Theodor Adorno (1903–69) may seem like an odd pair of thinkers to turn to when looking for a theory of tact. Both scholars returned from exile to Germany in 1949. Adorno came back from the United States where he had held several academic positions and spent some of the most intellectually productive years of his career.[3] Plessner returned from the Netherlands where he had taught at the University of Groningen, narrowly escaped the arrest by the Gestapo, and survived the years between 1943 and 1945 in hiding. Plessner and Adorno knew each other well and became temporary colleagues at the University in Frankfurt am Main. But they were also rivals who essentially stood for two competing and mutually exclusive schools of thought: the philosophical anthropology of modernity (Plessner) and the critical theory of society (Adorno).[4] This did not prevent Plessner from actively engaging with Adorno's work, while references to Plessner are notoriously absent from Adorno's writing.[5] And yet, the two texts that serve as the main material for this chapter – Plessner's uncompromising and occasionally aggressive essay *Grenzen der Gemeinschaft: Eine Kritik des sozialen Radikalismus* of 1924, and Adorno's highly stylized, contrapuntal (yet often equally aggressive) fragments of *Minima Moralia:*

63

Reflexionen aus dem beschädigten Leben, published in 1951 – make for
a surprisingly revealing combination. Plessner composed his book in 1923,
the year of the communist uprising in Hamburg (organized by factions of the
German Communist Party and modelled on the October Revolution in
Russia), and the failed National Socialist putsch in Munich led by Hitler and
Ludendorff. Plessner's text is a direct response to the politically and socially
unstable situation in the Weimar Republic, and a passionate warning against
the rise of social and political radicalism on either side of the political
spectrum.[6] Adorno wrote most of the *Minima Moralia* in the 1940s in
exile in the United States, contemplating the effects of fascism on German
society and exploring how the smallest occurrences in everyday life may
reflect the most catastrophic crimes in human history. Although the two texts
were written at different historical turning points of the twentieth century,
they both respond to times of immense social and political upheaval,
including growing radicalization of large parts of the German population
and, in the case of Adorno, ruling Nazism and war.

Situating both texts within their wider intellectual context, in this chapter
I plan to reconstruct how and why Plessner and Adorno started out from
conflicting theoretical assumptions, but came to draw surprisingly similar
conclusions. Both scholars fundamentally disagree on a series of key concepts
that shape their theories of tact. And yet, despite these differences, they share
a suspicion of certain forms of intimacy and touch, and a preference for
individual difference over communal identification. By offering
a comparative analysis of their writing, I hope to show that Plessner's and
Adorno's theories of tact contribute to an ethic of indirectness that allows us
to depart from conventional ideas of proximity and distance, and to develop
alternative and non-violent modes of interpretation.

Like so many well-known academics of their time, Adorno and Plessner
came from similar social and cultural backgrounds. Both were born into
affluent upper-middle class families of partly Jewish decent. Plessner's
father, Fedor Plessner, was the director of a private sanatorium for internal
and nervous diseases in Wiesbaden. Adorno's father, Oscar Alexander
Wiesengrund, was a wine merchant. And while the young Adorno thrived
in the sensual sphere of music created by his 'two mothers', Maria Calvelli-
Adorno della Piana, a former singer, and her sister Agathe, a pianist,
Plessner spent much of his childhood in the secluded world of the fin-de-
siècle sanatorium, eating at the table over which his father presided and
watching the patients, strangers to their neighbours, engage in polite
conversation.[7] Plessner's life-long fascination with salon culture that
informs his *Grenzschrift* may have its biographical roots here, as did his

first choice of academic subject, medicine, a discipline he chose against the advice of this father (who knew the theoretical mind of his son), and which he soon replaced with zoology and then philosophy. Like Adorno, who began to read philosophy at the age of seventeen only to complete his degree six terms later with the top mark for his dissertation on Husserl's phenomenology, Plessner had an outstanding academic career in very difficult times. But in contrast to Adorno who, although a life-long outsider to most disciplines, was quick to rise to the position of West Germany's 'exemplary intellectual',[8] the position Plessner inhabited for much of his life in relation to German academic discourse was, as he himself repeatedly emphasized, a marginal one.[9] Taking stock of his life's achievements in 1975, Plessner suspected the open character of his work to be the reason he had never quite managed to form 'a school'. But then, this might have been a good thing. For '*Schulen*', he went on to observe, '*verführen ... zur Fixierung auf Lehrmeinungen und Ideologien, um nicht zu sagen: Heilslehren. Und davon hatten wir schon genug*' (Schools lead to a fixation on scientific doctrines, not to mention redemption narratives. And of these we have surely had enough).[10] Indeed, Plessner's *Grenzschrift* addresses this very issue: what happens, the text also asks, when theoretical concepts congeal into eidetic units which, unquestioned, become ideological tools?

With *Grenzen der Gemeinschaft*, Plessner turns his mind, for the first time in his intellectual career, to socio-ethical questions. The essay is, like Adorno's *Minima Moralia*, a generic hybrid that oscillates between general philosophical inquiry, socio-ethical analysis, and literary-essayistic polemic. Plessner thus hoped to liberate himself from the '*Umständlichkeit und Konstruktion*' (intricateness and construction) that he believed to have contributed to the lack of attention his earlier work had received.[11] ('Plessner', Edmund Husserl reportedly proclaimed to the young man upon reading his doctoral dissertation, 'you forgot about the audience!')[12] Like Adorno, who sought to revitalize the long-lost tradition of philosophical thought dedicated to the 'teaching of the good life' (M 21/MM 15), Plessner conceptualized his argument '*vom Leben her*' (from life') (G 11/L 41). And just like his younger colleague, Plessner also addressed an audience that should ideally combine an academic with a more general readership. But while *Minima Moralia* sold more than 120,000 copies and was dubbed '*das letzte deutsche Volksbuch der Philosophie*' (the last German chapbook of philosophy),[13] the immediate impact of Plessner's *Grenzschrift* was, once again, limited. Although the book received a number of high-profile reviews,[14] it soon went out of print. Its wider academic reception was only triggered half a century later when the text came out in a reprinted edition in honour of the author's eightieth birthday in

1972.[15] The occasion prompted Plessner to observe that the topicality of his 'little book' had not only been ongoing since its first publication in 1924; drawing a direct line between the crisis that marked the Weimar Republic and West German society in the aftermath of 1968, it seemed to him that the critique of community he had offered back then was by no means outdated. It was, on the contrary, particularly acute.[16] In what follows, I shall consider this observation when reading Plessner's *Limits of Community* in close alignment with Adorno's *Minima Moralia*, reconstructing their respective contributions to the history and theory of tact.

Adorno's Tact

'Tact', Adorno observes in *Minima Moralia*, has its precise 'historical hour':

> *Es ist die, in welcher das bürgerliche Individuum des absolutistischen Zwangs ledig ward. Frei und einsam steht es für sich selber ein, während die vom Absolutismus entwickelten Formen hierarchischer Achtung und Rücksicht, ihres ökonomischen Grundes und ihrer bedrohlichen Gewalt entäußert, gerade noch gegenwärtig genug sind, um das Zusammenleben innerhalb bevorzugter Gruppen erträglich zu machen.* (M 39)

> [This] was the hour when the bourgeois individual rid himself of absolutist compulsion. Free and solitary he answers for himself, while the forms of hierarchical respect and consideration developed by Absolutism, divested of their economic basis and their menacing power, are still just sufficiently present to make living together within privileged groups bearable. (MM 36)

Unlike Norbert Elias, whose theory of the civilizing process focused on the phenomenon of politeness when thinking about the transformation of aristocratic courtliness (*Höfischkeit*) into courtesy (*Höflichkeit*) between the middle ages and the early modern period,[17] and in contradistinction to Foucault who, as we saw earlier, associates modern forms of tact and discretion with control over enunciation and the policing of statements,[18] Adorno locates the rising importance of tact in the Enlightenment and links it to the birth of the bourgeois subject. Moreover, he develops his theory of tact on the basis of what Roland Barthes would later refer to as 'novelistic simulations' of human interaction. One of his prime sources is *Wilhelm Meisters Wanderjahre*, the third and last volume of Goethe's genre-defining Bildungsroman cycle (1807–29). For Adorno, Goethe's novel thematizes the effects of unprecedented urbanization, industrialization, and population growth on human relations. It reveals how tact becomes important in times of rapid change, when established social hierarchies are collapsing, and norms and conventions disintegrating. Within this context tact serves as a means to buffer the effects of what Adorno perceives as the growing alienation between people. It results from what he calls a renunciation of original contact (as undiminished intimacy), of passion, and of unalloyed happiness (M 38/MM 35–36).

Adorno's argument is based on the hypothetical assumption of a polar tension between an alleged immediate human existence on the one hand, and alienation and objectification on the other. At first glance, this tension seems to indicate a mode of reasoning that ties in with Jean-Jacques Rousseau's theory of alienation based on a distinction between the so-called natural state of human beings and their social existence.[19] According to Rousseau, self-alienation is diagnosed whenever there is a discrepancy, or a contradiction, between natural being and historical existence: '*le sauvage*', we read in the *Discours sur l'origine et les fondements de l'inégalité parmi les hommes*, '*vit en lui-même; l'homme sociable, toujours hors de lui ne sait vivre que dans l'opinion des autres*' (the savage lives within himself; the sociable man, always outside of himself, knows how to live only in the opinion of others).[20] Building on this idea, the evolution of human social existence can be described, alternatively, as a continuous history of decay, or in view of a potential overcoming of alienation.[21] Within this context, the idea of self-sufficiency – more specifically, the ideal of authenticity as an untroubled correspondence with one's own 'self' and one's own 'nature' as epitomized in the '*être-en-soi*' of 'natural man' – can, paradoxically, signify a lost form of one's natural state *as well as* its future restoration.[22] But Adorno's apparent nod at Rousseau's notion of the 'original state of nature' in *Minima Moralia* is deceptive. A look at Rousseau's and Adorno's quite different uses of the term 'humaneness' not only serves to highlight the differences between the two thinkers at this point, it also helps to clarify the logic inherent to Adorno's mode of argumentation.

According to Rousseau, '*humanité*' results from the relational feeling of compassion or, as he later specifies, pity (*pitié*). For Rousseau, pity, like compassion, is a pre-reflective affect or drive. Like David Hume and Adam Smith before him, Rousseau defines pity as a natural quality which he associates with the concept of 'natural man'. Its basic function is to limit self-love. Pity is described as an immediate, spontaneous affect that is 'native to the human heart'. But, Rousseau later specifies, pity would remain eternally dormant unless it is activated by the act of imagination. Rejecting the commonly made distinction between emotion and reason, Rousseau explains that next to pity, as a pre-reflective mode of affection, there must be a second form of pity that is both reflective and imaginative.

This second form is based on the temporary dissolution of the emotional and physical boundaries between the compassionate self and the suffering other. It allows the self to merge temporarily with, and to inhabit, the object of one's compassionate affection: '*Comment nous laissons-nous émouvoir à la pitié? En nous transportant hors de nous-mêmes; en nous identifiant avec l'être souffrant*' (How do we let ourselves be moved to pity? By transporting ourselves outside of ourselves; by identifying ourselves with the suffering being).[23]

In Adorno's reading of Goethe's *Meister* novels, by contrast, '*Humanität*' is linked to neither compassion nor pity as a figure of intimacy and identification. Instead, it is associated with tact as a figure of distance and separation. In Adorno's interpretation, tact is presented as the saving reference (*rettende Auskunft*) between alienated human beings. In fact, in Goethe's work, tact and humanity, Adorno argues, are the same thing.[24] This does not mean that the humane dimension of tact consists in the idea of an overcoming of the boundary between the self and the other. It consists, on the contrary, in the conscious renunciation of the very idea of undiminished intimacy in the first place. The deliberate self-restriction that results does not resist but embraces what Adorno describes as the ineluctable course of history and the inhumanity of progress. It goes hand in hand with the 'withering of the subject' (*Verkümmerung des Subjekts*), its dissolution, and disappearance (M 14–15, 38/MM 16, 36). This means that although Adorno's argument originates, like that of Rousseau, in the assumption of a bipolar conflict between human nature and alienation, in contradistinction to Rousseau, salvation for Adorno cannot be achieved through the attempt to restore an original immediacy of human relations. For Adorno, such an attempt could only ever result in simulation. The key to the problem is to be found not in the restoration of intimacy and identification but in the cultivation of distance and dissociation. '*Nur Fremdheit*', writes Adorno in *Minima Moralia*, '*ist das Gegengift gegen Entfremdung*' (retention of strangeness is the only antidote to estrangement) (M 105/MM 94).

This seemingly paradoxical idea is further unpacked in Adorno's ensuing discussion of Henrik Ibsen's bourgeois drama *Hedda Gabler* (1891). Here, Adorno discusses the relation between two prominent bourgeois virtues which we already saw addressed (at least partially) by Proust: '*das Gute*' (goodness) and '*die Güte*' (benevolence). Benevolence, Adorno argues, is a deformation of goodness inasmuch as it separates the moral principle from the social principle, displacing the former into the realm of private conscience. Benevolence, he states, aims at the alleviation of social injustice but not at its overcoming. This is its limitation. Benevolence simulates the possibility of direct relations between individuals. Its 'guilt', Adorno writes, is intimacy and, indeed, touch. For '*Güte*', he explains,

> *überspringt die Distanz, in der allein der Einzelne vor dem Angetastetwerden durchs Allgemeine sich zu schützen vermag. Gerade im engsten Kontakt erfährt er die unaufgehobene Differenz am schmerzlichsten.* (M 105)

> [Benevolence] overrides the distance that is the individual's only protection against the infringements by the universal. It is precisely in the closest contact that he feels the unabolished difference most painfully. (MM 94)

Accordingly, for Adorno, one of the key problems of modern human existence is not the growing extension of distance between individuals but the elimination thereof, not the loss of intimacy but the expansion of intimacy in its perverted form. Adorno's argument hinges on the idea of touchability here, and its potentially negative repercussions. In his formulation, tact is being removed from its semantic connection with 'touch' and 'contact' ('*Antasten*' means 'to touch', but also: 'to infringe', 'to violate'; as in article 1 of the German *Grundgesetz* (1949): '*Die Würde des Menschen ist unantastbar*' (Human dignity is inviolable)). Tact appears as the reverse of touch. Or better, in a variation of Derrida's formulation referred to in the Introduction to this book, tact becomes a form of contact without touch.

For Adorno, tact does not simply mean 'the subordination to ceremonial convention'. In contrast to politeness, which follows an established code, tact determines difference. Although tact relates to convention and is shaped by formation, it is essentially based on '*wissenden Abweichungen*' (conscious deviations) from normative modes of behaviour (M 40/MM 37). This definition enables Adorno to discuss tact as a category to be employed both in ethical and in aesthetic terms. Pushing the boundaries of Kant's aesthetic of genius, according to which all fine art is the product of a negotiation between the originality of the genius and the more mechanical aspects of general principles and rules,[25] Adorno observes that the works of figures such as Goethe, Beethoven, and indeed Kant himself appear to him as eminently '*taktvoll*' inasmuch as they creatively perform what Adorno describes as the simultaneity of social convention and individual variation (M 39/MM 36). Tact, Adorno later explains in one of his 'Little Proust Commentaries' of 1958, emerges from a difference to the '*Konfektion des Gedankens, das vorgegebene und etablierte Cliché*' (ready-made thought, to the pre-given and established cliché).[26] Tact grows out of one's own personal strength to withstand the general flow of what everybody else says, does, or believes in. Tact implies that we are capable at times of standing alone: alone with ourselves and with others.

Adorno's association of human sociability with intellectual and artistic innovation follows the same antagonistic logic from which we already saw Kant's own conception of genius arise. This is the paradoxical dynamic that drives Kant's paradigm of 'unsociable sociability' (*ungesellige Geselligkeit*).[27] At the heart of human development, Kant explains in his 'Idea for a Universal History with a Cosmopolitan Purpose' (1784), lies the individual's desire to integrate with society combined with a constant thirst for isolation. This antagonistic dynamic is one of the key drivers that spur human social and cultural development. Kant uses the term '*Widerstand*' (resistance) here to qualify this human tendency for disintegration. It emerges from the paradoxical struggle of wanting to participate in collective culture while at the same time seeking to renounce it. Adorno makes a similar point when arguing that intellectual productivity presupposes the individual's involvement in collective culture precisely because it is this involvement that provides the individual with the strength to dismiss it (M 30–31/MM 29). And yet, there is a crucial difference. While the Kantian paradox follows a progressive narrative marked by belief in the human capacity for perfection,[28] Adorno's antagonism takes a negative turn. In fact, in a critical shift in his argument, Adorno describes reconciliation between the unconfirmed demands of convention and the unruly claims of the individual, which the exercise of tact demands, as actually impossible (M 39/MM 36).

Adorno is pessimistic when it comes to answering the question of how tact can become normative without undermining its own subjectivity. At first the decay of ceremonial convention in modernity appears to benefit tact, inasmuch as it opens up greater space for the subject's autonomous action. However, if tact, as an individual mode of deviation, emancipates itself from social convention to confront the individual as an absolute, without any general rule or principle in place from which this tact can still be distinguished, tact helps to produce the sense of domination it initially sought to subvert and, as a result, humaneness turns into repression (M 40–41). A brief look at Adorno's essay on the 'Classicism of Goethe's Iphigenie', delivered as a public lecture at the Freie Universität Berlin in 1967, helps to unpack this point.

In his polarizing interpretation of Goethe's drama (1779/1786) Adorno argues that what makes Iphigenie's humanity so infamously 'devilish' is the fact that it grows out of the experience of an antinomy. The dramatic plot of the play, Adorno observes, thematizes the precarious relation between the absolutist social order and the rebellious bourgeois subject, portrayed in the case of the female protagonist as a conflict between individual self-determination and mythical immaturity. But Iphigenie's rebellion, Adorno contends, is flawed. 'Boastful' (*auftrump-fend*) in its nature, it bears the traces of a seemingly liberated mind that must declare itself precisely because the humanity it proclaims is not entirely substantiated.[29] As the plot unfolds, Adorno detects a dynamic that threatens to turn Iphigenie's humanity into domination, and civilization back into the mythical context of guilt it initially sought to overcome. Indeed, Adorno observes, Iphigenie's humanity could only ever become truly humane if it ceased to insist on its right of privilege. Adorno's reading of the play's grand finale illustrates this. Despite its conciliatory tone, the agreement reached between Iphigenie and Thoas – namely for the Barbarian king to renounce all his demands and let Iphigenie and her fellow visitors return to their homeland, Greece – is unilaterally enforced upon him. And it is precisely the tactful nature of Iphigenie's speech, Adorno argues, that helps to conceal what is actually taking place. The words exchanged between Iphigenie and Thoas suggest friendship and hospitality while in reality Thoas, whose conduct has been much nobler than that of the Greeks, stays behind in isolation. Adorno concludes that, although Thoas acts as humanity's subject, he remains its object.[30] The alleged reconciliation on which Iphigenie's tact insists is, in truth, a flawed settlement:

> *Sie wird zur Leistung des Takts. Durch den Schein von Natürlichkeit verbirgt er die regieführende, sinngebende Hand; durch behutsames Polieren schleift er die Ungebärdigkeit der nicht länger eingefaßten Details ab.*

> It becomes something achieved by the means of tact. Through the semblance of naturalness, it conceals the hand that does the staging, the hand that gives meaning; through careful polishing it smooths off the unruliness of the now outlying details.[31]

In Adorno's reading of the tactful encounter between Iphigenie and Thoas, the paradoxical dynamic of tact articulates the painful dialectic that Adorno assigns to the civilizing process at large. Iphigenie's tact promotes the latent inhumanity of bourgeois culture that it initially helped to conceal, and serves to unfold its coercive potential. Simulating individual freedom while effecting control, Iphigenie's tact contributes to the decay of the humaneness that, in Adorno's earlier reading of Goethe's *Meister* at least, it originally helped to protect. Tact remains haunted by that which it seeks to overcome.[32]

Addressing this paradoxical dynamic, Adorno's chapter on the dialectic of tact in *Minima Moralia* concludes with a contemplation of what happens at a time when tact – even in the distorted version at work in the encounter between Iphigenie and Thoas – disappears. Adorno argues that the renunciation of convention as an outdated ornament leads to a life of direct domination. What remains is the triumph of intimacy over distance, and of directness over digression. Any form of individual agency, or difference, any intellectual activity, essentially understood as a form of resistance, becomes impossible. Tact and humanity give birth to what they initially set out to prevent. The modern subject, once seemingly enlightened and free, is crushed in what Adorno calls, in reference to Nazi Germany, a travesty of freedom that manifests itself in the potentially murderous culture of 'rib-digging camaraderie' ('*Kameraderie der Anrempelei*') (M 40/MM 37).

Plessner's 'Culture of Impersonality'

Just like Adorno with his *Minima Moralia*, Plessner, too, responded in *Grenzen der Gemeinschaft* to a specific historical moment in time. And yet, like his younger colleague, Plessner developed a line of argument that he maintained, in variations, throughout his entire academic career. With his essay, Plessner intervened in a debate that defined 'society' (*Gesellschaft*) and 'community' (*Gemeinschaft*) as dichotomous sociological terms, and challenged the preference for the term community over society that prevailed in German academic and public discourse at the time. Plessner criticized politicized definitions of community as an original and natural state of identification that might offer protection from society, portrayed as a harsh and cold sphere marked by distraction, separation, and alienation, '*eine Zone', in short, 'in der [man] sich fremd wird*'.[33] This does not mean that *Grenzen der Gemeinschaft* was directed against all notions of community. Instead, the essay set out to limit widespread expectations that, based on the belief in the possibility of direct relations between individuals, promote idealized ideological conceptions of community as a space within which alienation would dissolve.[34] In fact, in his essay, Plessner attacked the '*bald international, bald völkisch getönte Verklärung der Schrankenlosigkeit im Miteinander*' (idealization of seamless togetherness, tainted by both internationalist and ethnic-nationalist (*völkisch*) colours)[35] that he saw as dominant in the intellectual and public debate of the 1920s. Responding to the rising levels of social and political radicalization that characterized German society at the time, Plessner's argument anticipated Adorno's later concerns about a community marked by 'rib-digging camaraderie', and defended an idea of society – defined as an open communication system between unconnected people (G 95) – that could offer a space in which distance affords every human being their own dignity.[36]

Plessner shares with Adorno a concern about the decay of ceremonial convention since the Enlightenment. In contrast to Adorno, however, Plessner does not assess the emancipation of the subject that coincides with it in particularly positive terms. While Adorno associates the emergence of tact as a specific form of sociability with the rise of the bourgeois subject in the aftermath of the French Revolution, Plessner goes further back in time to find his model for orientation in the aristocratic salon culture of the seventeenth and eighteenth centuries. The code of conduct Plessner recommends combines aspects of Gracián's courtly code of conduct (1647) with Nietzsche's 'pathos of distance' (1887) and the Moralist ideal of the *'honnête homme'*, portrayed by La Rochefoucauld in his *Maximes* (1665) as a master of communication who derives his talents from character traits that combine fortitude and courage with an infallibility of judgement, taste, and tact.[37] Even more rigorously than Adorno, Plessner emphasizes the ongoing need for a code of conduct. It appears to him as a necessary framework to counterbalance, and contain, the rise in significance of the concept of 'personality' that coincided with the decline of the *ancien régime*, and the potential overvaluation, as Plessner sees it, of personal freedom and originality that came with it (G 86–87).[38] The liberation of the individual from social and cultural constraints, Plessner argues, created a need to establish new means of protection, to shelter the intimate self from public exposure, and to maintain its 'hygiene' and health by protecting it from violation and humiliation. In contradistinction to Adorno, the allegiances Plessner expresses here are anti-bourgeois and aristocratic. Plessner's defence of the value of ceremonial codes predating the age of bourgeois revolutions, fuelled by his fervent critique of rationalism, is, as Lucia Ruprecht observes, 'paradoxically conservative, and at odds with its own historical moment'.[39] And yet, we shall see that Plessner finds his allies in seemingly unlikely figures such as Richard Sennett and Roland Barthes.[40]

The variation in judgement between Plessner and Adorno is linked to a fundamental difference between their wider theoretical orientations. Adorno's reading of Goethe's *Wilhelm Meister's Travels* illustrated that his dialectical theory of tact retains the theoretical possibility of a *'Wahrheit übers unmittelbare Leben'* (truth about life in its immediacy) when scrutinizing everyday lived experience in its contemporary, alienated form (M 15/MM 13). Despite the negative dialectic it pursues, Adorno's text is still composed from the – at least hypothetical – standpoint of redemption (*Erlösung*) (M 283/MM 247). For Plessner, by contrast, this hypothetical standpoint does not exist. According to him, the very concept of an 'immediate form of human existence' (however utopian it may be) is inconceivable in the first place. Against all negative theories of alienation that start with Rousseau and take much of their inspiration from a potentially reductive Hegelian-Marxist dialectic, Plessner argues that alienation is not a temporary state of human existence that could potentially be overcome. For him, the idealist axiom according to which '*der Mensch mit sich identisch werden müsse, weil er es einmal gewesen sei*' (humans must become identical to their original selves, because that is what they once were) is wrong.[41] In contradistinction to Rousseau's differentiation between historical existence and essence, Plessner posits that alienation is an inherent part of the human essence.[42] Based on the assumption that the human position is marked by a constitutive 'mediacy' (*Vermitteltheit*), Plessner develops his two fundamental concepts of 'natural artificiality' and 'eccentric positionality'. Eccentric positionality manifests itself in the ontological gap between 'being a body' (*Leibsein*) and 'having a body' (*Körperhaben*). 'Natural artificiality' helps us to compensate for this fundamental dissociation. Humans are essentially '*Doppelgänger*' inasmuch as they are split into an outer personality, the public self which Plessner also calls the 'irrealized' or 'de-realized self', and an inner personality, the 'real' or private self. Following Plessner, any forms of direct, immediate, organic relationship with others, and with ourselves, are potentially destructive. It is only through performing a social role, by wearing a metaphorical mask, that we can create and protect our own private existence.

With his theory, Plessner calls into question the terminological significance of the concept of alienation that, although controversial today, was one of the unquestioned theorems of critical theory at the time.[43] For someone like Adorno, for example, there was no doubt that the social role we play in society was the result of alienation and objectification. Blending Marxist and existentialist motifs, Adorno argued that, in the modern consumer society the idea of the '*an sich seiende[] und unabhängige[] Persönlichkeit*' (personality as existing independently and in itself) becomes an illusion. This means that we do not find ourselves alienated *from* society. Instead, it is our integration into society itself that we experience as a loss of authenticity: '*Ohnmächtig in der überwältigenden Sozietät, erfährt der Einzelne sich selber nur noch als gesellschaftlich vermittelt*' (powerless within an overpowering society, the individual can only experience himself as socially mediated) (M 288).[44]

For Plessner, by contrast, the conflict between authentic existence and alienation may perhaps exist on a psychoanalytical level, but it certainly does not apply when we are trying to describe historical reality and its social conditions.[45] According to Plessner, our social persona does not abolish our private self. On the contrary, it is the social role that allows us to have a private existence in the first place. This is why, in a movement of thought that recalls the digressive dynamic of Hegel's concept of self-formation discussed earlier, Plessner can argue that alienation is the condition of identification.[46] In direct contradistinction to Adorno, alienation, Plessner tells us here, is not a deformation, or a deficit, but a potentiality. For it is in the realm of social coercion that we can find liberation, as it is only via the detour of being other that we can become ourselves.[47] This is the context in which Plessner's theory of tact as a way to permeate the boundaries between interior and exterior, private and public, the self and the other, can evolve.

Plessner's Tact

The facets of tact Plessner explores in *Grenzen der Gemeinschaft* bear a number of resemblances to those we have encountered in earlier chapters. Like Proust before him, Plessner defines tact in distinction to politeness and diplomacy. Politeness follows a code. Tact negotiates between this code and individual expectation. Politeness is associated with convention and tradition. It is nostalgic. It faces the past. Tact, in turn, is an individual variation. It is linked to the spontaneity of the individual person. Tact is a situational form of handling that occurs in the here and now of the actual moment (G 110). The idea of tact is to create an equilibrium between the persons involved. This equilibrium is temporary and fragile, as it is located beyond the rules of convention. Like diplomacy, tact follows the logic of play. But while the former is predominantly associated with the world of affairs, the latter is linked to the realm of sociability. Diplomacy occurs between largely de-realized persons, while tact negotiates between the roles we play in society and our private selves.[48] Diplomatic behaviour is target-oriented. It may operate with ruse and threat but must respect the freedom of all people involved. Its principle is reciprocity, its goal to reach an agreement (G 101). Tact, by contrast, is distinct from tactics. It differs from diplomacy in that it escapes calculation. Tact is irrational and intuitive, a way of 'finding one's way in the dark' (G 107). Tact is an open form of communication, based on an attentiveness towards otherness, and the willingness to measure the other person by their own standards rather than our own. And it takes time for tact to evolve. In this sense, Plessner's tact is essentially anti-modern and anti-capitalist. It resists the developments of the technological world, the acceleration of time and the shrinking of space. Plessner's tact defies any sense of tactility and follows the aesthetics of disguise. It is a way of playing hide-and-seek, based on the art of not coming too close and not being too open (G 106). Escaping the logic of efficiency and determination, it is essentially without purpose (*grundlos*) (G 111), cautious in its expression (*gedämpft*) (G 110), nuanced, uncertain, and, most importantly, indirect. This indirectness appears as a means for Plessner to achieve the highest possible degree of reciprocal protection (G 107/L 163).

Plessner's verdict against any direct, immediate forms of human expression not only contributes to the cultural-conservative aspects of his position, it also fuels his radical critique of contemporary aesthetics. For Plessner, art, design, and literature should refrain from any claims to honesty and authenticity that would threaten to expose the intimate sphere of the subject. Instead, they should help prevent any direct forms of representation and promote an aesthetic that subscribes to the creation of distance and dissimulation. Seen from this angle, Expressionism appears as the aesthetic of tactlessness while the clean-cut surfaces of New Objectivity (*Neue Sachlichkeit*) look like manifestations of a morality that is marked by what Plessner calls a reckless honesty combined with a principled practice of hurting oneself and others (G 110/L 167).

For Plessner, tact and diplomacy are separate in theory yet intertwined in practice (G 112). Together, they offer the individual a strategy to safeguard themself against any forms of authenticity and fusion. Tactful behaviour serves as a provision against rational and emotional overflow. It helps to reconstruct boundaries where unrestricted and immediate forms of communication with others, as well as with oneself, may currently exist. As a well-tempered compromise between hot and cold, tact regulates the social and emotional distance between the self and the other. Tact thus contributes to what Plessner, in a key passage, describes as

> *das gesellschaftliche Benehmen, die Beherrschung nicht nur der geschriebenen und gesatzten Konvention, die virtuose Handhabung der Spielformen, mit denen sich die Menschen nahe kommen, ohne sich zu treffen, mit denen sie sich voneinander entfernen, ohne sich durch Gleichgültigkeit zu verletzen.* (G 80)

> societal conduct, the control not only of written and established conventions, the virtuous mastery of forms of play where persons come close to each other without meeting and where they establish distance without damaging each other through indifference. (L 131)

The particular choreography this passage evokes is based on a moderate form of social and physical distancing. It recalls the spatial dynamic performed by

Schopenhauer's freezing porcupines described in the parable we mentioned before in relation to Proust's experiments in proxemics.⁴⁹ Whenever the porcupines try to huddle together in search for warmth they end up hurting each other with their spikes. And whenever they move apart, they get cold. In the end, they settle on a form of middle distance ('*mittlere Entfernung*') that protects them from both injury and isolation. In the case of us humans this middle distance, Schopenhauer explains, is created by way of politeness and genteel custom (*Höflichkeit und feine Sitte*). Following the English call to 'keep your distance', it helps to ensure a peaceful coexistence in society.⁵⁰ But there is a critical edge to the association of Plessner with Schopenhauer. For Schopenhauer's model of sociability is based on a pessimistic assumption. It presumes that humans are essentially egoistic and driven by inclinations of aggression. Within the context of this line of argument, tact and politeness contribute to a mode of social disciplining that exists to protect the self from exposure to the potentially repulsive selves of others.⁵¹ Reading Plessner with Schopenhauer thus contributes to an interpretation of Plessner's anthropology as a theory that, in the words of Carl Schmitt, leans 'closer to evil than to goodness'.⁵² The image repertoire Plessner draws upon as his argument proceeds seemingly supports this interpretation. Evoking a Hobbesian concept of society as '*Kampf aller gegen alle*' (a struggle of all against all) (G 81/L 131) – whereby modes of roleplay serve to provide us with a ritual mask of sociability in the form of an armour, '*eine Rüstung gleichsam*', with which we enter the 'battlefield of the public sphere' (G 82/L 133) – Plessner presents the individual person as someone who is always in a position of attention, '*tastend, sichernd, das Gesicht wahrend*' (feeling, securing and saving one's face on the outside⁵³) (G 108/L 164). Plessner's subject, as Helmuth Lethen observes, is a '*Duellsubjekt*', someone who is proving to be an expert in division.⁵⁴ At the same time, however, I would argue that Plessner's portrayal of society as a battlefield is complemented by an idealist terminology that allows for an alternative interpretation. Note, for example, that Plessner introduces the passage quoted above with the words, '*Hier gibt es kein stabiles Gleichgewicht des Lebens mehr, hier herrscht labiles Gleichgewicht, hier gilt tänzerischer Geist, das Ethos der Grazie*' (What governs here is a fragile counterweight; here a dance-like spirit – the ethos of grace – counts as valid) (G 80/L 130). The association of sociability with the spirit of dance and the ethos of grace brings another reference to mind. Like Schopenhauer's parable, the author I am thinking of makes reference to English society. This time, however, it is not the English call to keep your distance, serving Schopenhauer as an illustration of sociability, but the even more complex mode of distance regulation performed within the context of an English dance. In a famous passage drawn from his letter to Christian Körner (23 February 1793) Friedrich Schiller describes the ideal of aesthetic society as follows:

> *Ich weiß für das Ideal des schönen Umgangs kein passenderes Bild als einen gut getanzten und aus vielen verwickelten Touren komponierten englischen Tanz. Ein Zuschauer aus der Galerie sieht unzählige Bewegungen, die sich aufs bunteste durchkreuzen und ihre Richtung lebhaft und mutwillig verändern und doch niemals zusammenstoßen. Alles ist so geordnet, daß der eine schon Platz gemacht hat, wenn der andere kommt, alles fügt sich so geschickt und doch wieder so kunstlos ineinander, daß jeder nur seinem eigenen Kopf zu folgen scheint und doch nie dem andern in den Weg tritt. Es ist das treffendste Sinnbild der behaupteten eigenen Freiheit und der geschonten Freiheit des andern.*

I can think of no more fitting image for the ideal of social conduct than an English dance, composed of many complicated figures and perfectly executed. A spectator in the gallery sees innumerable movements intersecting in the most chaotic fashion, changing direction swiftly and without rhyme or reason, yet never colliding. Everything is so ordered that the one has already yielded his place when the other arrives; it is all so skilfully, and yet so artlessly, integrated into a form, that each seems only to be following his own inclination, yet without ever getting in the way of anybody else. It is the most perfectly appropriate symbol of the assertion of one's own freedom and regard for the freedom of others.[55]

Schiller's scenario, as Plessner's description, follows a choreography that is cautious of any direct physical contact and careful to prevent any form of collision. Where we saw Plessner highlight the 'virtuous mastery of forms of play', Schiller writes of a 'wilful change'. Both emphasize the close association between artificiality and naturalness ('*geschickt*' and '*kunstlos*') and, like Schiller before him, Plessner also draws on the notion of protection (*Schonung*). Reading Plessner with Schiller, whose name is only mentioned once in Plessner's essay but whose terminology reverberates throughout Plessner's entire text,[56] shines a light on a certain aspect of Plessner's theory of tact that the reading with Schopenhauer failed to reveal: namely, the particular tension, already described by Kant and Adorno, that arises from the simultaneity of general norms and individual variation. Whereas Schopenhauer's parable of the porcupines focuses on the key role of manners within the context of civilization, Schiller's ideal aesthetic society is not simply based on a dynamic of reciprocal attraction and repulsion, but on a particular form of attentive co-operation. The grace (*Anmut*) Schiller's dancers create does not grow out of a precise obedience to the (physically and socially distanced) choreography prescribed, but arises from their individual and intuitive response to the singularity and concreteness of the communicative situation. In resonance with Goethe's portrayal of the tactless maestro in Venice who, as we saw in 'Tact's History' (Chapter 1), by beating the correct time did not advance but destroy the harmony of the musical performance,[57] Schiller highlights the difference between '*Takt*' as mechanical accuracy and tact as individual deviation or, as Barthes later puts it, between tact as a prescribed 'rhythm' and tact as its individual interpretation in the form of an '*idiorrythmie*'.[58] This individual interpretation is understood, in a nod to Kant, as an ethical act of individual freedom, a freedom that grows out of the respect for, and in accordance with, the freedom of others. In both Plessner's and Schiller's model of an ideal sociability, it is thus the sensitivity to tact – defined as a fragile, temporary equilibrium between individuals established outside, albeit not entirely detached from, prescribed forms of interaction – that avoids domination, collision, and touch, making room for the ethical dimension of grace.

It is true that Plessner's works are, as Lethen notes, '*Mischräume heterogener Diskurse*' (mixed spaces of heterogeneous discourse) that reflect the general intellectual climate in Weimar Germany.[59] But reading Plessner in the light of the idealist vocabulary it employs makes it difficult to reduce Plessner's anthropology to the code of 'cool conduct' that Lethen so suggestively describes in his book of the same title.[60] And despite Plessner's frequent recourse to the medical register of health and hygiene, he also escapes, I would argue, Roberto Esposito's classification as a 'theoretician of the preventive immunisation of all social forms'.[61] Plessner's emphasis on the ethos of grace and his references to the idealist category of the 'beautiful soul' that, despite its unresolved ontological ambivalence, appears in his essay as a potentially redemptive vanishing point, indicate otherwise – and so does Plessner's introduction of the term '*Zartheit*' as the 'most important symptom of tact' (G 107).

The word '*Zartheit*' carries connotations of delicacy, tenderness (*Zärtlichkeit*), gentleness, harmony, weakness, and fragility. Associated with affection and with the idea of (maternal) care and protection, '*Zartheit*' is also linked with femininity, forming, like Schiller's dignity and grace, a counterprinciple to '*Roheit*' (crudeness, rudeness) (G 28) and masculine strength.[62] Within the context of Plessner's argument, we find '*Zartheit*' related to warm-heartedness and the notion of curing. As a distant, light, and elusive form of contact, not a grip (G 110), '*Zartheit*' appears as the only means to render social intercourse possible and agreeable. Together with the other two symptoms, 'naturalness' and 'grace', it is the manifestation of '*Zartheit*' that contributes to the healing power of Plessner's tact (G 107–109).

Plessner's theory of tact bears traces of the traumatic repercussions of the First World War for German society and the fundamental social and cultural crisis that followed. The post-war individual Plessner describes in *Grenzen der Gemeinschaft* struggles to strike a balance between the 'immeasurable chilling of human relationships by mechanical, commercial, and political abstractions', and the equally 'immeasurable' reaction this chilling provokes 'in the ideal of a glowing community overflowing through all of its supporters' (G 28/L 65). The '*Kultur der Unpersönlichkeit*' (culture of impersonality) Plessner advocates in response to this dilemma grows out of the spirit of tact as a configuration of distance (G 133/L 194). This does not mean that the members of this culture are isolated or indifferent to each other. On the contrary, I would argue that Plessner's model of sociability combines an idealist notion of sensitivity and fragility with a post-war sense of firmness and resistance. The agents of Plessner's society thus form part of a complex and delicate network of multiple spatial, social, and emotional associations that - if they work - exist to guarantee their reciprocal protection, with and against each other. In Plessner's essay, the metaphors of the dance hall and the fencing arena, the beautiful soul and the duellist, stand side by side in an unresolved tension.

Conclusion

In their theories of tact, both Plessner and Adorno draw on a paradigm that dates back to the late seventeenth century: namely the idea that we exist in two separate spheres, each of which requires different forms of communication.[63] Barthes will much later address this paradigm in his lecture course of 1977–78, *Le Neutre*, as '*le mythe public/privé*' or, more specifically, '*le mythe historique des deux hommes dans un même sujet*' (N 183). According to this classic dichotomous model, we are split into an exterior personality and an interior self. Our exterior personality is social, worldly, and open to the judgement of others. It constitutes itself on the basis of our performance of the various roles we play in the course of our lives. Our interior self, on the other hand, the 'real me', resists any form of signification, abstraction or classification. It is fleeting, tangible, unfathomable, and, potentially, free. We saw that both Plessner and Adorno critically refer to this dualist distinction between self and role. And yet they offer rather different interpretations. Adorno conceptualizes the social persona in terms of alienation and objectification. For Plessner, by contrast, it is this very state of alienation that carries the potential for individual freedom. To Plessner, the metaphorical mask we put on when entering society is not a sign or symptom of deformation or distortion. Nor does it inflict any sense of rupture. On the contrary, our private self can only come into existence in response to, and by way of a detour via, the other. '*Am anderen wird der Mensch seiner habhaft*', Plessner writes. '*Diesen anderen trifft er auf dem Umweg über die Rolle, genau wie der andere ihn*' (The human being gets hold of himself in the other. This other he meets on a detour via the role. And so does the other meet him.)[64] In the context of this argument, tactful behaviour negotiates between social expectations and individual variation, the self and the other, mask and face. The idea is not to hide the face behind a shield, but to facilitate its truthful expression under protected conditions. The goal is to uphold the mask in order to keep face. Plessner resolves this apparent contradiction by introducing the term 'nimbus'. Latin for 'luminous vapour', '(dark) cloud', 'storm', or 'halo', the word is used to signify a person's good reputation and social prestige. For Plessner it is the nimbus of the individual that may offer him distance in proximity, mask *and* face: '*Der künstliche Zauber des unzerstörbaren Nimbus bringt den Widerspruch zur Lösung*', Plessner observes. '*Er schafft seinem Träger zugleich Raum und Anziehungskraft, Maske und Gesicht*' (G 85). In *Minima Moralia*, Adorno introduces the related concept of 'aura'. Latin/Greek for 'breeze' or 'air', 'aura' is semantically linked to 'nimbus'. And, like Plessner's nimbus, Adorno's aura describes a processual dynamic based on a dialectical tension between nearness and distance. While Plessner's nimbus abolishes the conflict between mask and face, however, within the context of Adorno's theory of tact, aura is associated with the intimate sphere of the self. Aura appears as the medium of the individual's singularity and difference. As such, and in consistency with Benjamin's earlier understanding of the term as '*einmalige Erscheinung einer Ferne, so nah sie sein mag*' (unique apparition of a distance, however near it may be),[65] aura corresponds to what Adorno calls '*das Menschliche*' (the humaneness) in the subject (M 207/MM 182). Threatened by the demands of intimacy and public incorporation, aura determines the condition of the subject *as* individual. We shall see that the utopian lifestyle Barthes envisages in his lectures convened in the 1970s follows a logic that complies with Adorno's idea.

Plessner's and Adorno's theories of tact were developed at different critical turning points of the twentieth century and start out from different methodological assumptions. Plessner introduces tact as an antidote to the rising social and political populism and radicalism in interwar Germany. Adorno, in turn, sketches a dialectical theory of tact as a concept that also contributes to the collapse of the humaneness it initially helped to defend. Despite these fundamental differences, however, Plessner and Adorno come to reach unexpectedly similar conclusions. The theories of tact they propose share a suspicion of intimacy and touch, and a preference for singularity and difference over communal sameness and identification. On a hermeneutic level, their theories allow us to develop new modes of non-violent contemplation. On a social and political level, they contribute to the idea that keeping your distance and wearing a mask (literally or metaphorically) does not necessarily have to be interpreted as a dystopic sign of isolation. It can also be seen as an act of co-operation (not fusion), of solicitude and care. The next chapter, 'Individuation', will carry some of these ideas over to the year of 1968 and explore how they play out in the work of François Truffaut.

CHAPTER 4

Individuation (Truffaut)

J'aime beaucoup de gens hypocrites. L'hypocrisie, c'est le tact.

I love plenty of hypocritical people. Hypocrisy is tact.

François Truffaut, 4 May 1967[1]

When François Truffaut filmed *Baisers volés* (*Stolen Kisses*) in Paris he was not happy. 'I will not be sending you a copy of my script for *Stolen Kisses* which I am shooting at the moment', he wrote to Alfred Hitchcock on 19 February 1968, 'because it is just a nostalgic, romantic comedy, budgeted at 250,000 Dollars and largely improvised!'[2] Two years later, Truffaut would still emphasize the strong sense of unease that had tainted his work on the film:

> *J'ai failli abandonner* Baisers volés *quinze jours avant le tournage, tellement j'avais honte, je me sentais inconfortable. J'avais déjà le script de* L'Enfant sauvage *et celui de* La Sirène du Mississippi. *Je me disais: quand même, j'ai deux bons scripts à tourner; il y a des romans magnifiques et je vais tourner dans quinze jours un film où on ne raconte rien du tout!*

> I almost abandoned *Stolen Kisses* fifteen days before shooting began, I was so ashamed, and felt so uncomfortable about it. I had already written the script for *The Wild Child*, and that for *Mississippi Mermaid*. I said to myself, 'Hell, I have two good scripts to shoot; there are magnificent novels to do, and in fifteen days I am going to make a film that deals with nothing at all!'[3]

It is true that, on the surface at least, *Stolen Kisses* appears to be a romantic comedy that seduces its audience with a sweet nostalgia and a lightness of touch. Contemporary reviewers thus lauded the film's 'cinematic grace',[4] praised the plot as an 'insightful meditation on love ... (and second thoughts)',[5] and admired the optimistic charm of the young Claude Jade in the role of Christine.[6] More than half a century later, however, the film reveals a different dimension that, at the time of its making, might not even have been so obvious to its creators. A seemingly timeless story of young love and its discontents, the film can also be interpreted as a response to the all-pervading sense of crisis that marked the year of its production, and the challenge this crisis posed to normative modes of sociability and co-habitation.[7]

Stolen Kisses was filmed in the months running up to one of the most violent conflicts post-war France had ever seen: the street protests in Paris of May 1968. When a group of students from the University of Nanterre occupied the Sorbonne on 3 May and a few hundred students engaged in a street battle with units of the *Compagnies républicaines de sécurité* (CRS), the shooting of *Stolen Kisses* was complete. The film premiered in the autumn of 1968. At that point, the dust of the 'night of the barricades' (10–11 May) had settled. The industrial action involving seven million French citizens, which had briefly paralysed the entire country, and the mass rallies had ceased. When on 29 May President Charles de Gaulle announced the dissolution of the National Assembly, hundreds of thousands of people marched down the Champs-Élysées, demonstrating the solidarity of the hitherto silent majority of the French population with de Gaulle and his conservative government. At the end of June 1968, the election of the National Assembly resulted in the victory of the Gaullistes and the Independent Republicans, while the number of seats previously occupied by the Left was practically reduced to half. A year later, in June 1969, the conservative prime minister, Georges Pompidou, was elected successor of President Charles de Gaulle. At that point, the Parisian May had already turned into a legend. And yet, 'Mai '68' had irrevocably changed French society.[8]

Truffaut was generally sympathetic to the student movement although, like his contemporary Roland Barthes, he did not define himself as a political activist.[9] But while Barthes was successful in staying clear of any direct political involvement, moving to Morocco in the immediate aftermath of 1968, Truffaut got caught up in '*une double vie de cinéaste et de militant*'[10] precisely at the time when the filming of *Baisers volés* was about to begin.[11] His involvement was sparked by the politically motivated dismissal of Henri Langlois, the founder and director of the Cinémathèque française in Paris, and an intellectual father figure to many of the young film makers involved with the *Nouvelle Vague*.[12] On 12 February 1968, between 200 and 300 film personalities and enthusiasts – including Truffaut and many of the cast and crew of *Stolen Kisses*, notably the two protagonists, Claude Jade and Jean-Pièrre Léaud – blocked the entrance of the Cinémathèque in rue d'Ulm. Two days later the protest culminated in a violent confrontation on L'Esplanade de Trocadéro between 3000 protestors and the police. On 26 February, Truffaut, at the time a member of the Cinémathèque's board of directors, created the 'committee for the defence of the Cinémathèque française'. He began to act as its treasurer and started writing a series of outraged articles in *Combat*. On 11 March 1968, when the filming of *Stolen Kisses* was coming to a close, Truffaut published an article that not only spurred the political side of the conflict but also implies a first and interesting use of the notion of tact. 'Autrefois', Truffaut wrote,

> *les gaffeurs, les maladroits, les malappris, le gouvernement s'en débarrassait en expédiant celui-là en Algérie, celui-ci en Nouvelle-Calédonie. Dans la France de 1968, les Moinot, les Barbin s'accrochent à Paris, ils tiennent à bouffer chez Lipp, à clôturer les festivals, à distribuer des petites médailles aux étrangers de passage et des bouquets de fleurs aux vedettes, ils sévissent, ils s'incrustent, ils irritent, ils aggravent leur cas.*

> Formerly, the government used to get rid of blunderers, tactless fools and boors by sending them to Algeria or New Caledonia. In the France of 1968 the Moinots and Barbins cling to Paris, they want to eat at Lipp's, bring festivals to a close, hand out little medals to visiting foreigners and bouquets of flowers to female stars; they dig in their heels, take root, irritate, and they aggravate their cases.[13]

As an aesthetic and social category, tact, we said in Chapter 1, has the potential to overthrow existing hierarchies and traditional social and cultural norms. At the same time, however, tact can also lead to new forms of social distinction within the newly formed elites. Tact can be simultaneously inclusive and exclusive. It may integrate those people who are believed to have tact – in Truffaut's particular case the Parisian avant-garde intellectuals and film makers engaged in the political conflict – and single out those who do not, here the '*maladroits*', the newly instated and allegedly provincial government officials. Tact serves as a means to forge coherence within one particular group of people and erects boundaries for those who seem incapable of reading and actively using its unwritten codes, the people who dare invade a certain social space and 'dig in their heels' where they, allegedly, do not belong. Like Bourdieu's taste, Truffaut's tact classifies. And, by extension, it classifies the classifier.[14] At the same time, however, it is precisely this sense of classification and the idea of identification it entails that, for Truffaut at least, was also always an object of contestation.

The interviews Truffaut gave around 1968, in which he reflects on his films and the contemporary social and political situation, show his ambivalent position in relation to the May protests. Contemplating, for example, his participation in the street rallies, Truffaut distanced himself from the comrade-rhetoric employed by some of its most prominent leaders.[15] Apprehensive towards any ideological and politicized notion of community,

Truffaut's thinking displays certain parallels to Plessner's critique of the term. Plessner, we saw in Chapter 3, identified striking parallels between the political debates marking the 1920s and those post-1968. Pointing to the renewed accuracy of his original argument of 1924, Plessner emphasized in the 1970s that, now and then, the celebrated ideal of a communal absorption in some form of overall organic commitment does not help to protect the individual person but, on the contrary, puts their singularity, and hence their humaneness, at risk.[16] Truffaut's statements thus offer a contradictory picture. On the one hand, they reveal the film maker as an individualist who, like Plessner and Adorno before him, is suspicious of any form of collective identification and believes in the principle of individual divergence. On the other, Truffaut's comments also articulate a strong desire to conform to existing societal norms and conventions. '*On se croit toujours coupable*', he repeatedly observed.

> *Par exemple, manifester devant la Cinémathèque, aller m'asseoir au conseil d'administration, passer dans la même rue, c'est ahurissant. Quand je manifeste, je me retrouve en pleine enfance. Après, j'ai l'impression de m'immiscer dans un monde en cachette, et je dis dix fois trop: 'Bonjour, monsieur' à tout le monde!*

> You always feel as if you are guilty.... For example, for me to demonstrate in front of the Cinématèque, to go and sit on a board of directors, to go down the same street, is astounding. I realize that I haven't crossed the other side. When I demonstrate, I find myself back in my childhood. Afterwards, I get the feeling of having secretly pried into someone's world, and I say 'Good morning, Sir' ten times more than is necessary to everyone!'[17]

The interviews Truffaut gave around 1968 portray him as a figure who abstains from taking sides, who dreads the very idea of collective identification and confrontation. Life, he maintained, was not to be seen 'in terms of power relations'. 'It is not a settling of scores.' Instead, he argued, once more emphasizing the idea that would also shape the character of the male protagonist in *Stolen Kisses*, life is 'an attempt to make oneself accepted'.[18]

Stolen Kisses reflects the ambivalence of Truffaut's position. The film's opening shot shows the blocked entrance gate of Langlois' Cinémathèque to which the film is dedicated. And, throughout the film, allusions are made to the ongoing collective upheaval in the streets of Paris: in conversations between characters, within the context of Christine's academy of music being closed, or in the news reels flickering on TV screens in the background. At the same time, however, the overall design of *Stolen Kisses* avoids clear periodization and reflects Truffaut's preference for individualism over communality. Commenting on the first version of the screenplay, drafted by his two co-script writers Claude de Givray and Bernard Revon, Truffaut insisted on staying away from collective scenes and avoiding social parody. He explicitly rejected settings that might be associated with mass gatherings ('I hate stadiums', 'No table football, nothing collective')[19] and replaced scenes that aimed to portray the social dynamics within larger groups of people – a reception in a bourgeois salon for example – with encounters that did not involve more than two or three characters at a time. In stark contrast to the ideal of a passionate identification with a certain group of people or a particular ideology, and in clear opposition to any notion of seamless togetherness that may coincide with it, the film introduces its male protagonist, Antoine Doinel, as an anachronistic hero who takes his main inspiration from reading romantic nineteenth-century novels, and who responds to the news of the collective upheaval in the streets of Paris with incomprehension and indifference. Antoine is an individualist, and a social misfit who grapples with social norms and conventions, and yet, like his creator, he wants to belong. '*Je vois bien*', Truffaut observed in an attempt to characterize his alter ego,

> *qu'Antoine n'est certainement pas un antisocial. Il est sûrement un asocial, mais il n'est pas révolutionnaire à la façon d'aujourd'hui. A partir de ce constat, j'admets que mes films soient condamnés politiquement. Doinel n'est pas un type qui veut changer la société; il se méfie d'elle, il s'en protège mais il est plein de bonne volonté et désireux, me semble-t-il, de se faire 'accepter'.*

> I can see that Antoine is certainly not an antisocial type. He is definitely asocial, but he is not a revolutionary of the sort that is fashionable today. In that regard, I do admit that my films are condemned politically. Doinel is not the type who wants to change the world; he despises society, he protects himself from it, but he is full of good will, and I think he really wants to be 'accepted'.[20]

This chapter takes as its starting point the assumption that Truffaut's conception of tact arises from an antagonism we saw Kant describe as the human tendency for disintegration (Chapter 1). This antagonism is based on the paradoxical struggle of wanting to participate in collective culture while at the same time seeking to renounce it. I suggest that one of the key concerns motivating *Stolen Kisses* is precisely the question that, from Kant to Barthes, runs through this entire book, forging an underlying bond between the individual encounters I describe. As Proust, Plessner, and Adorno before him, Truffaut, too, reacts to a sense of crisis when addressing the following problem: at a time when existing norms and conventions fall apart, how can we approach one another without colliding, and how can we part without hurting each other through indifference? In other words, how do we reconcile the Kantian paradox of wanting to be alone while wanting to be with others? Mapping *Stolen Kisses* against the historical and political background to which it responds, this chapter argues that the film occupies a bystander position in relation to either side of the social and political parties involved. Against politicized ideologies of fusional collectivity – a symbiotic form of existence in which we experience ourselves as one with others – Truffaut experiments with new forms of individuality, freedom, and communication. Using Antoine's romantic entanglement with the two female lead characters, Fabienne and Christine, as my main example, in this chapter I follow the ways in which Truffaut's protagonist struggles with the tension between fading social norms and individual deviation, assimilation and dis-similation. I highlight the ways in which the film oscillates between getting too close (staging moments of intrusion, fusion, exposure, and ridicule) and seeking to (re)create distance (erecting barriers through manners, silence, blindness, hypocrisy, dissimulation, and lying), a safety zone, as it were, against the potential onslaughts of directness, frankness, empathy, and identification.[21] In so doing, I shall also revisit Truffaut's parable on the difference between tact and politeness with which this book began: the story about the gentleman caller and the naked lady in the bathroom, read out by Fabienne in one of the signature scenes of the film. In what follows, I reconsider this story, and the initial interpretation I offered in the introduction to this book, to place it more carefully within the context of the film and the director's political engagement that coincided with its making. Truffaut's tact, I shall argue, simultaneously undermines and confirms existing (and disintegrating) structures of power and domination. It is a particular mode of divergence that resists confrontation, coincidence, and conflict. Not distinct from, but synonymous with hypocrisy and lying, Truffaut's tact is an amoral category that helps to create a non-committing play with distance and proximity, sensibility and sensuality, amour and politesse. Linked to the un-immediate, the artificial, the provisional, the inconsequential, and the free, Truffaut's tact may perhaps have the capacity to cause an exaltation of existing norms and conventions. It may even succeed in creating a temporary equilibrium between two people outside the rules of convention. But, like Swann's tact, it will always fall short of a revolution.

Handling Doors

Mapped against the politicized dream of community as a symbiotic mode of existence in which the individual person can experience him/herself as united with others, Truffaut's *Stolen Kisses* is not about the abolition of distance but about feeling out the space as it expands between his characters as isolated individuals. In resonance with the ever-changing character constellations in Proust's *Recherche*, the figures that populate Truffaut's film are constantly negotiating their positions in relation to each other. And as with Proust's *Recherche*, Truffaut's *Stolen Kisses* consists of a series of different test arrangements in which the characters are either getting too close to each other (as in the scene in which Antoine tries to kiss Christine in her parents' house on the way down to the wine cellar) or they are drifting apart from each other (for example when Christine escapes through the side exit of her parents' house at exactly the moment her mother greets Antoine at the front door). Humans, wrote Georg Simmel in 1917, are *'grenzbestimmte[] Gebilde'*,[22] suggesting that each of us is surrounded by a boundary that exists to protect our personal sphere from outward intrusion (by other people). In Simmel's reading, this boundary does not simply appear as a line in space that relates to our psyche and, by extension, to our innermost moods and feelings. Instead, the concept of the boundary itself, and with it the aspect of an expansion or a collapse of distance it implies, takes on a psychological valence. Simmel's boundary is a psycho-spatial category, a mental and sociological occurrence (*'ein seelisches, näher: ein soziologisches Geschehen'*) that comes into being whenever we are exposed to other people, taking on shape and substance through collisions, rejections, disappointments, and adaptations.[23] Produced about half a century later than Simmel's essay, *Stolen Kisses* can be read as the metaphorical elaboration of this idea. But the boundaries erected in Truffaut's film are not always drawn to prevent direct contact between the characters involved. On the contrary, at times they are put into place in order to be playfully overcome.[24] The first re-encounter between Antoine and Christine after his disreputable dismissal from the army is significant within this context. It involves Christine wanting to visit Antoine during one of his shifts as a night watchman in a hotel lobby. At first the camera lingers in a medium-wide shot on Christine, seen through the glass door from inside the hotel where Antoine is placed at the reception. In graceful pantomime communication, Christine makes a few helpless gestures. Antoine waves, smiles, and encourages her to enter with a tilt of his head. ('This is when I fell in love with her', Antoine will later recall in the last film of the Antoine Doinel cycle, *L'amour en fuite* (*Love on the Run*, 1979). What Christine does not understand at this point in *Stolen Kisses* is that if you want to open the door you need to push it. Her temporary rival, Fabienne Tabard, performed by Delphine Seyrig with fabulous poise, is for much of the time the only character in the film who appears to know the art of handling doors. You do not leave them closed for too long, as Christine does. Nor do you break them down, as Antoine does on occasion in his capacity as a night watchman and, later, in his subsequent job as an informer at the detective agency. You open and close them, like the gentleman caller in Fabienne's story, with the well-tempered distance created by tact.

Tact and Tactlessness

This is, you will remember, how the story goes:

> *Quand j'étais au collège, mon professeur expliquait la différence entre le tact et la politesse. Un monsieur, en visite, pousse par erreur la porte d'une salle de bains et découvre une dame absolument nue; il recule aussitôt, referme la porte et dit: 'Oh pardon, Madame!' Ça c'est la politesse! . . . Le même monsieur, poussant la même porte, découvrant la même dame absolument nue et lui disant: 'Oh pardon, Monsieur!' Cela, c'est le tact.*

> When I was at school, my teacher explained the difference between tact and politeness. A gentleman caller accidentally opens a bathroom door and sees a naked lady. He quickly withdraws and, closing the door, he says: 'Pardon, Madame!' This is politeness. Should the same gentleman open the same door, discover the same naked lady and withdraw by saying: 'Pardon, Monsieur!' – that would be tact. (1:05, 1:12)[25]

This, we said in the Introduction to this book, is a story about tact. But is it also a tactful story?

When Truffaut asked Givray and Revon to produce a first draft of the script for *Stolen Kisses*, he gave them a set of key motifs from which the plot should arise: the protagonist's dishonourable discharge from the military service, the film's title, borrowed from the 1942-song by Charles Trenet, the outline of a scene describing 'Antoine's nightmare',[26] and the failed encounter between the infatuated young working-class man and the attractive, married, older, middle-class lady that culminates in Antoine uttering the unfortunate words 'Oui, Monsieur'. Written in its final version by Truffaut himself, the scene mirrors a very similar scene in Anatole France's semi-autobiographical novel *Le Livre de mon ami* (1885).[27] In France's version the 17-year-old narrator, Pierre Nozière, first sets eye on the object of his romantic infatuation during a reception at his family home. Mme Alice Gance, who shares with Mme Fabienne Tabard '*un air de bonté*' mixed with a touch of '*coquetterie*' and '*tristesse*'[28] is the beautiful widow of a well-known pianist. At one point during the reception Mme Gance is invited to play a piece on the grand piano. When she finishes, Pierre escorts her to her seat and sits down beside her. The dialogue he recalls corresponds precisely to the words exchanged between Mme Tabard and Antoine in the Tabard's apartment:

> *Elle me demanda si j'aimais la musique; sa voix me donna le frisson. Je rouvris les yeux et je vis qu'elle me regardait; ce regard me perdit. 'Oui, monsieur', répondis-je dans mon trouble.*

> She asked me if I was fond of music, her voice sent a thrill through me. I opened my eyes again, and I saw that she was looking at me. That look was my undoing. 'Yes, sir,' I answered in my confusion.[29]

Like Mme Tabard and Antoine, Mme Gance and Pierre have reached a critical point in their face-to-face encounter at which it no longer makes sense for the flustered participant to conceal or downplay his level of distress. The small social system they had, for a fleeting moment at least, created for themselves, has collapsed. The gaffe mars what, for either young man, could have turned into a euphoric situation. France does not tell us exactly how the collision between Pierre and Alice is dissolved. But we see (and feel, since embarrassment is contagious) that in Truffaut's version the level of distress has what Goffman calls 'an abrupt, orgasmic character',[30] a description that corresponds to Truffaut's close-up on the coffee spilling across the tray. Overwhelmed by embarrassment and gender confusion (by calling Fabienne 'Monsieur' he has just masculinized her while feminizing himself, although she is the woman he desires as a man),[31] and incapable of restoring the smooth transmission and reception by which a sense of propriety would generally be sustained,[32] Antoine dashes to the nearest exit. The face-to-face encounter has collapsed. Both characters must assume a new set of roles if they want to reengage in any form of future interaction. With Antoine having (temporarily) abdicated his role as someone who is capable of sustaining a 'normal' encounter, Fabienne assumes the position of the tactor to mend what is no longer intact, and to help the tactee, Antoine, who has fallen, back onto his feet. This, Truffaut shows, cannot be done directly. It can only be achieved indirectly, via the detour of writing. ('Wrong' Truffaut notes on the margins of an early draft of the film script. 'She would definitely talk about something else, except by letter'.)[33]

Tact, we said earlier, has the capacity to create, or restore, an equilibrium between individuals beyond the constrictions posed by existing hierarchies, norms, and (gender) conventions. Tactful behaviour, if we once more follow Simmel, is a form of communication that facilitates a frictionless co-operation between equals.[34] Tact, we saw Simmel suggest, is so important in a society because it guides the self-regulation of the individual in their personal relation to others, creating a communicative situation where '*keine äußeren oder unmittelbar egoistischen Interessen die Regulative übernehmen*' (no outer or directly egoistic interests provide regulation).[35] But tact, as Fabienne's use of the letter reveals if we consider its various possible implications in context, can also be seen merely to conceal rather than abolish the power imbalance that may temporarily exist between the people involved in the tactful encounter. And it may be strategic. (Indeed, we witnessed the same ambivalent relation between tact and power before, namely in the tactful encounters between Goethe's Iphigenie and Thoas as read by Adorno (Chapter 3), and between Andrée and Marcel as portrayed by Proust (Chapter 2).) Tact is a game of hide and seek. Based on the tension between display and disguise, freedom and effectiveness, it can quickly turn into an amorous game the goal of which is the erotic encounter. Fabienne's parable, and the strategic use she makes of it to advance her case, can be interpreted to this end. The parable reverts the existing power imbalance between Fabienne and Antoine, and 'sets straight' the gender reversal that occurred, by portraying Fabienne in the role of the naked lady, vulnerable and exposed in her desire for Antoine, and Antoine in the role of the gentleman caller, tactfully ignoring her desire while concealing his own.[36] At the same time, however, Fabienne's tactful retelling of the failed encounter does not abolish the 'offence against propriety'[37] Antoine had inadvertently committed by calling her 'Monsieur'. On the contrary, Fabienne's story amplifies rather than gracefully sublimates the erotic tension that had caused Antoine's slip in the first place. It re-inscribes intimacy into distance, touch into tact, and concludes by proposing an empathetic, yet rather tactless, threat of intrusion (of Antoine's mind and, as we shall see, of his bedroom): '*J'ai compris votre fuite, Antoine. À demain*' (I know why you fled, Antoine. See you tomorrow[38]) (BV 1:12).

It is not quite clear at this point in the film to what extent Antoine understands any of this. Fabienne's letter could be interpreted as benevolent, intended to mend the broken communicative situation and to heal the flustered state of Antoine's mind. At the same time, it could also be understood as strategic, and motivated by egoistic rather than altruistic concerns, save that, as in the tactful encounter between Andrée and Marcel, none of this is openly addressed. The systemic uncertainty Fabienne's message thereby creates is further intensified by the imbalance in class affiliation between Fabienne and Antoine that the film does not tire of underscoring.[39] Tactful communication, we saw Sartre observe, can only take on its full meaning between people of similar social and cultural background who share the same values, mores, and customs.[40] If we want to follow this argument, the same can be said for situations like the present one, where the limits of tact are momentarily challenged, stretched, and potentially outrun: situations, in short, in which, as is the case with Fabienne's letter, the grey zone between tact and tactlessness is playfully explored. It is one thing to know tact's unwritten rules so as to bend them. It is another to know these rules so as to detect their bending. '*Le tact dans l'audace*', Jean Cocteau once observed, '*c'est de savoir jusqu'où on peut aller trop loin*' (Tact in audacity is knowing how far you can go without going too far).[41] And so, from the moment Fabienne delivers her paradoxical letter to Antoine's doorstep, we start watching both characters treading a very fine line.

Tact, Touch, and the Media

Antoine responds – and like Fabienne, he responds indirectly, in writing. But while she advances by reinscribing touch into tact, he retreats, increasing rather than diminishing the social and physical distance that exists between the two of them, formulating feelings that are seemingly cleansed of all their bodily traces, and avoiding any expression of physical desire that Fabienne's letter may have aroused. We see him late in the evening, writing at his desk, and listen to his voice-over:

> *Ceci est une lettre d'adieu. Vous êtes magnanime et je ne mérite pas votre indulgence. Vous ne me reverrez plus. . . . Je suis un imposteur bien au-delà de ce que vous pouvez imaginer . . . J'ai rêvé, un moment, que des sentiments allaient exister entre nous. Mais ils mourront de la même impossibilité de Félix de Vandenesse pour Madame de Mortsauf dans* Le Lys dans la vallée. *Adieu.*

> This is a farewell letter. You are magnanimous, and I don't deserve your generosity. You will never see me again.. . . I am much more of an impostor than you can even imagine . . . I dreamt, for a moment, that there might be feelings between us. But they died of the same impossibility as those by Félix de Vandenesse for Madame de Mortsauf in *The Lily of the Valley*. Adieu. (BV 1:12:20/AD 247)[42]

By quoting Balzac's 1835 novel that, like France's account of Pierre Nozière and Mme Gance, tells the autobiographically inspired story of an unconsummated love between a young man and an older, married woman, Antoine not only takes refuge behind the romantic protagonists of Balzac's *Lys dans la vallée*;[43] in the act of writing the letter, he also seeks to translate sensuality back into sensibility, sublimating his own physical desire into the non-corporeal emotional culture of a nineteenth-century novel where touch as tact signifies a psychological sensitivity more than a physical desire.[44] And yet, while we listen to Antoine's voice reading the letter, we also watch him walk down the street. We witness him pass by the mailbox and see his hand in close-up dropping the letter into another box instead, a box that is marked with a word we then hear his voice very slowly pronounce, emphasizing every single syllable it contains: '*pneu – ma – tique*'.

'Every history of politeness is a history of technology', Jacques Derrida observed in 1992 during a series of interviews revolving around questions concerning the technicity of presentation, the preservation of memory, and the volatile nature of the authorial subject.[45] To underline his point, Derrida quotes Heidegger, who in his lectures on Parmenides of 1942–3 made the point that 'in the time of the first dominance of the typewriter, a letter written on this machine still stood for a breach of good manners. Today a handwritten letter is an antiquated and undesired thing. It disturbs speed reading.'[46] While Heidegger was contemplating the relation between manners, technology, and time, Truffaut is more interested in exploring the connection between manners, time, and space, bringing into play a communication technology that, although outdated at the time, was still in use in the Paris of 1968: the pneumatic post system.[47] Consisting of a vast underground network of tubes (467 km in total length since 1934), the system was used for the fast delivery of urgent messages and stretched out like a giant web all across the city. The '*petit bleu*' or '*pneu*', as the letter card was called, was posted in mailboxes especially designed for this purpose and arrived at the telegraph office nearest to the addressee. From there it was delivered by a messenger directly to the recipient's address. Once Antoine has posted his '*pneu*', the camera follows the letter's journey, encapsulated in a small cylindrical container, as it propels through the network of pressurized air tubes, zigzagging all the way from rue Lépic in the 18th arrondissement to the avenue de l'Opéra in the 1st arrondissement, the address nearest to its final destination. On the one hand, Truffaut's detailed staging of the pneumatic system visualizes the idea of a distanced connectivity between the two characters involved, with the different arrondissements (working class and bourgeois) emphasizing the spatial distance and social difference between Antoine and Fabienne. On the other, the tone of Antoine's voice-over, echoing the breathless sensuality of Fabienne's timbre, the hissing sound of the air in the tubes, the steam and the rhythmic beat of the cylinders suggest a physical connection between the sender and the recipient that is even further enhanced by the close-up on the series of hands touching the letter throughout the course of its journey, creating a physical bond between Antoine's hand sliding the letter into the slit of the box, via the various different hands of the postal officers that help direct the letter through the pneumatic system, to Fabienne's hands (with painted red finger nails, as Truffaut points out in the script[48]), unrolling the '*pneu*' early in the morning, when it has finally been delivered to her apartment. We could say that Antoine's letter, as a pastiche of a romantic letter of renunciation, signifies the evacuation of physical desire into the secondary world of a non-corporeal circulation of signs. We could also argue, however, that the letter functions as the carrier medium with the help of which he can stay in touch with Fabienne across the physical and emotional distancing regulations that Antoine, on the surface at least, had sought to impose on their relationship.[49] By choosing the pneumatic post system as a means of communication, Truffaut simultaneously confirms and undermines the idea of tact as a touchless form of sociability the aim of which is to confirm respect for the inaccessibility of the other person.[50] For if the letter's alleged intention was tact and discretion, its actual effect is touch and intrusion. Its arrival not only interrupts the recipient quite rudely in her sleep; it also provokes another and even more radical breach of privacy when, in yet another kaleidoscopic turn of Truffaut's game of gender role reversals, we see what happens when the gentleman caller, now played by Fabienne, upon opening the door and spotting the lady, now represented by Antoine lying naked in bed, decides not to withdraw while closing the door, but to enter the room to stay.

Frankness

The systemic uncertainty that characterizes the paradoxical communication between Fabienne and Antoine is not a cause for lasting anxiety. After her rendezvous with Antoine in his apartment, (once they have slept together), Fabienne disappears from the film as if her character had never existed.[51] At this point Truffaut's treatment of tact differs from that by Proust. In *Stolen Kisses*, neither tact nor tactlessness (and there is plenty of the latter in the film) are perceived as potentially unsettling. The threat lies elsewhere, in a concept that over the course of its intellectual history has largely been discussed as a virtue: '*sincérité*' or, as Truffaut calls it synonymously, '*franchise*'. In *Stolen Kisses* we find the concept personified by a character whose absence is vital for the amorous encounter between Antoine and Fabienne to succeed, the rather unpleasant figure of Fabienne's husband, M. Tabard, performed by Michael Lonsdale. '*J'ai une faute très grave*' M. Tabard announces quite aggressively when approaching Antoine's detective agency to help him find out why nobody loves him: '*C'est la franchise*' (BV 0:45:42).

Were we to consider some of the key philosophical debates on sincerity, we would find that in the course of its history the advocates of the word have repeatedly triumphed over its critics. Beginning with Aristotle, who argued that truthfulness is a desirable mean between the deficiency of self-deprecation and the excess of boastfulness,[52] the concept became a key virtue in seventeenth-century Europe,[53] gaining even further momentum in the Romantic period, whose representatives, in the wake of Rousseau, tended to reject any so-called artificial forms of sociability in the name of personal integrity, authenticity, and the '*droiture du cœur*'.[54] For Truffaut's M. Tabard, by contrast, frankness poses a problem – but not for ethical reasons. Unlike Kant or Proust, Truffaut is not interested in thinking about tact within the context of a debate about the potential link between a person's moral decorum and their moral disposition. Proust's question of whether a tactful person is also a good person, or if a person who has no tact is morally bad, is of no importance to him. Nor is the Kantian didactic thought that a person's good moral decorum, if only practised for long enough, may facilitate an improvement of their moral disposition.[55] For Truffaut, tact takes precedence over sincerity because it helps to maintain the smooth transmission and reception of information between all interlocutors involved. Sincerity, in turn, interrupts the flow of communication. It can break an encounter between two or more people that may formerly have been intact. '*Moi je ne suis pas absolument sincère*', Truffaut declares in an interview of 1967:

> *J'aime beaucoup de gens hypocrites. L'hypocrisie, c'est le tact. Par exemple: je connais des gens sincères qui sont invivables. ... Quelqu'un avec qui je ne parle jamais, comme Simone Signoret, je la laisse parler, mais je ne lui dirai jamais quoi que ce soit, parce que c'est une femme sincère. Et sa sincérité va vers une espèce de muflerie. ... je préfère ... sentir quelqu'un qui fait des réserves sur vous, qui ne vous aime pas mais qui vous ne le dit pas ... Ce critère de la franchise absolue, n'est pas un critère pour moi. J'aime les gens, je mets le tact au-dessus de tout, et quelqu'un qui a du tact, c'est-à-dire, quelqu'un qui ... ne dit ce qu'il pense qu'au moment où il pense qu'il faut le dire, c'est pour moi une plus grande valeur que quelqu'un qui dit toujours ce qu'il pense par exemple. Je crois qu'il y a des heures où on ne doit pas dire ce qu'on pense ... et des pensées qu'on doit cacher.*

> I love plenty of hypocritical people. Hypocrisy is tact. For example, I know some sincere people who are unbearable ... Someone, I never talk to, such as Simone Signoret, I let her speak, but I would never tell her anything, because she is a sincere woman. Her sincerity tends towards a kind of boorishness. ... I ... prefer to feel that someone has reservations about you, does not like you but does not tell you. ... This criterion of absolute

sincerity is not one of my criteria . . . I place tact above everything else. And someone who has tact, that is, someone who doesn't say what he thinks at the time when he thinks he must say it, that for me is of greater value than someone who always says what he thinks, for example. I believe that there are times when you shouldn't say what you think . . . thoughts you should hide.[56]

If ever we feel the need to convey a certain point to another person, Truffaut tells us here, we should do so by using an indirect means of communication: talk or write about something else, as Fabienne does with Antoine, or remain altogether silent.[57] For Truffaut, characters like M. Tabard who are sincere, authentic, and direct, are not only difficult to bear. They are also impossible to be with, '*invivable*'. The modes of sociability we live by, politeness and tact, are part of a game the written and unwritten rules of which we must know so as to be able to participate in society. Sincerity, frankness, and authenticity are harmful because they interrupt this game. They interfere with the keeping away from each other and talking past each other on which it depends.[58] '*Nackte Ehrlichkeit*', writes Plessner in implicit agreement with Truffaut, is '*Spielverderberei*' (Naked honesty . . . has the effect of spoiling the game) (G 83/L 135). The daily falsities we exchange with each other, by contrast, are essential in that they help us protect the social fabric. They keep the game going. They are, with Plessner, what makes us human: '*Direkt und echt im Ausdruck ist schließlich auch das Tier; . . . Im Indirekten zeigt sich das Unnachahmliche des Menschen*' (Ultimately, the animal, too, is direct and honest in its expression; . . . The incomparability of humans is revealed in their indirectness) (G 106/L 162).

Truffaut's categorical rejection of frankness and his preference for tact as hypocrisy have to do with the notion of identity and the idea of civilization that underlie *Stolen Kisses*. Although Antoine spends his life reading romantic novels, there is nothing romantic about Truffaut's conception of the individual person. In contrast to someone like Rousseau, for example, Truffaut does not distinguish between potentially alienated modes of human existence and an immediate original essence we may have lost. There is no soul-searching in *Stolen Kisses*, no authentic intimate self the characters may want to uncover or need to restore. Truffaut's critique of frankness and his eulogy of tact as hypocrisy reveal as much. Truffaut, like Plessner, opposes '*diese romantische Meinung von der Zivilisationsfeindlichkeit des menschlichen Herzens*' (this romantic opinion that the human heart is hostile to civilization) (G 104/L 160). Although critical of contemporary society, Truffaut, like Plessner, embraces the virtues of civilization: 'My life, my experiences, and my ideas', he observes, 'all tend in that direction'.[59] And yet, Truffaut's rejection of a romantic philosophy of inwardness and introspection does not prevent the film from communicating a strong sense of alienation. A look at the following signature scene helps to explore this point.

Antoine, still in his pyjamas, stands in front of the mirror. We watch him from behind, slightly from the left, sharing the direction of his gaze and witness him fixating the reflection of his face while beginning to exclaim, repeatedly, compulsively, and hypnotically, overacting with great theatricality, the names 'Fabienne Tabard', 'Christine Darbon', 'Antoine Doinel', rhythmically emphasizing the second and third syllables of the name he concludes with: 'AnTOIne DOInel, AnTOIne DOInel' etc (BV 0:59:46/AD 233–4). One could interpret the scene in psychoanalytical terms, as a search for identity, or the lost maternal gaze in which Antoine might find his own self reflected.[60] With equal justification, however, one could look at it from an anthropological point of view and read it, with Plessner, as an allegory of the human condition.

In his 1948 essay on 'The Anthropology of the Actor', Plessner once more mobilizes his aforementioned theory that humans are naturally artificial and eccentric to argue that, when thinking about the category of the self, we should not do so in terms of a confrontation between an 'immediate interior essence' and an 'alienating exterior world', but in the sense of a productive relation between the private and the public aspects of our existence.[61] Humans, Plessner argues, are essentially doubles. Like actors, we can only ever experience ourselves through the roles we play in society. This means that our self does not simply exist. Our identification with our self is preceded by an act of abstraction that allows us to assume an ex-centric position in relation to ourselves. The split of the self that results is constitutive inasmuch as our sense of self is not essential but relational. Our self can only ever come into being in its relation to the other (person). And it is only through this detour via the other person that we can become ourselves.[62] Thus, the goal of Plessner's search for identity does not consist in a rejection, or an overcoming of the role, but in the reciprocal complementation of self and role. 'Er ist nur', Plessner concludes, portraying the actor as the epitome of the human being, 'wenn er sich hat' (Only if he has himself can he be).[63] Not that Truffaut's character Antoine ever achieves this goal. All five films in the Antoine Doinel cycle are about the protagonist's failure to create and embrace his role in society, to form a productive relationship with the other characters he appears to love, and, in so doing, succeed in establishing a productive relationship with himself. But the desire to achieve this goal is there. It drives all the films. And it is closer to Plessner's anthropological worldview than it is, as we shall see, to that developed by Barthes.

Conclusion

When *Stolen Kisses* was released in French cinemas in late 1968 and 1969 it became, to the great surprise of its makers, a remarkable critical and commercial success. After a four-month run 335,000 tickets had been sold in Paris alone. The film received the Prix Louis Delluc and the Prix Méliès. It came eighth on the *Cahiers du Cinéma* annual top ten list in 1968 and was nominated for the Golden Globe Awards and the Academy Awards as best foreign language film in 1969. Overall, *Stolen Kisses* brought in three times its investment.[64] The film's favourable reception was arguably linked to its appeal as a delightful, nostalgic comedy that had the potential to appease the collective upheaval of minds and bodies after a turbulent summer, and to reconcile the audience with the changes to come. But, as I have tried to show in this chapter, *Stolen Kisses* is more than just a lyrical crowd pleaser. Grappling with the antagonistic desire for both dissimilation *and* assimilation, the film reacts to an all-pervading sense of crisis when responding to the question of how we can create a society in which we approach each other without colliding and part again without ending in isolation. Truffaut's notion of tact arises from the tension addressed in this question. As an exaltation of conventional modes of politeness, as Barthes will have it, Truffaut's tact may allow its practitioners to reach across existing social boundaries. It may mobilize, bend, and occasionally outstretch, but never quite overthrow, existing norms and codifications. Evading confrontation and resisting conflict, it may help to negotiate an Aristotelian mean between collective modes of identification and incorporation on the one side and individual alienation and isolation on the other. But Truffaut's tact is not a moral category; it does not belong to the sphere of good or bad, true or false. Its value lies elsewhere. It consists in creating a particular form of well-being based on a well-tempered and well-balanced mode of co-existence. While Truffaut's tact thus resonates with much of what has been said about tact in the previous chapters, *Stolen Kisses* also introduces a significant variation. By reinscribing the hidden traces of touch into tact, the film simultaneously confirms and undermines the modern conception of tact as a touchless form of sociability. The outcome results in a mode of impassioned distance. This paradoxical category defies the misgivings about touch shared by Plessner and Adorno, and helps us prepare for what Barthes will describe as

> un 'monstre' logique, le bon dosage de l'émoi et de la distance: ... reconnaissance du désir, ancrage dans le corps (non refoulé) et distance, garantie qu'on n'écrase pas l'autre sous une demande poisseuse, qu'on ne lui fait aucun chantage à l'attendrissement → en somme, un Éros bien conduit, 'retenu', 'réservé ... (LN42)'

a logical 'monster': the right mix of emotion and distance . . ., acknowledgement of desire, (unsuppressed) anchorage in the body, and distance, guarantee that one doesn't crush the other under the stickiness of a demand, that
one in no way blackmails him into tenderness → in short, a well-behaved
Eros, 'restrained', 'reserved' . . . (N 15–16)

Truffaut's tact describes a provisional, useless, and ornamental form of
pleasure. It abstains from any direct forms of expression, aggression,
domination, or fusion. At once natural and artful, it aspires to the ideal
of a fragile and temporary emotional and cognitive balance between the
interlocutors involved. Distant and sympathetic, hopeful yet non-
committing (we sense that this balance will never last for long), we find
it summarized in a particular facial expression that features in one of the
closing scenes of the film.

Antoine and Christine have spent the night together. At breakfast in
her parents' house, they begin to exchange a series of notes. The content
of these notes remains hidden to the audience, but we can assume that
Antoine has proposed. Then their hands draw towards each other.
Gently, Antoine takes Christine's hand and, lightly, he slips the top of
a bottle opener over her ring finger. The script describes what we see
next in the film: '*Il regarde longuement cette alliance improvisée et il
sourit*' (He takes a long look at this improvised alliance and he smiles)
(BV 1:28.27/AD 261).[65]

CHAPTER 5

Approchement *(Barthes)*

... 'tact' (a somewhat provocative word nowadays).
Roland Barthes, 4 May 1977[1]

When Roland Barthes in the concluding session of the first lecture course he convened at the Collège de France, *Comment vivre ensemble* (1976–7), established tact as one of the key values on which to base his fantasy of alternative forms of living together, his audience was seriously concerned. What could be more reactionary to the minds of the demographically diverse clientele at the Collège in post-May 1968 Paris than resuscitating the dusty vocabulary of bourgeois etiquette? But the fact that Barthes, by this time one of the most prominent figures of the French intellectual avant-garde, referred to the unfashionable concept of tact, was not the only aspect of his lecture that made for a provocation. It was also *the way* he did it. To many of his listeners the mode by which Barthes proceeded seemed suspiciously de-theorized and unsystematic, leaving questions unanswered and problems unsolved.[2] At the same time, the notion of tact Barthes appeared to introduce did not bear much resemblance to one of the very few potentially acceptable ways of discussing the word in the 1970s, namely as an indicator for class affiliation. In contradistinction to Sartre's by now familiar use of the term in *Anti-Semite and Jew* (1944) and Bourdieu's exemplary analysis of the neighbouring concept of taste in *La Distinction* (1979), in his lecture course Barthes took no interest in explaining tact with the help of a theory according to which different forms of communication were, like modes of cultural consumption, 'predisposed, consciously and deliberately or not, to fulfil a social function of legitimating social differences'.[3] Although Barthes shared with many of his contemporary scholars a longstanding interest in analysing and exposing the workings of power, an interest he emphasized throughout his lecture course on

How to Live Together, in the concluding lecture Barthes positioned himself as an untimely figure (in the Nietzschean sense of the word), as someone who, like Helmuth Plessner before him, was at odds with his own historical moment to which he, at the same time, was responding. Instead of considering tact, with Bourdieu, as a 'marker of class',[4] Barthes proposed to think about tact as a concept that might, on the contrary, derive its strength from its radical resistance to any form of classification. As Barthes would explain in the lecture course that followed, *Le Neutre* (1977–8), we should try to see tact as a value that can be associated neither with domination nor with submission. Instead, Barthes would suggest, tact consists of the art of abstaining from both. Just as the 'degree zero' in the context of morphology and phonology is distinct from the negative and the positive, defining itself precisely through making no use of this relation,[5] Barthes' tact is characterized by a special form of neutrality. And it is from this neutrality that tact, established as a different mode of sociability and an alternative practice of interpretation, derives its utopian potential as – and again Barthes calls upon a seemingly outdated concept here – *'une forme du Souverain Bien'* (CVE 180/HLT 132).

In this chapter I want to engage with Barthes' conception of tact by situating it within a wider philosophical landscape that expands from the West (Kant, Rousseau, Schopenhauer, Nietzsche) to the East (Okakura, Suzuki). In so doing, I wish to reconstruct some of the ways in which Barthes explores the manifold connections between human forms of cohabitation and intellectual productivity in view of their ethical and aesthetic potential. I hope to demonstrate that while Barthes' 'non-method' is based on the assumption of an opposition between semiology (as *'écriture de la variation'*) and hermeneutics (as *'une voie de remontée verticale vers un objet central'* (a vertical route ascending toward a central object)),[6] the conception of tact on which it rests bears unexpected similarities to those put forward by Adorno and Gadamer before him. I suggest that Barthes' theory of social and aesthetic tact, although deemed unfashionable at the time of its invention, is crucial to the ongoing debates that challenge the hermeneutics of suspicion and stretch the limitations of 'critique'.[7] Within this context, I also explore if and how the intuitive, digressive, and radically egalitarian notion of tact Barthes proposed in the 1970s can help us resolve the antagonism that marked most of the theories of tact we previously considered, inasmuch as they risked reproducing the sense of distinction they originally sought to escape.

Peripheral Thinking

The two lecture courses, *Comment vivre ensemble* and *Le Neutre*, that Barthes convened at the Collège de France between 1976 and 1978, reflect his ambivalent position within the French academic community as a trendsetter and a misfit. While Barthes had been actively cultivating this double role since the publication of *Mythologies* in 1954, it was also a side-product of the (not always) deliberately unconventional trajectory of his academic career. As an intellectual with no doctoral degree or *agrégation* – his only academic qualification was a classics degree from the Sorbonne – Barthes was an unusual scholar who had spent most of his career abroad (in Romania, Egypt, and Morocco), or on the margins of the French academic system. And yet, in 1976, secured by just one single vote, Barthes was elected into the Collège de France, one of the most prestigious academic institutions in Europe, where he would deliver his lectures and seminars until his untimely death in 1980.[8]

As an avid reader of Hegel, Marx, and Brecht, Barthes was an intellectual who shared with Plessner and Adorno a concern for the formation of totalitarian forms of knowledge and power – and like Adorno, Barthes, too, took a particular interest in the role language might play as their potential arena. But surprisingly, and in contrast to the works of his German contemporaries, Barthes' writing is largely devoid of allusions to the experience of fascism and war.[9] Barthes had lost his father in the First World War and was thirty years old when the Second World War ended. But while Plessner and Adorno's theories of tact are characterized by a strong sense of historical continuity and, in the case of Adorno, a dialectical inevitability of evil, Barthes' approach to the concept is marked by the notion of discontinuity and rupture. Barthes' contemplations on the historicity of his own body help to illustrate this point. Like Proust, Barthes suffered from pulmonary tuberculosis as a young man and spent much of the 1940s withdrawn from the world in the secluded communities of various sanatoria. And, in resonance with the memories of Plessner – who, as we saw earlier, passed much of his childhood observing the peculiar forms of sociability cultivated by the upper-class patients in his father's sanatorium – for Barthes, too, his time spent as a patient was a life-forming experience that gave inspiration to the particular sense of community that is one of the leitmotifs of *Comment vivre ensemble* and *Le Neutre*. At the same time, and in stark contrast to Plessner and Adorno, Barthes' thoughts on the matter were driven by a rather radical sense of renewal. '*My own body*' of 1942, the body suffering from tuberculosis, '*was historical*',[10]

Barthes tells his audience in his inaugural lecture at the Collège de France on 7 January 1977, for example. In fact, he adds, it is more contemporary to Hans Castorp's body in Thomas Mann's *Magic Mountain* pre-1914 than the present world, where tuberculosis has largely been vanquished. In the conclusion Barthes draws from this observation, he replaces the notion of memory, marked by a moral obligation to remember, with the figure of forgetting, proposing an idea that culminates in substituting a consideration of the past with an exclusive focus on the present. '*Si donc je veux vivre*', Barthes exclaims,

> *je dois oublier que mon corps est historique, je dois me jeter dans l'illusion que je suis contemporain des jeunes corps présents, et non de mon propre corps, passé. Bref, périodiquement, je dois renaître. . . . J'entreprends donc de me laisser porter par la force de toute vie vivante: l'oubli.*

> If I want to live I must forget that my own body is historical. I must fling myself into the illusion that I am contemporary with the young bodies present before me, and not with my own body, my past body. In short, I must be periodically reborn. . . . I undertake therefore to let myself be borne on the force of any living life, forgetfulness.[11]

Barthes' line of argument is not only characteristic of his attitude towards his own corporality. It is also symptomatic of his thinking more generally. It helps to explain why Barthes – like his contemporary Truffaut, who waited until late in life before making a film about France under German occupation[12] instead of considering the long-term repercussions of fascism, war, and occupation on contemporary forms of sociability – decided to experiment with new forms of individuality and sociability as he saw them emerge in the aftermath of the student revolution. While we found Plessner emphasizing the potential similarities between the intellectual climate in Germany after the First World War and post-1968, for Barthes, by contrast, '*la rupture de mai 1968*'[13] becomes a major reference point that not only affects the ways he thinks about the historicity of corporality but also motivates him to consider an epistemological paradigm shift that concerns his understanding of semiology altogether. Before 1968, Barthes argues in his inaugural lecture, the primary object of semiology was '*la langue travaillée par le pouvoir*'. After 1968, he contends, the object of semiology is still politics, but the image of the social and speaking subject has changed, and so has the nature of power. Divided and multiplied into various different individual pressure groups, most of the '*libérations*' proposed have, in themselves, turned into discourses of power. '*On se glorifiait*', Barthes observes, '*de faire apparaître ce qui avait été écrasé, sans voir ce que, par là, on écrasait ailleurs*' (We took credit for restoring what had been crushed, without seeing what else we crushed in the process).[14] As a consequence, our method must change with the object. Since we can no longer work under the assumption that exposure offers a pathway to liberation (replacing untruth by truth), our only way forward is to suspend the negative dialectic this involves. In order to transgress the logic of power and subversion we need to invent a third term, a term that can help to capture the sense of what Barthes introduces as a certain mode of dis-empowerment. He calls it '*dépouvoir*' or, indeed, tact.

Barthes' lectures at the Collège de France were composed at a time that was marked, we saw Plessner critically observe in 1975, by the renewed belief in the possibility, and the significance, of immediate relations between people. This, Plessner argued, gave rise to ideological notions of community that helped to fuel a variety of illusions:

> *vom Rückzug aus der Gesellschaft im Sinne der Hippies – bis zum langen Marsch durch die Institutionen … Der leitende Gedanke auf allen Fronten war und ist die Befreiung des Menschen aus seiner Entfremdung, an welcher je nach Bedarf und Lage der Kapitalismus, bald der Kommunismus schuld sind.*

> beginning with the retreat from society according to the Hippies, and ending with the 'long march through the institutions' … the overarching idea was, and remains, the liberation of the human being from alienation, allegedly caused, depending on purpose and situation, by capitalism or communism.[15]

In his lecture course Barthes, too, toys with escapist fantasies in response to what he depicts as a particular sense of alienation. We shall see, however, that the scenarios he proposes as a possible solution differ quite distinctly from the anti-societal ideologies and communities that were the object of Plessner's critique.

Barthes' lectures are less openly political than Plessner's essay. Like Adorno, who was under severe attack in 1968–9 for refusing to engage directly with the political challenges of the time, Barthes stayed away from immediate political discourse.[16] This does not mean, however, that his lectures do not have political implications. On the contrary, Barthes concurs with Plessner and Adorno in thinking that aesthetics is an essential component in the consideration of social conditions.[17] This is why Barthes' lectures do not aim to incite direct political activism but take their inspiration from a critique of language. At the same time, like Adorno, who sought to revitalize a tradition of philosophical thought as a teaching of the good life, and like Plessner, who wrote his essay from the perspective of lived experience, Barthes, too, aims for '*une introduction au vivre, un guide de vie*' (N 37). In the '*projet éthique*' that emerges, Barthes, again like

Adorno, draws on literature as a tool to investigate problems of communality, searching, like his German counterpart, for a utopian balance
between community and autonomy, social integration and intellectual
independence. In the process, all three authors chose to occupy an off-
centre position. Adorno, although strongly influenced by Hegel, criticized
the prioritization of the general over the individual that he found to be
a dominant feature of post-Hegelian thought (M 14–15/MM 16–17).
Plessner, with his radical critique of the limits of community, consciously
wrote on the margins of the intellectual spectrum of the Weimar Republic.
And by referring, as does Adorno, to Hegel, Barthes also knows that to
valorize the individual at the expense of the communal deviates significantly from the collective undercurrent of the post-1968 French intellectual
debate.[18] It is within this context that Barthes gradually defines tact as one
of the key concepts of his lectures, or, as he prefers to call it – in a turn of
thought that chimes with Plessner's use of the term '*Zartheit*' as a sign and
symptom of tact – '*délicatesse*'.[19]

Tact as a Figure of Compassion

Barthes offers a first detailed discussion of tact in *Le Discours amoureux*, his
lecture course on '*épisodes de langage*' as structural patterns that shape the
minds of lovers, convened at the École pratique des hautes études between
1974 and 1976.[20] In the session of 11 March 1976, Barthes introduces the
term within the context of a wider contemplation on different forms of
compassion. The experimental arrangement that interests Barthes in this
session features a compassionate subject and a loved object who feels
unhappy for a reason that is exterior to their relationship. At the heart of
this constellation is the idea of the subject's violently affective and physical
identification with the object '*qui devient une partie, un organe du corps du
sujet*' (who becomes a part, an organ of the subject's body) (DA 521). To
further explore this position, Barthes runs through a list of various possible
concepts: '*sympathie*' (good in its etymological sense but outdated, and
potentially verging on insincerity); '*commisération*' (good in that it emphasizes with Rousseau the aspect of identification, but bad because it con-
notes condescension); and '*empathie*' (good in that, again, it captures the
idea of identification, but bad inasmuch as it has been corrupted by social
theory). The German word '*Einfühlung*' sounds better, notes Barthes, as it
accentuates the notion of empathetic coalescence in terms of what he calls
an 'oneiric hallucination'. Towards the end of this exercise Barthes decides,
however, that the only term that may hold after all is a polyphonic

umbrella term that depicts the identification of distress without embarrassing or interfering with the compassionate subject. This is the term *'amour'* (DA 521;) or, more precisely, 'maternal love', since, in a surprising turn, Barthes identifies the position of the compassionate subject with that of the *'Mère'* as an abstract principle that could also be masculine or neutral and is essentially defined as 'celui *qui a du souci'* (*the one who is concerned*) (DA 522;). The peculiar blending of the maternal with the erotic taking place here is further complicated by the assumption that in the course of an amorous relationship, the positions (of the subject as Mother and the object as child) are potentially exchangeable. Moreover, this Mother is essentially a *'Mère imparfaite'* insofar as she is associated with narcissism. In a final turn of argument Barthes dissolves the constellation of complete affective and corporeal identification that fascinated him earlier, into a constellation based on radical separation and exclusion: if the other suffers without me, Barthes' amorous subject concludes, why suffer for them (DA 522)?

The structural pattern of Barthes' experimental arrangement is marked by a growing sense of separation and distance. Initially, the figure of 'compassion' is thought to be based on the affective and corporeal identification of the compassionate self with the suffering other person. Yet the very idea that we can and indeed should identify with this other person turns out to be misleading. In the end, the recognition of the other person is of no interest here, and neither is the actual nature of their distress. Both are beyond the horizon of our understanding. Both only matter in relation to the compassionate self. In the end, Barthes presents a non-dialectical relationship between the self and the other, where the compassionate self fails to reach out to the other person and collapses back into his original state of narcissistic isolation.

In the revised version of the session that appears in *Fragments d'un discours amoureux*, the best-selling book Barthes published in 1977 while writing his lectures for *Comment vivre ensemble*, Barthes further radicalizes this point. In the section with the symptomatic title, *'J'ai mal à l'autre'* (I have an Other-ache), he does so by dropping all references to Rousseau's definition of compassion, introducing instead Nietzsche and, through him, Schopenhauer's more recent (and more radical) theory of *'Mitleid'*. Schopenhauer develops this concept as a remedy against human egoism and aggression, defining *'Mitleid'* as *'Einleid'* or *'Einleidigkeit'*, understood as the self's complete and utter identification with the other's distress (OC V 87–88).[21] Following Nietzsche's polemical (and ill-justified) rejection of Schopenhauer's concept, Barthes argues in *'J'ai mal à l'autre'* that

Schopenhauer's understanding of the term is misleading. Rather than feeling self-hatred when the other feels self-hatred or turning mad when the other turns mad, for Barthes, being compassionate means to preserve a certain distance from the other. For Schopenhauer, the recognition of the other person's distress leads to the recognition of our own (and equally valuable) distress. This in turn reveals the essential identity of all living beings as sufferers. Barthes draws the opposite conclusion. Compassion does not lead us to realize identity, but difference. What we learn when trying to identify with the other person's distress is, according to Barthes, that this distress takes place without us. In fact, their suffering is an act of betrayal, since we are neither its origin nor its end. Schopenhauer writes that compassion demolishes the wall between 'you' and 'I.'[22] In Barthes' constellation the exact opposite is the case. This is why, for the Barthes of *Fragments d'un discours amoureux,* the only plausible consequence lies precisely in what Schopenhauer sought to defy: a celebratory act of egoism.[23] Since the suffering of the object threatens to annihilate me as the compassionate subject, I had better annihilate the suffering object. This leads Barthes to the following exclamation: '*Que surgisse le mot refoulé qui monte aux lèvres de tout sujet, dès lors qu'il survit à la mort d'autrui: Vivons!*' (Let the repressed word appear which rises to the lips of every subject, once he survives another's death: Let us live!) (OC V 88).[24] The ethical compromise Barthes consequently proposes is a conception of compassion in terms of a well-tempered mélange between nearness and distance, passion and reason. He calls this mélange '*délicatesse*' (tact) (OC V 88).

While Schopenhauer's '*Mitleid*' has to do with the affective and corporeal fusion of the self and the other person, Barthes' transformation of compassion into '*délicatesse*' is motivated by a desire for separation. Schopenhauer's '*Mitleid*' is altruistic; Barthes' tact is egocentric. Tact enables the self to protect himself from empathetic identification and hence from being harmed, '*angetastet*' (touched, violated), by the misery of the other person. While Schopenhauer celebrates the breakdown of the boundary between 'you' and 'I' in the act of compassionate identification, Barthes aims to resurrect it.[25] Tact thus helps to reinstate the difference between the self and the other. For Barthes – as for Proust, Plessner, Adorno, and Truffaut before him – this distinction between the individuals involved is associated with protection. And, like Plessner's '*Zartheit*', Barthes' '*délicatesse*' is linked to the control of emotions, to 'culture', 'art', ('artificiality'), and to (psychological) 'health'.[26]

Whereas in *Fragments d'un discours amoureux* the figure of tact triggers a relapse into a non-dialectical, self-centred construction of thought, in the lecture series that followed, *Comment vivre ensemble* and *Le Neutre*, tact is by contrast transformed from a figure that helps confirm the boundary between 'I' and 'you' to a concept that assists in erecting this boundary in order to overcome it. In his lectures, Barthes is no longer thinking about a dual model (the couple), nor is he simply replacing that dual model with a plural or collective model (the family, the crowd). Instead, he explores what we could call a very personal fantasy of a lifestyle: '*Quelque chose comme une solitude interrompue d'une façon réglée: le paradoxe, la contradiction, l'aporie d'une mise en commun des distances – l'utopie d'un socialisme des distances*' (Something like solitude with regular interruptions: the paradox, the contradiction, the aporia of bringing distances together – the utopia of a socialism of distance) (CVE 37/HLT 6). The motif that sets this fantasy to work is the small group of coenobitic monasteries on Mount Athos in Greece: monks both isolated from and in contact with one another, within a particular type of structure based on '*agglomérats idiorrhythmiques*' (CVE 37).[27] In his lecture course, Barthes' interest thus shifts from an individual ethic that focuses on the idiosyncrasies of the 'I' to a social ethic that actively takes into consideration the space of the other.

Tact Replaces Compassion

In *Comment vivre ensemble* and *Le Neutre*, Barthes abandons the idea that tact may be a particular kind of compassion.[28] In fact, in *Le Neutre*, compassion no longer even appears among the thirty figures discussed.[29] The notion of tact Barthes continues to develop in its stead further explores the idea of a spatial and emotional distance between oneself and other people, or oneself and the world at large. Barthes does this in a deliberately associative way, taking growing inspiration from a combination of Western literature and thought, with Eastern ethical and aesthetic concepts as introduced to the West through the works of Kakuzō Okakura, D. T. Suzuki, Alan Watts, and Jean Grenier. By mobilizing a number of concepts drawn from traditional Japanese ethics and aesthetics, the aim of Barthes' 'Japonisme'[30] is not to interrogate Japanese thought, nor to incite an actual dialogue between 'the East' and 'the West'. Instead, the philosophical detour via Japan allows Barthes to revisit established conventions and concepts of Occidental thought and see them anew with a defamiliarized eye. Barthes thus presents to his audience a series of surprising correspondences that help to subvert existing paradigms and frequently lead to novel and unforeseen constellations while, at the same time, a number of continuities remain.

Like Proust, Plessner, Adorno, and Truffaut before him, Barthes defines tact in relation to its neighbouring concept, politeness. Politeness, Barthes argues, at least in its conventional Western, class-oriented use, is based on education.[31] It depends on a set of norms and regulations. Critically understood as a mode of social disciplining, politeness consists of '*une gangue conformiste d'habitudes*' (a conformist straitjacket of habits), channelling the individual by a series of can'ts and musts (N 62/TN 33).[32] Tact, on the other hand – and here too Barthes chimes with his (Western) predecessors – is described as an individual deviation from habitual norms and forms of social consent. If politeness follows a mathematical sense of correctness, then tact grows out of the spirit of individual sensitivity and intuition. As a spontaneous and situational form of social handling, tact parries generality with non-normative and inventive modes of behaviour (N 61–62/TN 32–33). Politeness, Barthes observes, relies on the principle of repetition. It is superficial, conservative and nostalgic by nature. Tact, by contrast, occurs in the here and now of the singular moment. Tact, Barthes claims, is oblivious of history and tradition. Unlike politeness, tact is associated with an elevated state of attentiveness and suspension that may allow us to form a particular connection with another person, with the world that surrounds us, or simply experience the intense pleasure of being alive (N 79/TN 47).[33]

While Barthes associates Western politeness with norms, class, and convention, he is not interested in exploring tact within the context of its bourgeois appropriation as another potential marker of class and distinction. Instead, the figure of tact that fascinates him is socially atopic, '*au-delà des classes: sans marque*'.[34] Rather than casting judgement and placing people according to their cultural background or social status, in the manner of Proust's great-aunt, Barthes' tact is inspired by a (broadly conceived) Oriental resistance to modes of abstraction and categorization, whereby things are reduced to their general outlines with the help of symbols and signs. By contrast, Barthes' tact is based on an intuitive sensitivity for the concrete paired with an attentiveness towards the unfathomable singularity of the subject. '*Chaque fois*', Barthes notes,

> *que dans mon plaisir, mon désir ou mon chagrin, je suis réduit par la parole de l'autre ... à un cas qui relève très normalement d'une explication ou d'une classification générale, je sens qu'il y a manquement au principe de délicatesse.* (N 66)

> Every time that in my pleasure, desire, distress, the other's discourse ... reduces me to a case that fits an all-purpose explanation or classification in the most normal way, I feel that there is a breach of the principle of tact. (TN 36)

Barthes merges motifs associated with the Japanese tea protocol, described in Okakura's famous *Book of Tea* (1906), as a particularly sophisticated '*art du supplément inutile*' (N 59/TN 30), with quotations drawn from the Marquis de Sade, Baudelaire and the Sophists to show how tact is not only a marginal and 'ex-centric' mode of behaviour, but also 'socially obscene', inasmuch as it is, like Fabienne's and Antoine's short-lived affair, offensive in relation to form and transgressive in view of convention. Tact, Barthes observes, is distinct from tactics. Unlike diplomacy, which is target-oriented, tact is an ornamental figure, aimless, useless, futile, and effeminate (N 58/TN 34). With the help of a rare reference to Walter Benjamin – who, under the influence of hashish, is hesitating over what to eat, '*non par goinfrerie*', as Benjamin explains in the French translation, '*mais par expresse politesse à l'égard des plats, de peur de les froisser en les refusant*' (not from greed, but from an extreme politeness towards the dishes that I did not wish to offend by a refusal) – Barthes portrays tact, like Proust before him, as an exaltation of politeness, an intensely pleasurable form of excess (N 62/TN 35).[35]

This does not mean, however, that Barthes' tact is associated with the onslaught of strong emotions. Linked to the Japanese *sabi*, described by Alan Watts as the detached yet highly sensitive mood of the 'solitary and quiet',[36] Barthes' tact appears as an amorous state that, distinct from any forms of virility, is essentially non-invasive and withstands the desire to possess (N 35). As a mode of aloneness and inwardness, tact appears in Barthes' contemplations as a sublimated form of sexuality. Neither intimate nor remote, neither hot nor cold, tact is described as creating an equilibrium that – like the Taoist principle of *wu-wei* as a particular mode of non-interference – abstains from the '*vouloir saisir*' (will-to-grasp) (CVE 172/HLT 126).[37]

Barthes' tact is complicit with the implicit, the silence of '*tacere*' (N 53/ TN 25). It is a particular way of concealing something so that the addressee may discover it, of merely suggesting what one dare not reveal.[38] As a non-linear form of signification it follows the logic of shifting. Like metaphor, tact isolates a feature and lets it '*proliférer en langage, dans un mouvement d'exaltation*' (proliferate as language, in a movement of exaltation) (TN 63/ TN 34). In this way, tact abstains from any direct modes of expression that appear to Barthes as forms of aggression. In contrast to frankness (N 53/TN 24) or blackmailing, for example, tact does not crush the other '*sous une demande poisseuse*' (under the stickiness of a demand) (N 42/TN 16). Defined both as natural and artful, Barthes' tact is thus gradually developed as a value based on a particular mode of emotional and cognitive balance. Significantly, Barthes concludes his lecture course *Le Neutre* in the final session of 3 June 1978 with the evocation of the same facial expression that is also the concluding motif of Okakura's *Book of Tea*. We saw it feature in one of the final scenes of Truffaut's *Baisers volés* (Chapter 4). For Plessner, it summarizes the human position (in relation to ourselves, and the world at large). Distant yet sympathetic, promising but erratic: '*le sourire*' (the smile) (N 244/TN 195).[39]

Mask and Face

In his contemplations on tact, Barthes draws on a paradigm we already encountered when visiting Plessner and Adorno's theories of tact in Chapters 3 and 4 of this book. This is the idea that our existence is split into a self we inhabit and a role we perform when entering the public sphere. We saw that Plessner describes the public sphere in terms of a theatre where individuals enter into an artificial, impersonal and trans-formative relationship with each other. When seen by other people, we cease to be ourselves. Instead, we begin to play a role, become other. Plessner does not describe this process of alienation in negative terms. On the contrary, he argues that becoming other is not only a condition for the formation of the self; it also allows for an encounter between the self and other people under protected conditions. Adorno, by contrast, dis-agrees with Plessner's unconditional affirmation of the role. Unlike his colleague, he does not define our daily role-playing in terms of a productive process but as a form of impoverishment, associating the various personae we assume in society with distortion, hypocrisy, and commodification. Within this context, Adorno's relation to the idea of a rupture between self and role is ambivalent. On the one hand, he rejects the idea that underneath our social personae may hide an original and authentic self (M 174–176) because it is due to pathological modes of role-play that we are unable to form a self in the first place, a self that is capable of actively relating to other people, to itself, to the world. On the other hand, Adorno also conjures the image of us humans as beings who, however diminished and impoverished in our essence, still seek to resist the spell that threatens to transform us into mere façades (M 13/MM 15). While the former argument implies the potentially unsettling idea that behind the roles we play in our daily lives there may be nothing, the latter is based on the more assuring conception of our self as an ontological ground, distinct from its social existence, a self in its non-alienated state, as it were, in relation to which we must measure our current condition. Within the context of Plessner's theory of sociability, tact helps to negotiate between social expect-ations and individual variation, the self and the other, the mask and the face.

For Adorno, in turn, tact is associated with a glimpse of hope inasmuch as it may offer a potential remedy for the alienation and commodification that these social expectations produce in a capitalist world. For tact, Adorno concludes, referring, like Plessner before him, to '*Zartheit*' (delicacy) as one of its symptoms, '*ist nichts anderes als das Bewußtsein von der Möglichkeit zweckfreier Beziehungen, das noch die Zweckverhafteten tröstlich streift*' (is nothing other than the awareness of the possibility of relations without purpose, a solace still glimpsed by those embroiled by purposes) (M 45/MM 41).

The utopian lifestyle Barthes envisages in his lecture course follows a logic that complies more with Adorno's idea than it does with Plessner's point. The 'principle' of tact, Barthes observes in the final session of *Comment vivre ensemble*, is as follows:

> *Ne pas manier l'autre, les autres, ne pas manipuler, renoncer activement aux images (des uns, des autres), éviter tout ce qui peut alimenter l'imaginaire de la relation = Utopie proprement dite, car forme du Souverain Bien.* (CVE 179–80)

> not to direct each other, other people, not to manipulate them, to actively renounce images (the images we have of each other), to avoid anything that might feed the imaginary of the relation = Utopia in the strict sense, because a form of Sovereign Good. (HLT 132)

Inflected by a Lacanian vocabulary, Barthes' use of the 'image' is marked by a negative understanding of alienation (in terms of a deficit) that shares many of its traits with Adorno's use of the term. For Barthes, as for Adorno, tact is essentially motivated by a respect for the private sphere of the self. It offers a form of defence against potential commodification. Yet in contrast to Plessner, for Barthes, liberation cannot be found in the social sphere but in the individual's retreat from the public. As he points out in *Le Neutre*, mobilizing, as Adorno did before him, a Marxist notion of commodity fetishism:

> *le mythe public/privé ...; on a dit: idéologiquement capitaliste: mais c'est l'utilisation du 'public' qui est aliénée dans un marché (photos, interviews, racontars, etc.): le 'privé' est une défense naturelle contre la transformation du public en marchandise* (N 183)

> the public/private myth ... it has been said: ideologically capitalist: but it's the use of the 'public' that is alienated in a market society (photos, interviews, gossip etc.): the 'private' is a natural defense against the commodification of the public (TN 141)

The fantasy of an alternative mode of living together which Barthes subsequently develops in *Le Neutre* returns to Rousseau as an example.

Rousseau, Barthes tells his audience on 13 May 1978, withdrew from society to nature (more specifically, to a tiny island in Lake Bienne, Switzerland) with the aim, in Rousseau's own words, to '*interdit toute espèce de communication avec la terre ferme de sorte qu'ignorant tout ce qui se faisait dans le monde j'en eusse oublié l'existence et qu'on y eût oublié la mienne*' (forbid any communication with the mainland so that being unaware of all that went on in the world I (Rousseau) might forget its existence and that it might also forget mine) (N 180/TN 138–139).[40] In Barthes' interpretation, Rousseau's '*retraite*' signifies an exemption from social responsibility and a return from role to self. But then Barthes begins to digress. What interests him in this example is not the either/or-ism of the nature/culture divide we generally tend to associate with Rousseau's philosophy of alienation, but the description of Rousseau's relations with the tax collector and his family, who also lived on the island, as well as the limited number of visitors from the mainland who would come to the island on Sundays. In Barthes' reading, these individuals are ideal companions inasmuch as they are described as (personally and intellectually) '*insignifiants*'. This makes them non-intrusive, non-invasive cohabitants, allowing them to provide just the right dose of otherness, '*l'altérité légère donc au besoin plate*' (the light and thus if needed flat otherness) (N 181/TN 139) that makes Barthes' phantasmatic vision of a retreat work. This is not a retreat from society into the intimate sphere of the family (for Barthes just another trap with no exit). Nor is it one of those anti-societal communities that were the object of Plessner's critique. What Barthes develops here on the basis of his reading of Rousseau is a form of community that foils the binary structure on which the '*mythe public/privé*' depends. Once more, Barthes associates his notion of tact with *wu-wei* as a form of abstaining from dualistic choice, of 'doing nothing', to create a third model of human cohabitation that is neither social nor solitary, strange or familiar, but where a light and non-intrusive form of communication based on the idea of a suspension of the image, and an exemption of meaning, prevails (N 181/TN 139).[41] This social utopia is as close to Barthes' figure of tact as can be: '*identification logique du clandestin (ou de l'anonyme) et du libre*' (N 141/TN 183).

Conclusion

More explicitly than Adorno, Barthes reflects in his lectures on his own position as an intellectual in society. Seeking to reconcile the paradox '*de vouloir vivre seul et de vouloir vivre ensemble*' ((of) wanting to live alone and wanting to live together) (CVE 35/HLT 5), Barthes explores, in a loose adaptation of the above-mentioned Kantian antagonism of unsociable sociability,[42] the connection between human sociability and intellectual productivity in view of its cognitive potential. Tact, within this context, offers a way to disestablish the intellectual self as a public figure and to deconstruct habitual patterns of thought (N 140). In this way, Barthes succeeds in translating the idea of ethical tact into a form of aesthetic perceptivity that resides at the heart of an alternative practice of interpretation. Recalling Nietzsche's opposition between method and *paideia* ('culture'), or, in Barthes' words, 'non-method', Barthes' general idea is not to pursue a clearly marked path but to let the mind roam, and to present one's findings as one goes along.[43] For Barthes, as for Adorno, the practice of culture is defined by an engendering of forces essentially understood as an *'écoute des différences'* (an attentiveness to differences).[44] Intellectual practice means to not speak *'la langue de "tout le monde"'* (the language 'everyone else' speaks) (CVE 50/HLT 18). Defined, with Adorno, as a form of resistance that diverts from the *'vertraute[] Strom der Rede'* (familiar flow of speech), intellectual inquiry is based on conscious deviations from normative thought patterns, abstract principles, and categorizations. It must not succumb to any sense of belonging or original contact (M 114/ MM 100). Instead, for Barthes, as for Adorno, it is marked by an intimate sensitivity to the particular and a non-dogmatism that does not aim at the consolidation, stabilization, and fixation of concepts, but advocates lightness, volatility, and a flexibility of thinking. Feeling for the finest nuances and quickest shifts of meaning, it follows the principle of inexactness, indirection, and digression. Deliberately undetermined and unfinished, this is a non-linear form of engagement that avoids establishing the shortest connection between two points by approaching the object of one's desire in a plurality of digressions.[45] As Barthes notes in *Le Neutre*, tact is

> *une jouissance d'analyse, une opération verbale qui déjoue ce qui est attendu . . . une perversion qui joue du détail inutile . . . c'est ce découpage et ce détournement qui est jouissif → on pourrait dire: jouissance du 'futile'. . . . En somme, délicatesse: l'analyse . . . qui ne sert à rien.* (N 58–9)

> a pleasure in analysis, a verbal operation that frustrates expectation . . . a perversion that plays with the useless . . . it's this cutting and rerouting that is the source of pleasure → one could say: pleasure in the 'futile'. . . . In short: tact: analysis . . . when aimless. (TN 29–30)

Barthes' introduction of tact as a mode of deviation contributes to notions of critical engagement that do not define the act of reading as a form of *empathetic* identification or appropriation, nor as a kind of decoding or classification. Instead, it is understood as an act of respect and discretion, rather than suspicion and exposure, of giving space rather than coming close, of building on rather than digging into.[46] More than a mode of contact and comprehension (grasping), it is a way of letting go. The idea is to create a balance, however precarious, between the self and other people, objects, and texts. This balance arises from a notion of distance that does not signify a 'safety-zone' that protects us by keeping us apart, but a shared space in which we actively take the risk to expose ourselves to otherness. In fact, it may help to think of this shared space, with Adorno, as a 'field of tension' that does not manifest itself 'in relaxing the claim of concepts to truth, but in the delicacy (*Zartheit*) and fragility (*Zerbrechlichkeit*) of thinking' (M 144/MM 127).

More rigorously than most of the authors previously encountered (and more successfully, I would argue), Barthes proposes a notion of tact that is not, as he writes in *Sade, Fourier, Loyola*, '*un produit de classe, un attribute de civilisation, un style de culture*' (OC III 859–60) but a mode of engagement that bypasses the bourgeois appropriation of tact as a tool of privilege and exclusion and transcends the logic of power and submission on which it depends.

In the *Le Neutre* seminar of 6 May 1978, Barthes introduces a term we first encountered in Chapter 1 when engaging with the philosophical baselines of a tactful hermeneutics proposed by Gadamer in *Wahrheit und Methode* based on the Greek ethic of measure. We saw that, within the context of Gadamer's argument, Aristotle's *mesotes*, the middle way or middle ground, was understood as a situation or, more specifically, as an ethical possibility for action that resists conflict, and with it the dynamic of domination and submission. Thus, *mesotes* was mobilized by Gadamer as a concept that allows us to appreciate a distant feeling for individuality combined with an awareness of the limits of what we can know. It is based on our respect for the 'mystery', as we witnessed Gadamer observe in reference to Schleiermacher, 'of the inwardness of the other person'.[47] Although Barthes develops his semiology as a fundamental critique of the '*inventaire du code herméneutique*'[48] for which Gadamer stands, his reflection on an art of interpretation that grows out of the spirit of tact chimes with Gadamer's idea. I argued in Chapter 1 that in *Wahrheit und Methode* Gadamer did not quite succeed in bridging hermeneutics and ethics, inasmuch as the notion of tact he developed remains entangled in the historicity of the concept as a bourgeois virtue. In *Le Neutre*, Barthes, by contrast, manages to contrive ways to sideline the term's prevalent association with social distinction, refinement, formation, and class.

On 6 May 1977, Barthes first mobilizes the grammatical neutral, the *oudétéron* that derives its meaning from taking no side. Then, he introduces the political neutral, the *mesos* that escapes the binary logic of conflict. Further specifying this line of thought, Barthes continues by distinguishing between the formal 'neutral' (without value or judgement), and the ethical neutral (relating to an option). Letting his mind roam, he then moves on in his play with words, spinning his associations further than Gadamer did and introducing yet another concept, *hétérorropos,* meaning, firstly, the one *'qui penche d'un côté et de l'autre'* (who leans to one side and the other) and, secondly, words whose declension proceeds from different themes, 'irregular' words (N 171/TN 130). In so doing, Barthes not only mobilizes the concept of the mean understood as a productive tension between the self and the other that results from a reciprocal cancelling of forces, effecting a suspension of meaning; he also emphasizes the idea of the unpredictable that grows out of the notion of irregularity, *'du tour à tour en désordre'* (of the one following the other without order) (N 171/TN 130). To cancel and to scramble, to stir: at the end of his lecture course in May 1978, Barthes' tact emerges as a word that suggests openness, denoting the unforeseeable, the surprising, the new. It signifies *possibility.*

Coda

The social practice of tact can be linked to the ability to empathize with another person. In order to be tactful, it helps to be able to imagine how the other feels so as to alleviate their – and possibly our own – state of distress. But while empathy is an important pathway to tact, it may not always be necessary. A last look at Truffaut's story about the gentleman caller and the naked lady in the bathroom reveals as much. To handle the situation creatively, in slight but essential deviation from the general code of politeness, the gentleman does not necessarily have to be able to feel how the lady feels in the very moment he opens the door. Although it may help if he does, it suffices for him to know that it is generally deemed an embarrassment for a lady to be caught naked in the bathroom by a (not yet quite known) representative of the other sex. Tact, like empathy, is based on a certain form of mutual understanding. But while empathy implies the idea of entering someone else's mind, inasmuch as it is linked to the presumption that 'I know how you feel', tact exists to create a form of bonding between individuals that is not based on the idea of intrusion but, conversely, on the respect for existing boundaries, and on a willingness to not always assume that one knows. While empathy requires resonance and proximity, tact is there to restore distance, and to accept the difference between the individuals involved, to protect and preserve their dignity. Tact is based on an attention towards otherness. It functions as a way to negotiate the space between different horizons of experience in the same way as it facilitates an *approchement* between the horizons of readers and texts. Tact, understood with Proust and Adorno as an ethical sensitivity to form, is based on an individual digression from the norm that may, at least in the case of Barthes and Truffaut, arouse pleasure (of interpretation).

In visiting the five theories of tact advanced by Proust, Plessner, Adorno, Truffaut, and Barthes, we saw that the notion of crisis gives rise to the figure of tact. Tact flourishes at times when established codes and conventions deteriorate but have not yet disappeared. The challenge is, then, to develop new forms of communication that enable individuals to approach each other without colliding, and to depart from each other without ending in isolation. While Proust's, Plessner's, Adorno's, Truffaut's, and Barthes' theories of tact were produced at different turning points in the history of the twentieth century and – at least in the case of Plessner, Adorno, and Barthes – are characterized by conflicting methodological assumptions, they share a suspicion towards certain forms of intimacy and tactility, and a preference for individual difference, distance, and deviation over communal identification. The five variations of an ethic of indirectness that result are based on forms of communication that defy immediacy (Proust), authenticity (Plessner), frankness (Truffaut), directness (Barthes), and touch (Adorno). In this way, they seek to resist any possible strategies of incorporation. Defined, with Barthes and Adorno, as a form of resistance that diverts from the familiar flow of speech, tact, as a particular form of understanding, must not obey any sense of belonging and contact (M 114/MM 100). Instead, it is marked by a sensitivity for the particular and a non-dogmatism that avoids establishing the shortest connection between two points. Described by Plessner as a distanced feeling (*Fernfühlung*) or distant touching (*Ferntastung*) (G 110/L 167), and by Barthes as '*une distance amoureuse*', tact is based on a form of attentiveness that resists the pressure of nearness inasmuch as it approaches the object of one's desire by way of a plurality of digressions. The outcome consists in a form of non-violent contemplation that is, in the words of Adorno, 'the source of all the joy of truth'. It presupposes 'that he who contemplates does not absorb the object into himself: a distanced nearness' – '*Nähe an Distanz*' (M 100/MM 90).

Acknowledgements

I wrote much of this book in solitude, but rarely in isolation. Of the many people who generously offered their support, I am particularly thankful to Andreas Corcoran, who read large sections of the manuscript at various stages of its emergence and hugely helped me to improve it. I am also immensely grateful to Ian Cooper, Emma Gilby, David Caron, Shohini Chauduri, Ben Hutchinson, Lucy O'Meara, Lucia Ruprecht, Tom Baldwin, and Shane Weller for sharing their thoughts and insights on individual draft chapters, and for commenting on the project as a whole. I thank Kate Briggs, Ariane and Luc Boltanski, Martin Crowley, Hannah Freed-Thall, Tobias Heinrich, Katherine Ibbett, Marie Kolkenbrock, Tim Mathews, and David Russell for highly stimulating conversations on tact, empathy, and other related matters. Beatrice Blucke did a great job in proofreading an earlier version of the manuscript. Marieke von Bernstorff gave me some wonderful advice on the cover design. And Marine Authier, Andreas, and Frank Corcoran were equally brilliant in helping me with some of the quotations and their translations. Responsibility for any shortcomings is, of course, entirely mine.

I was delighted when Bethany Thomas at Cambridge University Press offered to take the manuscript under her wings, and am grateful also to the press's two anonymous readers for providing such useful and perceptive feedback. I thank Ginevra House for copyediting the manuscript and for taking great care of the index.

The origins of this book go back to May 2016, when I first presented the idea in the shape of a research paper at the University of Kent. I kept coming back to the project in the spring term of 2017, when I held a research grant from the Gerda-Henkel Foundation, and really should have thought more about mothers' milk and breastfeeding instead. A Leverhulme Trust Research Fellowship in 2019–20 helped me finish the book. I thank both institutions for their kind and generous support.

Sections of the Introduction, Chapter 3, Chapter 5, and the Coda draw on an article published in *The Modern Language Review*, 114:1 (2019), pp. 1–21. One section of Chapter 5 draws on an article published in *L'Esprit créateur*, 55:4 (2015), pp. 131–47. I am grateful to both journals for granting me permission to reuse this material here in a different context and in slightly modified form.

Notes

Epigraph

1. From *The Neutral* by Roland Barthes, trans. Rosalind E. Krauss and Denis Hollier. Copyright © 2002 by Éditions du Seuil. English translation copyright © 2005 Columbia University Press. Reprinted by permission of Columbia University Press and Georges Borchardt, Inc., on behalf of the author's estate. N 65/LN 98.

Introduction

1. Kant, 'Idee zu einer allgemeinen Geschichte in weltbürgerlicher Absicht', in *Schriften zur Anthropologie, Geschichtsphilosophie, Politik und Pädagogik I, Werkausgabe*, ed. by Wilhelm Weischedel, 12 vols. (Frankfurt: Suhrkamp, 1977), vol. XI, pp. 31–50 (p. 40)/translated by H. B. Nisbet as 'Idea for a Universal History with a Cosmopolitan Purpose', in *Political Writings*, ed. by Hans Reiss, (Cambridge: Cambridge University Press, 1991), pp. 41–53 (pp. 44–5).
2. See also the script version of *Baisers volés* in Truffaut's *Les Aventures d'Antoine Doinel* (AD 147–263 (246)). My translation.
3. Amy Coplan defines empathy as a 'complex imaginative process in which an observer simulates another person's situated psychological states (both cognitive and affective) while maintaining clear self-other differentiation'; 'Understanding Empathy: Its Features and Effects', in *Empathy: Philosophical and Psychological Perspectives*, ed. by Amy Coplan and Peter Goldie (Oxford: Oxford University Press, 2011), pp. 5–18 (p. 5).
4. Wollheim introduces the term to describe how a person who looks at an artwork is simultaneously aware of the object represented and of the fact that they are looking at its representation, in *Art and Its Objects* (Cambridge: Cambridge University Press, 1980).
5. Heinz Kohut, 'Introspection, Empathy, and the Semicircle of Mental Health', in *The Search for the Self: Selected Writings of Heinz Kohut: 1978–81*, ed. by P. H. Orstein (Madison, CT: International Universities Press, 1981), pp. 537–67 (p. 543).

6. Coplan, 'Empathy', p. 18.

7. Günther Gödde and Jörg Zirfas, 'Die Kreativität des Takts', in *Takt und Taktlosigkeit: Über Ordnungen und Unordnungen in Kunst, Kultur und Therapie*, ed. by Günther Gödde and Jörg Zirfas (Bielefeld: transcript, 2012), pp. 9–30 (p. 19). In addition, see Carl von Clausewitz's tractatus *Vom Kriege* (1812) for an exploration of the military connotations of tact.

8. Jacques Derrida, *On Touching – Jean-Luc Nancy*, trans. by Christine Irizarry (Stanford: Stanford University Press), p. 296.

9. Niklas Luhmann, 'Soziologie der Moral', in *Theorietechnik und Moral*, ed. by Niklas Luhmann and Stephan H. Pfürtner (Frankfurt: Suhrkamp, 1978), pp. 8–116 (p. 55). My translation.

10. Luhmann, *A Sociological Theory of Law*, trans. by Elizabeth King and Martin Albrow, ed. by Martin Albrow (London: Routledge & Kegan Paul, 1985 (1975)), p. 27.

11. Erving Goffman, *The Interaction Ritual: Essays in Face-to-Face Behaviour* (New Brunswick, NJ: Aldine Transaction, 2005), p. 97.

12. Max Scheler makes the distinction between '*Sozialperson*' and '*Intimperson*' in *Der Formalismus in der Ethik und die materielle Werteethik – neuer Versuch der Grundlegung eines ethischen Personalismus* (Bern: Francke, 1954), pp. 563–4. Goffman, in a similar vein, differentiates between the 'individual and his role' in 'Role Distance', in *Encounters: Two Studies in the Sociology of Interaction* (Harmondsworth: Penguin, 1972), pp. 73–134 (p. 95).

13. '*Takt*', K. Gratiolet observes in 1918, '*ist schlechthin nicht erlernbar*' (Quite simply, tact cannot be learned), *Schliff und vornehme Lebensart* (Berlin: Holzinger, 2013), p. 7. My translation.

14. Jean-Paul Sartre, *Anti-Semite and Jew: An Exploration of the Etiology of Hate*, trans. by George J. Becker (New York: Schocken, 1995), p. 124.

15. This has been argued by Sartre, among others, in *Anti-Semite and Jew*, p. 124. We will return to this idea in Chapter 1: Tact's History, and Chapter 2: Proxemics (Proust).

16. For a more detailed discussion of this point on which I draw here, see David Caron, *The Nearness of Others: Searching for Tact and Contact in the Age of HIV* (Minneapolis: University of Minnesota Press, 2014), p. 262.

17. See, again, Caron, *The Nearness of Others*, p. 264.

18. Theobald Ziegler, *Das Gefühl: Eine psychologische Untersuchung* (Stuttgart: Göschen, 1893), p. 177. My translation.

19. See Slavoj Žižek, 'Good Manners in the Age of Wikileaks', *London Review of Books*, 33:2 (20 January 2011), pp. 9–11. For more recent references to Truffaut's scene, see the above-cited Caron, who builds much of his argument in *The Nearness of Others* around it, and Haruki Murakami, whose Dr Tokai, the protagonist of one of his short stories, is associated

with Fabienne's principle of tact. See 'An Independent Organ', in *Men without Women* (2014), trans. by Philip Gabriel and Ted Goossen (London: Harvill Secker, 2017), pp. 77–103; the reference to Truffaut is on p. 87. Caron's observations in particular have inspired my own reading of Fabienne's letter set out in this introduction, and I will return to his book time and again. See also, within this context, Richard Sennett's argument about 'the tyrannies of intimacy' first presented in *The Fall of Public Man* (Cambridge: Cambridge University Press, 1977), a work that resonates particularly well, as we shall see in Chapter 3, with some of Helmuth Plessner's ideas on tact.

20. To my knowledge the present book is the first attempt to bring these five authors together. For rare examples of comparative work on Adorno and Barthes see Doris Kolesch, *Das Schreiben des Subjekts: Zur Inszenierung ästhetischer Subjektivität bei Baudelaire, Barthes und Adorno* (Vienna: Passagen, 1996); Lucy O'Meara, '"Not a Question but a Wound": Adorno, Barthes, and Aesthetic Reflection', *Comparative Literature* 65:2 (2013), pp. 182–99; and, more recently, adding Plessner to her discussion, Corina Stan, *The Art of Distances: Ethical Thinking in Twentieth-Century Literature* (Evanston: Northwestern University Press, 2018).

21. Note that *À la recherche du temps perdu* features prominently in Barthes' lecture courses at the Collège de France, and that the opening section of *Minima Moralia* is dedicated to Marcel Proust; (M 21/MM 21).

22. Truffaut, letter to Nicole Stéphane (1964) in *Correspondance*, ed. by Gilles Jacob and Claude de Givray, preface by Jean-Luc Godard (Rennes: Hatier, 1988), p. 321/*Letters*, trans. by Gilbert Adair (London: Faber, 1989), pp. 250–1. However, Proust was supposed to feature as a character in Truffaut's *Belle Époque*, a film that, due to the director's premature death, never materialized.

23. An exception is Adorno's essay 'Filmtransparente: Notizen zu Papas und Bubis Kino', in *Die Zeit*, no. 47 (18 November 1966), p. 24, in which he alludes to Truffaut's formulation 'le cinéma de papa', coined to distinguish big-budget films as products of the culture industry ('*Papas Kino*') from independent cinema ('*Bubis Kino*').

24. I draw on the following formulation by Claude Coste here, who notes in his introduction to Barthes' lecture course, *Comment vivre ensemble*, '*A quelle distance dois-je me tenir des autres pour construire avec eux une sociabilité sans aliénation, une solitude sans exil?*', 'Préface', pp. 19–28 (p. 28).

25. Note that Barthes speaks of an '*éthique (ou une physique) de la distance*' in *Comment vivre ensemble* (CVE 110/HLT 72).

26. I draw on Johannes Unold here, who defines tact as '*sittliches Formgefühl*' (an ethical sense of form), allowing us to appreciate and to practise the Good *as* the Beautiful. Tact, he concludes, is the '*ästhetische Seite des Sittlichen*' (the

aesthetic side of the ethical), *Grundlegung für eine moderne praktisch-ethische Lebensanschauung* (Leipzig: Hierzel, 1896), p. 203.

27. For a seminal study in this context, see Keith Thomas, *In Pursuit of Civility: Manners and Civilization in Early Modern England* (Newhaven: Yale, 2018).

28. Note that David Heyd in his otherwise significant contribution to the debate discusses the term in the alleged 'absence of previous theoretical treatment of the concept of tact', 'Tact: Sense, Sensitivity, and Virtue', *Inquiry*, 38:3, (1995), pp. 217–31 (p. 218).

29. 'Interview' (from 1970) in *Le Cinéma selon François Truffaut*, ed. by Anne Gillain (Paris: Flammarion, 1988), p. 195/Gillain, Anne (ed.), *Truffaut on Cinema*, trans. by Alistair Fox (Bloomington, IN: Indiana University Press, 2017), p. 150.

30. *Cinéma selon Truffaut*, p. 193.

31. Barthes, *Leçon*, OC V 429–450 (p. 440).

32. '*Wir möchten, gerade in Zeiten der Not, einander nah sein. Wir kennen Zuwendung als körperliche Nähe oder Berührung. Doch im Augenblick ist leider das Gegenteil richtig. Und das müssen wirklich alle begreifen: Im Moment ist nur Abstand Ausdruck von Fürsorge*' (Of course we wish to be close to another, especially in times of adversity. We recognize another's affection through bodily nearness and touch. But unfortunately, in these times the opposite is the case. And this is something really everybody needs to come to accept: right now, it is only through keeping our distance that we can truly express our care for another); Angela Merkel, *Speech to the Nation* (18 March 2020), bit.ly/3J4141t. My translation.

1 Tact's History

1. See, as one of the earliest examples, the Middle English dialogue, *Vices & Virtues* (ca. 1225): 'Ða fif wittes.þat is, *visus, auditus, gustus, ordoratus, et tactus*, þat is ʒesihthe, ʒeherhþe, smac, and smell, and tactþe', 'tact, n.', in *OED Online* (Oxford University Press, September 2022), www.oed.com/view/Entry/196957.

2. '*Est il home qui ait le tact si soubtil comme l'areigne, qui sent le doit avant que le doit le touche?*', *Le livre du roi Modus et de la reine Ratio*, 1354–77, f° XXV, verso, Littré, https://gallica.bnf.fr/ark:/12148/bpt6k54066991/f739.

3. See 'Tact' in Johann Heinrich Zedler, *Großes vollständiges Universal-Lexicon aller Wissenschafften und Künste*, 68 vols. (Halle und Leipzig, 1731–54), vol. XLI, p. 687, column 1348, www.zedler-lexikon.de and 'Der Tact', in Johann Christoph Adelung, *Grammatisch-kritisches Wörterbuch der hochdeutschen Mundart*, 4 vols. (Vienna, 1811), vol. IV, columns 512–13, bit.ly/3leimAN.

4. See www.zeno.org/Brockhaus-1911/A/Takt.

5. On some of the theoretical premises of conceptual history, and on the significance of the '*Sattelzeit*' [threshold period] (1750–1850) in particular, see

Reinhart Koselleck's essay, 'On the need for theory in the discipline of history' in R. Koselleck, *The Practice of Conceptual History: Timing History, Spacing Concepts* (Stanford: Stanford University Press, 2002), pp. 1–19, (p. 5)

6. See 'tact, n.', in *OED Online*, www.oed.com/view/Entry/196957. The *Littré* quotes the following passage from Voltaire to illustrate tact's metaphorical turn: '*Pour la vérité dans les sentiments, pour le tact de certains ridicules, je serais assez votre homme*', letter to Mme du Deffant of 8 March 1769, *Littré*, www .littre.org/definition/tact.

7. As a synonym of '*toucher*' and '*l'attouchement*', '*tact*', Chevalier de Jaucourt explains, is '*la sensation la plus générale*' that helps distinguish humans from automatons; 'Tact, le', *L'Encyclopédie*, vol. xv (1765), pp. 819b–22b, (p. 820), bit.ly/3wWBZQv.

8. Dugald Stewart, *Outlines of Moral Philosophy: For the Use of Students in the University of Edinburgh*, 2nd. ed., enl., 2 vols. (Edinburgh: printed for Creech, sold by Cadell jun. & Davies, 1801), vol. 1, p. 6; I cite from the entry on 'tact, n.', in the *OED Online*, www.oed.com/view/Entry/196957.

9. Sidney Smith, 'On Taste', *Elementary Sketches of Moral Philosophy* (London: Longman, Brown, Green & Longmans, 1850), p. 154; I cite from the entry on 'tact, n.', in the *OED Online*. For a more detailed account which I draw on here, see David Russell, *Tact: Aesthetic Liberalism and the Essay Form in Nineteenth-Century Britain* (Princeton: Princeton University Press, 2018), p. 6.

10. 'Takt, m.' (1890), *Deutsches Wörterbuch von Jacob und Wilhelm Grimm*, digitized edition in the *Wörterbuchnetz des Trier Center for Digital Humanities*, version 01/21, www.woerterbuchnetz.de/DWB?lemid=T00647. For the Kant quotation, see Kant, *Anthropologie in pragmatischer Hinsicht*, in *Werkausgabe*, ed. by Wilhelm Weischedel, 12 vols. (Frankfurt: Suhrkamp, 1977), vol. XII, (§ 6) p. 424, edited and translated by Robert B. Louden as *Anthropology from a Pragmatic Point of View* (Cambridge: Cambridge University Press, 2006), (§ 6) p. 28. Translation modified. We will shortly return to Kant's concept.

11. Johann Wolfgang Goethe, *Die Wahlverwandtschaften* (Frankfurt: Insel, 1972), p. 194/*Elective Affinities*, trans. by David Constantine (Oxford: Oxford University Press, 1994), p. 189.

12. In 'Blindheit und Takt in Goethes *Wahlverwandtschaften*', Caroline Torra-Mattenklott traces Goethe's use of tact back to the year 1807. Some of the quotations from Goethe's work below are drawn from her wonderfully wide-ranging article in *German Life and Letters* 70:4 (October 2017), pp. 491–505. For more research on tact in Goethe, see also Elisa Ronzheimer, 'Eine Frage des Takts: Zur Übereinstimmung in Goethes *Unterhaltungen Deutscher Ausgewanderten*', in *Stimmungen und Vielstimmigkeit der Aufklärung*, ed. by Silvan Moosmüller, Boris Previšić, and Laure Spaltenstein (Göttingen:

Wallstein, 2017), pp. 277–91. For a detailed discussion of tact in relation to mathematics and the natural sciences, see Lutz Danneberg, '"*Ein Mathematiker, der nicht etwas Poet ist, wird nimmer ein vollkommener Mathematiker sein*": Geschmack, Takt, ästhetisches Empfinden im kulturellen Behauptungsdiskurs der Mathematik und der Naturwissenschaften im 19., mit Blicken ins 20. Jahrhundert', in *Zahlen, Zeichen, und Figuren: Mathematische Inspirationen in Kunst und Literatur*, ed. by Andrea Albrecht, Gesa von Essen and Werner Frick (Berlin: de Gruyter, 2012), pp. 600-57.

13. 'Leute von dem feinsten geselligen Tact', conversation with Eckermann, 22 March 1825, cited in Torra-Mattenklott, 'Blindheit und Takt', p. 498.

14. Goethe, *Vorarbeiten zu einem Deutschen Volksbuch*, cited in Torra-Mattenklott, 'Blindheit und Takt', p. 498.

15. Goethe, *Vorarbeiten*, cited in Torra-Mattenklott, 'Blindheit und Takt', p. 498.

16. Goethe, *Instruction für die Beobachter bei den Großherzogl. meteorologischen Anstalten*, cited in Torra-Mattenklott, 'Blindheit und Takt', p. 498.

17. 'Der Takt des Schrittes wird jeden Augenblick unterbrochen', Goethe, *Die Wahlverwandtschaften*, p. 29; '*ich fühlte wohl, dasz du [. . .] aus dem takt kamst*', *Der junge Göthe*, cited in Grimms' *Deutsches Wörterbuch*, www .woerterbuchnetz.de/DWB/takt.

18. Goethe, *Sprüche in Prosa*, cited in Grimms' *Deutsches Wörterbuch*, www .woerterbuchnetz.de/DWB/takt. My translation.

19. Goethe, *Italienische Reise* (Munich: Hanser, 1992), pp. 87–8/ *Italian Journey*, trans. by W. H. Auden and Elisabeth Mayer (London: Penguin, 1962), p. 83.

20. '*Es ist aber der Tact eine richtige Bewegung mit der Hand, nach welcher sich die Sänger und Instrumentisten richten müssen*', 'Tact', in *Zedler*, p. 678, col. 1348.

21. In his *Versuch Über Wagner*, Adorno writes of the '*totale Herrschaft der Taktiervorstellung*' that characterizes the composer's work. Adorno's argument is a different one, but his misgivings about a '*Gestik des Schlagens*' resonate, I think, with the concerns raised by Goethe in this passage, *Versuch über Wagner* (Frankfurt: Suhrkamp, 1981), pp. 25-9. I thank Lucia Ruprecht for alerting me to this passage.

22. In this point I divert from David Caron's interpretation of the concert scene which I otherwise follow in most of my own reading; Caron, *The Nearness of Others*, p. 294.

23. 'Ich weiß', Goethe's narrator observes, '*die Franzosen haben es an der Art, den Italiänern hätte ich es nicht zugetraut, und das Publikum scheint daran gewöhnt*'; Goethe, *Italienische Reise*, p. 87/'I know this thumping out the beat is customary with the French; but I had not expected it from the Italians. The public, though, seemed to be used to it', *Italian Journey*, p. 83.

24. Goethe, *Die Wahlverwandtschaften*, pp. 62-3/ *Elective Affinities*, trans. by David Constantine (Oxford: Oxford University Press, 1994), p. 55.

25. Ian Cooper pointed this out and I thank him for discussing this passage with me.
26. See Chapter 3: Alienation.
27. Reginald Baliol Brett in *The Nineteenth Century: A Monthly Review* (22 January 1882). I cite from the entry on 'tact, n.', in the *OED Online*.
28. See, again, Stewart, *Outlines of Moral Philosophy*, vol. 1, p. 6.
29. Thomas quotes Montesquieu within this context, who observes in *The Spirit of the Laws* (1748) that 'the more people there are in a nation who need to deal with each other and not cause displeasure, the more politeness there is'; cited in Keith Thomas, *In Pursuit of Civility*, p. 112.
30. For a more comprehensive engagement with the history of manners, see again Thomas, *In Pursuit of Civility*. From my point of view, chapter 1 on 'Civil Behaviour' (pp. 1–64) is of particular interest. I draw on Thomas' critical engagement with Norbert Elias' theory of the civilizing process here, *Pursuit of Civility*, p. 19, and pp. 112–13.
31. Albrecht Koschorke uses this term in *Körperströme und Schriftverkehr: Mediologie des 18. Jahrhunderts* (Munich: Fink, 1999), p. 52.
32. Koschorke refers to Norbert Elias' concept of 'Langsicht' here, outlined in Elias, *Der Prozess der Zivilisation*, 2 vols. (Frankfurt: Suhrkamp, 1976), vol. II, pp. 336–41.
33. Koschorke, *Körperströme und Schriftverkehr*, p. 189.
34. Ernst Cassirer, *The Philosophy of the Enlightenment*, trans. by Fritz C. A. Koelln et al. (Boston: Beacon, 1955), p. 355.
35. Johann Gottfried Herder, 'Zum Sinn des Gefühls' in Hans Dietrich Irmscher, 'Aus Herders Nachlaß', *Euphorion* 54 (1960), pp. 286–90 (p. 287).
36. Cassirer, *Philosophy of Enlightenment*, p. 304. Torra-Mattenklott, who also refers to Cassirer within this context, reminds us that 'feelings' in the plural was a neology of the time, 'Blindheit und Takt', pp. 491–2.
37. Denis Diderot, *Lettre sur les aveugles, à l'usage de ceux qui voyent* (London: publisher not identified, 1749), pp. 101–2/*An Essay on Blindness, in a letter to a person of distinction* (J. Barker, No. 7, Little Russell-Court, Drury Lane, 1780?), pp. 51–2; Eighteenth Century Collections Online, bit.ly/3HBTYAv.
38. I follow Inka Mülder-Bach's interpretation here, in which she describes this dynamic beautifully and in more appropriate detail: 'Kommunizierende Monaden. Herders literarisches Universum' (23 January 2004) in *Goethezeitportal*. www.goethezeitportal.de/db/wiss/herder/muelder-bach_monaden.pdf, p. 11. For Herder's writings on *Plastik*, see Johann Gottfried Herder: *Sämtliche Werke*, ed. by Berhard Suphan, 33 vols. (Berlin 1877/ Hildesheim 1967), vol. VIII, pp. 1–87, 88–115, and 116–63.
39. See again Kant, *Anthropologie in pragmatischer Hinsicht*, §6, p. 424/ *Anthropology from a Pragmatic Point of View*, (§6) p. 28.

40. Kant, 'Von einem neuerdings erhobenen vornehmen Ton in der Philosophie' (1796), in *Kants Werke: Akademie-Textausgabe*, vol. VIII: *Abhandlungen nach 1781* (Berlin: de Gruyter, 1968), pp. 387–406 (p. 398); 'On a recently prominent tone of superiority in philosophy', in Immanuel Kant, *Theoretical Philosophy after 1781*, ed. and trans. by Henry Allison and Peter Heath, trans. by Gary Hatfield and Michael Friedman (Cambridge: Cambridge University Press, 2002), pp. 430–45 (p. 438). Translation modified. Interestingly, Allison and Heath translate '*mystischer Takt*' as 'mythical touch' here, a decision that, deliberately or not, obfuscates the term's connection to Kant's own '*logischer Takt*' (logical tact) as developed in the *Anthropologie*.
41. I draw on Gadamer's discussion of Kant's conception of taste as a kind of *sensus communis* here, in Gadamer, *Wahrheit und Methode* (Tübingen: Mohr, 1960), p. 35. For the relevant passage in Kant, see *Kritik der Urteilskraft*, *Werkausgabe*, vol. x, pp. 225–8. We shall shortly return to Gadamer's work.
42. In *The Practice of Everyday Life*, Michel de Certeau builds on Kant's conception of logical tact when establishing the distinction between theory and practice on which much of his argument rests. But the description of reading as poaching that follows is closer to the idea of *tactics* as a mildly impertinent mode of game playing than to the non-strategic ways of tactful reading I am interested in here. See Certeau, *The Practice of Everyday Life*, trans. by Steven Rendall (Berkeley: University of California Press, 1984), pp. 72–76, 165–176.
43. Kant, *Kritik der Urteilskraft*, § 46, pp. 241–2, ed. by Paul Guyer, trans. by Paul Guyer and Eric Matthews as *Critique of the Power of Judgement* (Cambridge: Cambridge University Press, 2000), § 46, p. 186.
44. Kant, *Kritik der Urteilskraft*, § 47, p. 245.
45. Kant, *Kritik der Urteilskraft*, § 47, p. 244.
46. Cassirer, *Philosophy of Enlightenment*, p. 321.
47. Kant, *Kritik der Urteilskraft*, § 60, pp. 299–300.
48. See Winfried Menninghaus, *Disgust: Theory and History of a Strong Sensation* (Albany, NY: SUNY Press, 2003), p. 4. Menninghaus does not use the word tact, though.
49. Cassirer, *Philosophy of Enlightenment*, pp. 297–303.
50. As Adorno does in *Minima Moralia* (M 39).
51. See Kant, *Kritik der Urteilskraft*, § 40, pp. 224–8.
52. For the latter in particular see, Proust, *À la recherche du temps perdu*, with the notoriously tactless Monsieur Bloch (and his sisters) as one example, and Sartre, *Anti-Semite and Jew*, p. 124.
53. I follow Menninghaus' argumentation here (pp. 4–5), in which he draws on Kant, *Critique of Judgement*, trans. by Werner Pluhar (Indianapolis: Hackett, 1987), pp. 69, 160, and Pierre Bourdieu, *Distinction: A Social Critique of Taste*,

trans. by Richard Nice (Cambridge, MA, Harvard University Press, 1984), pp. 488–91. Similar claims have been made by Gadamer, *Wahrheit und Methode*, pp. 31–3.

54. Menninghaus, p. 5. See also Keith Thomas, *In Pursuit of Civility*, for the wider cultural-historical implications of the above.

55. Helmholtz, *Über das Verhältniss der Naturwissenschaften zur Gesammtheit der Wissenschaften* (Tübingen: Mohr, 1862), p. 10.

56. Helmholtz, *Verhältniss*, p. 15.

57. See Keith Doubt, who points to the problems of this approach, in 'The Pedagogy of Tact in Theoretical Discourse', *Phenomenology + Pedagogy*, 8 (1990), pp. 103–17.

58. Gadamer, *Wahrheit und Methode*, xvi.

59. See again Doubt, 'The Pedagogy of Tact', p. 104.

60. See Hegel, *Phänomenologie des Geistes* (Stuttgart: Reclam, 2020), 'Der sich entfremdete Geist; die Bildung', pp. 375–408.

61. *Wahrheit und Methode*, p. 11/ *Truth and Method*, trans. revised by Joel Weinsheimer and Donald G. Marshall (London: Continuum, 2004), p. 13.

62. Gadamer, *Wahrheit und Methode*, p. 12.

63. Gadamer, *Wahrheit und Methode*, p. 12/ *Truth and Method*, pp. 13–14.

64. Gadamer, *Wahrheit und Methode*, p. 14.

65. Gadamer, *Wahrheit und Methode*, p. 12.

66. Gadamer, *Wahrheit und Methode*, p. 31.

67. Sartre, *Anti-Semite and Jew*, p. 124, my emphasis.

68. Gadamer, *Wahrheit und Methode*, p. 13/ *Truth and Method*, pp. 14–15.

69. Gadamer, *Wahrheit und Methode*, p. 14.

70. Habermas, Jürgen, 'Interpretive Social Science vs. Hermeneuticism', in *Social Science as Moral Inquiry*, ed. by Norma Hann, Robert N. Bellah, Paul Rabinow, and William M. Sullivan (New York: Columbia University Press, 1983), pp. 251–69, p. 269.

71. For his critique of a 'hermeneutics of suspicion', see, Paul Ricœur, 'Book I: Problematic: The Placing of Freud', in Paul Ricœur, *Freud and Philosophy: An Essay on Interpretation* (New Haven: Yale University Press, 1970), pp. 3–58, 30. Rita Felski uses the latter formulation in *The Limits of Critique* (Chicago: Chicago University Press, 2015), p. 12.

72. Gadamer draws on Aristotle's notion of *mesotes* in the context of his discussion of taste in *Wahrheit und Methode*, p. 37. See Aristotle, *The Nicomachean Ethics*, trans. by David Ross, ed. by Lesley Brown (Oxford: Oxford University Press, 2009), book IV, chapter 8, pp. 77–9.

73. Aristotle introduces the term ἐπιδέξιο (*epidéxios*) here as one particular mode of ὁ μέσος (*o mésos*), the 'middle state'. In this form, ἐπιδέξιο is an adjective and has the connotation of movement. It can mean many things: auspicious, clever, dexterous. It can even mean elegant, lucky, prosperous, or, as David

Ross suggests, catapulting the word into modernity, 'tactful', *Nicomachean Ethics*, p. 78. I thank Anne Alwis for advising me on this point.

74. I will return to this point in the concluding chapter of this book, *Approchement* (Barthes).

75. Felski, *Limits*, p. 176.

76. Felski, *Limits*, p. 12.

77. Felski, *Limits*, p. 6.

78. This is also what may have motivated Valentine Cunningham when pitting tactful modes of close reading against what he calls 'Theory-compelled interpretations', *Reading after Theory* (Oxford: Blackwell, 2002), p. 159.

79. Marielle Macé, 'Ways of Reading, Modes of Being', *New Literary History: The French Issue: New Perspectives on Reading from France* (Spring 2013), 44:2, pp. 213–29. The article consists of translated excerpts from Macé's book-length essay of the same title, *Façons de lire, manières d'être* (Paris: Gallimard, 2011).

80. Macé, 'Ways of Reading', p. 224.

81. Felski, *Limits*, p. 182.

82. Gadamer, 'The Hermeneutics of Suspicion', in *Phenomenology and the Human Sciences*, ed. by J. N. Mohanty (The Hague: Nijhoff, 1985), p. 316.

83. Gadamer, 'Hermeneutics', p. 321.

84. Roland Barthes, 'En sortant du cinéma' (1975), OC IV 778–82 (782). Trans. by Richard Howard as 'Leaving the Movie Theatre', in *The Rustle of Language* (Berkeley: University of California Press, 1989), pp. 345–49 (p. 349). I thank Sophie Eager for alerting me to this formulation.

2 Proxemics (Proust)

1. RTP III 656/SLT III, 134. Proust died in 1922. The third volume of *À la recherche du temps perdu*, *La Prisonnière*, cited here, was first published a year after his death. Translation modified.

2. See for example: '*L'affaire Dreyfus était pourtant terminée depuis longtemps, mais vingt ans après on en parlait encore*' (RTP III 548).

3. This is a topic that is only of late receiving growing attention. For an overview, see Adam Watt, 'État présent: Marcel Proust', *French Studies*, 72:3 (2018), pp. 412–24.

4. For relevant research in this area see, for example, Catherine Bidou-Zachariasen, *Proust Sociologue: De la maison aristocratique au salon bourgeois* (Paris: Descartes & Cie, 1997); Jacques Dubois, *Le roman de Gilberte Swann. Proust sociologue paradoxal* (Paris: Seuil, 2018); Edward J. Hughes, *Proust, Class, and Nation* (Oxford: Oxford University Press, 2011); Cynthia Gamble, 'From Belle Époque to First World War: The Social Panorama', in *The Cambridge Companion to*

Proust, ed. by Richard Bale (Cambridge: Cambridge University Press, 2001); and Michael Sprinker, *History and Ideology in Proust* (London: Verso, 1998).

5. The concept of tact in Proust has so far received relatively little scholarly attention. Notable exceptions are: Antonin Wiser : 'Le Tact, expérience de la littérature ou Proust lu par Adorno', *Philosophie*, 113:2 (2012), pp. 79–93 and Stéphane Chaudier, 'Tact et Contacts dans *La Recherche*', *Marcel Proust aujourd'hui* (2012), 9, pp. 69–95.

6. For more information on the manuscript's history see Nathalie Mauriac Dyer's excellent annotations in F 16–20.

7. See also F 75.

8. That social and moral distinction are not necessarily the same thing we learn in a conversation between Marcel's grandmother and his uncle, F 38. (See also RTP I 20.) We shall return to this point.

9. As an English translation was not yet available at the time of writing, all translations of the quotations from Proust's *Feuillets* are mine.

10. With homosexuality being one notable exception, as Mauriac Dyer points out in her annotations.

11. This is, I believe, what Tadié has in mind when he writes in the introduction: '*C'est le recours à la technique du roman qui donnera au monologue proustien une form, des limites, des procédés, une densité, une pudeur aussi, qu'il n'avait pas encore en ce début de 1908. . . . Ici, nous savons tout et éprouvons le sentiment d'une sorte d'impudeur*', Tadié, 'Le moment sacré', in F 11–5 (14–15).

12. Lukács, *Die Theorie des Romans: Ein geschichtsphilosophischer Versuch über die Formen der großen Epik* (Stuttgart: Luchterhand, 1971), p. 62.

13. Lukács only first mentions *La Recherche* in the introduction to the 1962 edition of his book, *Theorie des Romans*, p. 8.

14. Lukács, *Theorie des Romans*, pp. 62–3.

15. Lukács, *Theorie des Romans*, p. 63/ *The Theory of the Novel*, trans. by Anna Bostock (London: Merlin Press, 1978), pp. 73–4.

16. I allude to the title of Macé's book, as discussed in Chapter 1: Tact's History.

17. See Chapter 1: Tact's History.

18. Proust, 'Journées de lecture', in *Contre Sainte-Beuve*, ed. by Pierre Clarac and Yves Sandre (Paris: Gallimard, 1972), pp. 160–94 (p. 163)/'On Reading', in Proust, *On Reading Ruskin*, ed. and trans. by Jean Autret, William Burford, and Phillip j. Wolfe (Newhaven: Yale University Press, 1987), pp. 99–130 (p. 102).

19. 'Taste classifies, and it classifies the classifier', Bourdieu, *Distinction*, p. 6.

20. Foucault, *History of Sexuality*, vol. 1, pp. 17–18.

21. Rudolph von Jhering, *Der Zweck im Recht* (1877–83), reprint, ed. by Christian Helfer, 2 vols. (Hildesheim: Olms, 1970), p. 46.

22. Goffman, *Interaction Ritual*, p. 103.

23. Sartre, *Anti-Semite and Jew*, p. 124, my emphasis.

24. Sartre, *Anti-Semite and Jew*, p. 124.
25. Note that Swann's period of social glory is of a temporary nature, and that his decline is simultaneous with the rise of his counterpart, the notoriously tactless Monsieur Bloch. The fact that both are of Jewish decent and thereby prone to be excluded from the national community for their alleged 'lack of tact', as Sartre observes (*Anti-Semite and Jew*, pp. 124–5), would deserve a chapter of its own. For commentary on cultural contacts between people of different social and religious (Christian/Jewish) background in *La Recherche*, see Chaudier, 'Tact et contacts', p. 79.
26. See Arthur Schopenhauer, *Parerga und Paralipomena: Kleine Philosophische Schriften II*, in *Sämtliche Werke*. ed. by Wolfgang Frh. von Löhneysen in 5 vols. (Frankfurt: Suhrkamp, 1994), vol. V, (§ 396) p. 765. We shall look at Schopenhauer's parable in greater detail in Chapter 3: Alienation (Plessner – Adorno). Like many of his contemporaries, Proust was familiar with Schopenhauer's work. For research on the philosopher's influence on Proust's writing see, for example, Anne Henry, 'Proust und die Krise des Subjekts: Die Funktion des philosophischen Models in *À la recherche du temps perdu*', in *Marcel Proust und die Philosophie*, ed. by Ursula Link-Heer and Volker Roloff (Frankfurt: Insel, 1997), pp. 29–44.
27. As developed by Edward T. Hall in *The Hidden Dimension* (New York: Anchor Books, 1966).
28. Goffman, *Relations in Public: Microstudies of the Public Order* (Harmondsworth: Penguin, 1971), p. 385.
29. Goffman, *Relations in Public*, p. 415.
30. Note the association of 'mental derangement' with '*aliénation*' here, also reflected by the use of the term '*aliéniste*' for a psychiatric doctor in nineteenth-century French (and English), see David Leopold, 'Alienation', in *The Stanford Encyclopedia of Philosophy* (Fall 2018 Edition), Edward N. Zalta (ed.), bit.ly/3YecUeQ.
31. Sigmund Freud, *Beyond the Pleasure Principle* (New York: Liveright, 1961 (1920)), p. 18.
32. I draw on aspects of my more detailed analysis of 'Albertine sleeping' in conjunction with the scenes related to the grandmother's illness and death in *Regarding Lost Time: Photography, Identity, and Affect in Proust, Benjamin, and Barthes* (Oxford: Legenda, 2012), Part I, Ch. 3.
33. As discussed in Chapter 1: Tact's History.
34. Translation modified.
35. See 'What Is Tact?' in the Introduction.
36. Kohut, 'Introspection, Empathy, and the Semicircle of Mental Health', in *The Search of the Self: Selected Writings* of Heinz Kohut (1981), p. 540. For more

recent research into the 'dark side' of empathy see Paul Bloom, *Against Empathy: The Case for Rational Compassion* (New York: Vintage, 2016) and Fritz Breithaupt, *Die dunklen Seiten der Empathie* (Frankfurt: Suhrkamp, 2018).

37. Goffman, *Interaction Ritual*, p. 103.

38. We began to discuss this point in the Introduction.

39. Reportedly, Proust himself was involved in a duel with Jean Lorrain that took place on 6 February 1897 in the Bois de Meudon, southwest of Paris.

40. Gadamer, *Wahrheit und Methode*, p. 14/ *Truth and Method*, p. 15.

41. Proust's formulation resonates with the conception of empathy I proposed in the introduction to this book.

42. See Chapter 1: Tact's History.

43. Georg Simmel, 'Die Geselligkeit' (1917), in *Grundfragen der Soziologie: Individuum und Gesellschaft* (Berlin: de Gruyter, 1970), pp. 48–67 (pp. 54–5).

44. Goffman, *Interaction Ritual*, pp. 101–2.

45. See again Simmel, 'Geselligkeit', p. 54: '*Darum ist in der Gesellschaft das Taktgefühl von so besonderer Bedeutung, weil dies die Selbstregulierung des Individuums in seinem persönlichen Verhältnis zu anderen leitet, wo keine äußeren oder unmittelbar egoistischen Interessen die Regulative übernehmen*', *Geselligkeit* (It is for this reason that the sense of tact is of such special significance in society, for it guides the self-regulation of the individual in his personal relations to others where no outer or directly egoistic interests provide regulation), 'The Sociology of Sociability', trans. by Everett C. Hughes, *American Journal of Sociology*, 55:3 (November 1949), pp. 254–61, (p. 256).

46. See, again, Brett defining tact as a 'fine instinct in the management of men', cited in 'tact, n.', *OED Online*.

47. Barthes, CVE 179–180/HLT 132.

48. This interpretation of Albertine's character is of course short-lived. See, for example: '*par nature elle* [Albertine] *était . . . menteuse*' (RTP III 605).

49. Proust became acquainted with Kant's work during the 1890s thanks to his teachers Marie-Alphonse Darlu and Emile Boutroux, both of whom he held in high esteem. *La Recherche* contains a series of explicit and implicit references to Kant's philosophy. For research on Kant's influence on Proust, see, for example: Manfred Schneider, 'Das Ereignis der Zeit: Proust und die Theorie des Erhabenen', in *Proust und die Philosophie*, pp. 121–37.

50. Kant, *Anthropologie in pragmatischer Hinsicht*, (§ 12) p. 442/*Anthropology from a Pragmatic Point of View*, (§ 14) p. 42.

51. Kant, *Anthropologie*, (§ 12) p. 442, my emphasis.

52. Kant, *Anthropologie*, (§ 12) pp. 442–3/*Anthropology*, (§ 14) p. 42. For commentary on Kant's conception of beautiful appearance (*schöner Schein*) as a civilizing force, see, Helmuth Lethen and Caroline, Sommerfeld-Lethen: 'Schein zivilisiert', in

Höflichkeit: Aktualität und Genese von Umgangsformen, ed. by Brigitte Felderer and Thomas Macho (Munich: Fink, 2002), pp. 155–73.

53. Kant, *Anthropologie*, (§ 12)p. 445/*Anthropology*, (§ 14) p. 44.

54. Kant, *Anthropologie*, (§ 12) p. 444/*Anthropology*, (§ 14) p. 44. Translation modified.

55. Niklas Luhmann, 'Takt und Zensur im Erziehungssystem', in *Schriften zur Pädagogik*, ed. by Dieter Lenzen (Frankfurt: Suhrkamp, 2004), p. 246. My translation.

56. Luhmann, 'Takt und Zensur', p. 248.

57. Luhmann, 'Takt und Zensur', p. 253. My translation.

58. Luhmann, 'Takt und Zensur', p. 251. Original emphasis. My translation.

59. Luhmann, 'Takt und Zensur', p. 258.

60. Luhmann, 'Takt und Zensur', p. 255. My translation.

61. Luhmann, 'Takt und Zensur', pp. 257–8.

62. Luhmann, 'Takt und Zensur', p. 258. Original emphasis.

63. Gilles Deleuze famously described *La Recherche* as an 'apprenticeship in the interpretation of signs' in *Proust et les Signes* (Presses Universitaires de France, 1972).

64. Luhmann, 'Takt und Zensur', p. 247.

65. Proust, 'Préface du traducteur', in *Préface, traduction et notes à* La Bible d'Amiens *de John Ruskin*, ed. by Yves-Michel Ergal (Paris: Bartillat, 2007), pp. 23–4/'Preface to John Ruskin's *Bible of Amiens*', in *On Reading Ruskin*, ed. by Philip J. Wolfe and William Burford, trans. by Jean Autret, William Burford, and Philip Wolfe (London: Yale University Press, 1987), pp. 12–13. With minor emendations by Proust.

66. In Szondi's words: '*daß jedem Kunstwerk ein monarchischer Zug eigen ist*'; Peter Szondi, *Hölderlin-Studien. Mit einem Traktat über philologische Erkenntnis* (Frankfurt: Suhrkamp, 1970), p. 22.

67. '*Takt*', writes Walter Benjamin in a passage that chimes with Ruskin's scenario, emphasizing tact's theological implications, '*ist die Fähigkeit, gesellschaftliche Verhältnisse, doch ohne von ihnen abzugehen, als Naturverhältnisse, ja selbst als paradiesische zu behandeln und so nicht nur dem König, als wäre er mit der Krone auf der Stirn geboren, sondern auch dem Lakaien wie einem livrierten Adam engegenzukommen*' (tact is the capacity to treat social relationships, though not departing from them, as natural, even paradisal, relationships, and so not only to approach the king as if he had been born with the crown on his brow, but the lackey like an Adam in livery), Benjamin, 'Karl Kraus', in *Gesammelte Schriften*, ed. by Rolf Tiedemann and Gerhard Schweppenhäuser, 7 vols. (Frankfurt: Suhrkamp, 2003), vol. ii.1, pp. 334–67 (p. 339)/*Selected Writings, 1927–1934*, trans. by Rodney Livingston, eds. by Michael W. Jennings et al. (Cambridge: Harvard University Press, 1999), vol. ii, pp. 433–58 (pp. 436–37).

68. Proust, 'Préface', p. 24/'Preface', p. 13.
69. Proust, 'Préface', p. 24/'Preface', p. 13.
70. See Chapter 1: Tact's History.
71. See again Chapter 1: Tact's History.
72. See Ruskin: '*Les Vénétiens sont le seul peuple qui, en Europe, ait pleinement sympathisé avec le grand instinct oriental*'. I draw this quotation from Mauriac Dyer's annotations, F 356–7.
73. This is what Mauriac Dyer suggests in her annotations, F 356–7.

3 Alienation (Plessner – Adorno)

1. Theodor Adorno, M 45/MM 41. Modified translation.
2. Helmuth Plessner, G 107/L 163.
3. Adorno continued to divide his life between the United States and Germany until he was offered the position of extraordinary (and later ordinary) professor at the Goethe Universität at Frankfurt am Main, where he finally settled down in 1953.
4. Plessner's philosophical anthropology takes its starting point from a specific conception of the human condition to then explain modern society on the basis of this conception. Adorno's critical theory, by contrast, works the other way around: it deduces a conception of the human condition from a specific theory of modern society of which it is the result. For a more detailed comparative discussion see Joachim Fischer, 'Kritische Theorie der Gesellschaft versus Philosophische Anthropologie der Moderne: Alternative Paradigmen aus dem 20. Jahrhundert', in *Mensch und Gesellschaft zwischen Natur und Geschichte*, ed. by Thomas Ebke, Sebastian Edinger, Frank Müller, and Roman Yos (Berlin: de Gruyter 2016), pp. 3–28.
5. See Adorno's infamously derogatory comment on Max Scheler, one of the founding fathers of philosophical anthropology: '*Scheler: le boudoir dans la philosophie*', M 218. The pun is an allusion to Sade's *La Philosophie dans le boudoir* (1795).
6. Note that, as Fischer reminds us, an early working title of Plessner's manuscript was *Grenzen der Gemeinschaft: Eine Kritik des kommunistischen Ethos*, Fischer, 'Nachwort', in Plessner, G 135–42 (136).
7. Plessner, 'Selbstdarstellung' (Self Portrait) (1975), in *Gesammelte Schriften*, ed. by Günter Dux, Odo Marquard, and Elisabeth Ströker, 10 vols. (Frankfurt: Suhrkamp, 2003), vol. X, pp. 302–41 (p. 302).
8. Christian Schneider, 'Deutschland I: Der exemplarische Intellektuelle der Bundesrepublik', in *Adorno Handbuch: Leben – Werk – Wirkung*, ed. by Richard Klein, Johann Kreuzer, and Stefan Müller-Doohm (Stuttgart: Metzler, 2011), pp. 431–4 (p. 431).

9. One of the key leitmotifs of Plessner's 'Selbstdarstellung' is the apparent lack of recognition: '*Ohne jede Resonanz*' (Without any resonance), he writes of his first major work, *Die Einheit der Sinne* (1923), which he saw as his intellectual breakthrough on the way towards a philosophical anthropology. '*Mit keinem Wort erwähnt*' (Not mentioned with a single word), he comments on his second major book, *Stufen des Organischen und der Mensch* (1928), the reception of which not only suffered from Martin Heidegger's simultaneous publication of *Sein und Zeit* (*Being and Time*), but also from Max Scheler's (wrongful) accusation of plagiarism; Plessner, 'Selbstdarstellung', pp. 317, 330.

10. Plessner, 'Selbstdarstellung', p. 341. My translation.

11. Plessner, 'Selbstdarstellung', p. 322. My translation.

12. '*Plessner, Sie haben auf das Publikum vergessen!*'; Plessner, 'Selbstdarstellung', p. 312. My translation.

13. Ulrich Raulff, 'Nachwort', in '*Minima Moralia' neu gelesen*, ed. by Ulrich Raulff and Andreas Bernard (Frankfurt: Suhrkamp, 2003), pp. 123–31 (pp. 123–4).

14. Reviewers included Siegfried Kracauer, mentor of the young Adorno, and Ferdinand Tönnies, the doyen of German sociology at the time and one of the prime targets of Plessner's critique. Both Tönnies' and Kracauer's reviews can be found in Wolfgang Eßbach, Joachim Fischer and Helmuth Lethen (eds.), *Plessners 'Grenzen der Gemeinschaft': Eine Debatte* (Frankfurt: Suhrkamp, 2002), pp. 353–6, 357–62. Plessner himself described Tönnies' review as a '*liebenswürdig anerkennende Rezension*' (graciously appreciative review), 'Nachwort zu Ferdinand Tönnies' (Postscript to Ferdinand Tönnies), in Plessner, *Übergänge: Politik, Anthropologie, Philosophie*, ed. by Salvatore Giammusso and Hans-Ulrich Lessing (Munich: Fink, 2001), p. 178. My translation.

15. For an overview of the Plessner renaissance in German debate, see again *Plessners 'Grenzen der Gemeinschaft': Eine Debatte*. For a first documentation of Plessner's reception in English, mostly written by continental European scholars, see *Plessner's Philosophical Anthropology: Perspectives and Prospects*, ed. by Jos de Mul (Amsterdam: Amsterdam University Press, 2014). The most recent English translations of some of Plessner's work are *Political Anthropology* (orig. *Macht und menschliche Natur* (1931)), trans. by Nils F. Schott, intro. by Joachim Fischer et al. (Evanston, IL: Northwestern University Press, 2018), and *Levels of Organic Life and the Human: An Introduction to Philosophical Anthropology*, trans. by Millay Hyatt, intro. by J. M. Bernstein (New York: Fordham University Press, 2019). Most recent publications in German include Plessner's previously unpublished lectures of 1961: *Philosophische Anthropologie*, ed. by Julia Gruevska et al. (Frankfurt: Suhrkamp, 2019) and the *Plessner Handbuch*, ed. by Joachim Fischer (forthcoming, Stuttgart: Metzler, 2023).

16. Plessner, 'Selbstdarstellung', p. 322. We shall return to this point in the final chapter, *Approchement* (Barthes).

17. Elias, *Prozess der Zivilisation*, specifically vol. II, pp. 312–13.

18. Foucault, *History of Sexuality*, vol. I, pp. 17–18.

19. Although Rousseau rarely used the word '*aliénation*' itself, he famously offered all the key words that launched the term's subsequent career. See Rahel Jaeggi, *Entfremdung: Zur Aktualität eines sozialphilosophischen Problems* (Frankfurt: Suhrkamp, 2016), pp. 25–6, and her very brief history of the theory of alienation that follows, pp. 25–31; translated as *Alienation*, ed. by Frederick Neuhouser, trans. by Frederick Neuhouser and Alan E. Smith (New York: Columbia University Press, 2016); and Micha Brumlik, 'Entfremdung', in *Archiv für Begriffsgeschichte* (Sonderheft) (Hamburg: Meiner, 2015), pp. 145–64 (pp. 148–51).

20. Rousseau, *Discours sur l'origine et les fondements de l'inégalité parmi les hommes*, in *Œuvres complètes*, ed. by Bernard Gagnebin and Marcel Raymond, 5 vols. (Paris: Gallimard, 1959–95), vol. III, pp. 131–223 (p. 193)/*Discourse on the Origin and Foundations of Inequality Among Men*, in *The Collected Writings of Rousseau*, ed. by Roger D. Masters and Christopher Kelly, trans. by Judith Bush et al., 13 vols. (Hanover, NH: University Press of New England for Dartmouth College, 1992), vol. III, pp. 1–95 (p. 66).

21. Either by restoring the original state of nature or by (re)appropriating one's social existence. See Plessner for a critical evaluation of this idea, in 'Das Problem der Öffentlichkeit', pp. 212–26.

22. As argued by Martin Bauer, 'Das Ende der Entfremdung', *Zeitschrift für Ideengeschichte*, 1:1 (Spring 2007), pp. 7–29 (p. 12).

23. Rousseau, *Essai sur l'origine des langues*, in *Œuvres complètes*, vol. V, pp. 371–429 (pp. 395–6)/*Essay on the Origin of Languages*, in *On Philosophy, Morality, and Religion*, ed. by Christopher Kelly, trans. by John T. Scott (Hanover, NH: University Press of New England for Dartmouth College, 2007), pp. 102–46 (p. 119). For a discussion of Rousseau's concept of pity in relation to Roland Barthes, see my article, '"J'ai mal à l'autre": Barthes on Pity', *L'Esprit créateur*, 55:4 (2015), pp. 131–47 (pp. 139–40).

24. '*Takt und Humanität – bei ihm (Goethe) das Gleiche*' (M 39/MM 36).

25. See for a brief discussion of genius in relation to tact, Chapter 1: Tact's History.

26. Adorno, 'Kleine Proust-Kommentare', in Noten zur Literatur, ed. by Rolf Tiedemann (Frankfurt: Suhrkamp, 1974), pp. 203–15 (p. 205). Translated by Shierry Weber Nicholsen as 'Short Commentaries on Proust', in *Notes to Literature*, ed. by Rolf Tiedemann, 2 vols. (New York: Columbia University Press, 1991), vol. I, pp. 174–84 (pp. 175–6).

27. Kant, 'Idee zu einer allgemeinen Geschichte in weltbürgerlicher Absicht', in *Werkausgabe*, vol. XI, pp. 31–50 (pp. 37–9)/ 'Idea for a Universal History with a Cosmopolitan Purpose', in *Political Writings*, pp. 41–53 (pp. 44–5).

28. Kant, 'Idee', pp. 38, 40 'Idea',/pp. 44, 45.

29. Adorno, 'Zum Klassizismus von Goethes Iphigenie', in *Noten zur Literatur*, pp. 495–514 (p. 504); translated as 'On the Classicism of Goethe's *Iphigenie*', in *Notes to Literature*, vol. II, pp. 153–70. For a rare example of research on tact in Adorno, see Elisa Ronzheimer's article, published after I had already completed this manuscript: '"Der Takt der Hand": Adornos Taktbegriff und die Kritik des Klassizismus', in *Takt und Taktilität*, ed. by Andrea Erwig, Sandra Fluhrer, Jakob Gehlen, and Elisa Ronzheimer, special issue of *Sprache und Literatur*, 50:2 (December 2021), pp. 204–25.

30. Adorno, 'Iphigenie', p. 509.

31. Adorno, 'Iphigenie', p. 503/*Iphigenie*', p. 160.

32. We witnessed a similar dynamic on a socio-psychological level in the tactful encounter between Andrée and Marcel, as described in *La Recherche*, see Chapter 2: Proxemics (Proust). We shall return to this point in Chapter 4: Individuation (Truffaut).

33. Plesser, 'Das Problem der Öffentlichkeit', p. 213.

34. In his 'Selbstdarstellung' Plessner still criticizes the '*Glauben an die Möglichkeit unvermittelter Beziehungen von Mensch zu Mensch*' (belief in the possibility of immediate relations between humans), p. 323. My translation.

35. Plessner, 'Nachwort zu Ferdinand Tönnies', p. 177. My translation.

36. See Fischer, 'Nachwort', p. 137.

37. See, for Nietzsche's 'pathos of distance', for example, *The Anti-Christ, Ecce Homo, Twilight of the Idols and Other Writings*, ed. by Aaron Ridley and Judith Norman, trans. by Judith Norman (Cambridge: Cambridge University Press, 2005), pp. 40, 58, 212. François de la Rochefoucauld supplies the mottos for two chapters in Plessner's *Grenzen*. For his characterization of the '*honnête homme*', see *Maximes: suivies des Réflexions diverses, du Portrait de La Rochefoucauld par lui-même, et, des Remarques de Christine de Suède sur les Maximes*, ed. by Jacques Truchet (Paris: Garnier, 1967), especially pp. 99, 128. For a discussion of Plessner's relation to French moralism, see Dorothee Kimmich, 'Moralistik und Neue Sachlichkeit: Ein Kommentar zu Plessner's *Grenzen der Gemeinschaft*', in Eßbach, *Plessners 'Grenzen der Gemeinschaft'*, pp. 160–82. For the significance of Baltasar Gracián's *Oracle* of 1647, not only for Plessner but for the wider anthropology of the 1920s in Germany, see Helmuth Lethen, *Verhaltensweisen der Kälte: Lebensversuche zwischen den Kriegen* (Frankfurt: Suhrkamp, 1994), pp. 53–70.

38. In *Die verspätete Nation* (Frankfurt: Suhrkamp, 1994), Plessner argues that the civilizing wave that swept across early modern Europe was compromised in Germany by the period of confessional wars and economic demise. For this reason, Germany must repeat the missed seventeenth century as the age when the assimilation of aristocratic ethos and bourgeois self-confidence gave rise to

the new elites of the western European nation states. For further commentary, see Joachim Fischer, 'Plessner und die politische Philosophie der zwanziger Jahre', in *Politisches Denken. Jahrbuch 1992*, ed. by Volker Gerhardt, Henning Ottmann, and Martyn P. Thompson (Stuttgart: Metzler, 1993), pp. 53–77 (p. 63).

39. See the chapter on 'Gestural (In)visibility: Béla Balázs and Helmuth Plessner', in Lucia Ruprecht, *Gestural Imaginaries: Dance and Cultural Theory in the Early Twentieth Century* (Oxford: Oxford University Press, 2019), pp. 107–24 (p. 118).

40. Echoing Plessner's concerns, Sennett wonders in 1974, for example, if the 'contempt for ritual masks of sociability has not really made us more primitive culturally than the simplest tribe of hunters and gatherers'; *The Fall of Public Man*, p. 15. Correspondences between Plessner's and Barthes' work will be addressed in Chapter 5: *Approchement* (Barthes).

41. Plessner, 'Das Problem der Öffentlichkeit', p. 220. My translation.

42. See for Plessner's critique of Rousseau, the 'romantic flight from civilization' and the 'form-negativism of the soul', (G 25, 105/L 60, 160).

43. As Axel Honneth observes: 'Regardless of how untransparent and complicated social relations might be, Adorno, Marcuse, and Horkheimer regarded the alienated nature of social relations as a fact beyond all doubt'; 'Introduction', in Jaeggi, *Alienation*, pp. vii–x (p. vii). For further discussion see, again, Jaeggi, *Alienation*, and Bauer, 'Das Ende der Entfremdung'.

44. My translation – this section from the 'Anhang' (Appendix) is not included in Jephcott's translation.

45. Plessner, 'Idee der Entfremdung', p. 223.

46. See Chapter 1: Tact's History.

47. Plessner, G 94, and Plessner, 'Soziale Rolle und menschliche Natur' (1960), in *Schriften*, Vol. X, pp. 227–40 (p. 235).

48. Plessner uses the words 'Amtsperson' (official person) and 'Privatperson' (private person) here (G 82/L 133).

49. See Chapter 2: Proxemics (Proust).

50. Schopenhauer, *Parerga und Paralipomena*, p. 765. It is precisely this peaceful form of co-existence that M. de Charlus' unruly behaviour in public undermines, see Ch. 2: Proxemics (Proust).

51. Schopenhauer, *Parerga und Paralipomena*, p. 765.

52. Carl Schmitt, *The Concept of the Political* (1932) (Chicago: University of Chicago Press, 2007), p. 60.

53. Translation modified.

54. See Lethen, *Verhaltensweisen der Kälte*, pp. 75–95. For a detailed critique of Lethen's position see Fischer's and Eßbach's contributions in *Plessner's 'Grenzen der Gemeinschaft'*, pp. 63–79, 80–103.

55. Friedrich Schiller, *Kallias oder Über die Schönheit: Briefe an Gottfried Körner*, in *Schillers Werke in vier Bänden* (Frankfurt: Insel, 1966), ed. by Herbert Kraft, vol. IV, p. 108/*On the Aesthetic Education of Man, in a Series of Letters*, ed. and trans. by Elizabeth M. Wilkinson and L. A. Willoughby (Oxford: Clarendon Press, 1967), p. 300. I am grateful to Lucia Ruprecht for bringing this passage to my attention.

56. See, for example, the idea of human dignity described as '*die Harmonie der Seele und zwischen Seele und Ausdruck, Seele und Körper*' (the idea of a harmony within the soul and between soul and expression, soul and objectual body) (G 75/L 123), '*Würde und Anmut*' (dignity and grace) (G 76/L 123), and '*schöne Seele*' (beautiful soul) (G 65, 92/L 111, 145). Kai Haucke addresses Schiller's influence on Plessner's work in 'Plessners Kritik der radikalen Gemeinschaftsideologie und die Grenzen des deutschen Idealismus', in *Plessners 'Grenzen der Gemeinschaft'*, pp. 103–30 (pp. 120–1).

57. See Chapter 1: Tact's History.

58. Note that Barthes lists Goethe's *Wahlverwandtschaften* as an example of the 'idiorrhythmic novel' in CVE 57/HLT 24.

59. Lethen, 'Anleitung zur Schlaflosigkeit: Über den Formzwang in der Politischen Anthropologie von Helmuth Plessner und Arnold Gehlen', in *Kunst, Macht und Institution*, ed. by Joachim Fischer and Hans Joas (Frankfurt: Campus, 2003), pp. 89–103 (p. 92).

60. For a more detailed critique of Lethen's position that resonates with my own reading of Plessner, see Fischer and Eßbach's contributions in *Plessner's 'Grenzen der Gemeinschaft'*, pp. 63–79, 80–103.

61. Roberto Esposito, *Immunitas: The Protection and Negation of Life*, trans. by Zakiya Hanafi (Cambridge: Polity, 2011), p. 99.

62. 'Zartheit, *w.*', in *Deutsches Wörterbuch*, http://woerterbuchnetz.de/DWB/?lemma=Zartheit. For more information on the conceptual history of '*Zartheit*' as the elder relative of tact, see Astrid von der Lühe, 'Zart, Zärtlich', in *Historisches Wörterbuch der Philosophie*, vol. 12, ed. by Joachim Ritter, Karlfried Gründer, and Gottfried Gabriel (Basel: Schwabe, 2004), cols. 1149–55.

63. As Joseph Butler writes in his *Sermons* (1726): 'Every man is considered in two capacities, the private and the publick'. I cite from Sennett who reconstructs the history of the words 'private' and 'public' in *The Fall of Public Man*, pp. 16–24 (p. 16).

64. Plessner, 'Idee der Entfremdung', p. 224. My translation.

65. Benjamin, 'Das Kunstwerk im Zeitalter seiner technischen Reproduzierbarkeit', in *Gesammelte Schriften*, vol. I.2, pp. 471–508 (p. 479). Translated as 'The Work of Art in the Age of Its Technological Reproducibility', in *Selected Writings*, vol. VI, pp. 251–83 (p. 272).

4 Individuation (Truffaut)

1. *Pour le Plaisir: Numéro spécial Festivals Cinéma 1966, 1967* (4 May 1967), realization Guy Gilles © INA. See also, 'François Truffaut à propos du métier de réalisateur' (4 May 1967), Institut national de l'audiovisuel, bit .ly/4020d8s, 10:24. My translation.

2. François Truffaut, *Correspondance*, ed. by Gilles Jacob and Claude de Givray (Rennes: Hatier, 1988), p. 411/Truffaut, *Letters*, ed. by Gilles Jacob and Claude de Givray, trans. by Gilbert Adair (London, Faber, 1989), p. 322.

3. Interview (1970), in Anne Gillain (ed.), *Le Cinéma selon François Truffaut* (Paris: Flammarion, 1988), p. 193/ *Truffaut on Cinema*, trans. by Alistair Fox (Bloomington: Indiana University Press, 2017), p. 150.

4. Vincent Canby, 'The Screen: Truffaut's Lyrical "Stolen Kisses" Bows', *New York Times* (4 March 1969), p. 4.

5. Danny Peary, *Guide for the Film Fanatic* (New York: Simon and Schuster, 1986), p. 405.

6. Louis Chauvet, 'Les Films par Louis Chauvet. *Baisers volés*', in *Le Figaro* (12 September 1968), p. 24.

7. Contrary to Diana Holmes I do not think that Truffaut's films suffer from a 'lack of a socio-political dimension'; see Diana Holmes and Robert Ingram, *François Truffaut* (Manchester: Manchester University Press, 1998), p. 173.

8. See for more detail, Norbert Frei, *1968 – Jugendrevolte und globaler Protest* (Munich: Deutscher Taschenbuchverlag, 2008), and *Paris, 13 Mai 1968: Kulturprotest und Gesellschaftsreform* (Munich: Deutscher Taschenbuchverlag, 1999).

9. In an interview from 1968, Truffaut said: 'Je suis le désengagement personnifié, parce que j'ai l'esprit de contradiction poussé très fort' (I am disengagement personified, owing to the fact that I have a very intense streak of contrariness), *Cinéma selon Truffaut*, p. 201/ *Truffaut on Cinema*, p. 155.

10. *Cinéma selon Truffaut*, p. 195/ *Truffaut on Cinema*, p. 150.

11. More precisely, two days into the filming.

12. Together with Georges Franju, Henri Langlois founded the Cinémathèque française in 1936 to screen a wide variety of films to French audiences. During the 1940s and 50s it served as the primary educational venue for the young critics and film makers that would later form the *Nouvelle Vague*.

13. I cite from Baecque and Toubiana, *François Truffaut* (Paris: Gallimard, 2001), p. 470/trans. by Catherine Temerson (Oakland: University of California Press, 1999), p. 240. Pierre Moinot was an official from the Ministry of Cultural Affairs. He nominated Pierre Barbin, at the time the director of the Tours and Annecy Festivals, to replace Henri Langlois as the director of the Cinémathèque; see Baecque and Toubiana, pp. 235–6.

14. Bourdieu, *Distinction*, p. 6.

15. See, notably, Truffaut's comments on the young Daniel Cohn-Bendit in *Cinéma selon Truffaut*, p. 209/ *Truffaut on Cinema*, p. 161.
16. See Plessner, 'Selbstdarstellung' (1975), p. 323, and G 28 (1924).
17. *Cinéma selon Truffaut*, p. 191/ *Truffaut on Cinema*, p. 148.
18. *Cinéma selon Truffaut*, p. 266/ *Truffaut on Cinema*, pp. 208–9.
19. I cite from Carole Le Berre, *François Truffaut at Work*, trans. by Bill Krohn (London: Phaidon, 2005), p. 104.
20. *Cinéma selon Truffaut*, p. 266/ *Truffaut on cinema*, p. 208.
21. Adrian Martin observes that '[t]he correct distance is Truffaut's dialectic' in 'The Untimely Moment and the Correct Distance', in *A Companion to Truffaut*, ed. by Andrew Dudley and Anne Gillain (Malden, MA: Wiley-Blackwell, 2013). pp. 205–17 (p. 208).
22. Simmel, 'Geselligkeit', p. 55.
23. Simmel, 'Der Raum und die räumlichen Ordnungen der Gesellschaft, Exkurs über die soziale Begrenzung', in *Soziologie: Untersuchungen über die Formen der Vergesellschaftung* (Berlin: Duncker & Humblot, 1908), pp. 467–70 (p. 468), https://socio.ch/sim/soziologie/soz_9_ex1.htm. We saw a similar idea earlier explored by Freud when thinking about the metaphor of the amoeba in Chapter 2: Proxemics (Proust).
24. Wittgenstein famously writes about this in his *Philosophische Untersuchungen*: '*Wenn man aber eine Grenze zieht, so kann das verschiedenerlei Gründe haben. Wenn ich einen Platz mit einem Zaun, einem Strich, oder sonst irgendwie umziehe, so kann das den Zweck haben, jemand nicht hinaus, oder nicht hinein zu lassen; es kann aber auch zu einem Spiel gehören und die Grenze soll etwa von den Spielern übersprungen werden; oder es kann andeuten, wo der Besitz eines Menschen aufhört und der des andern anfängt, etc. Ziehe ich also eine Grenze, so ist damit noch nicht gesagt, weshalb ich sie ziehe*' (If I surround an area with a fence or line or otherwise, the purpose may be to prevent someone from getting in or out; but it may also be part of a game and the players be supposed, say, to jump over the boundary; or it may shew where the property of one man ends and that of another begins; and so on. So if I draw a boundary line that is not yet to say what I am drawing it for). *Philosophical Investigations: The German Text with a Revised Translation* by G. E. M. Anscombe (Malden, MA: Wiley-Blackwell, 2001), § 499 pp. 117–18e.
25. See also the script version in *Les Aventures d'Antoine Doinel* (AD 246). My translation.
26. Le Berre, *Truffaut at Work*, p. 103.
27. Le Berre points out the connection to France, but identifies *Mémoires de Jeunesse* as the source, Le Berre, *Truffaut*, p. 101. Truffaut might have come across the scene via Proust, who refers to it in his correspondence as the epitome of embarrassment although, surprisingly, and unlike Truffaut,

Proust does not pick up on the erotic overtones of the scene, nor the gender confusion it implies: '*C'était il y a cinq ans chez vos parents qui m'avaient adorablement accueilli, à Cabourg. Monsieur votre Père me demanda: De quelle province êtes-vous originaire?' Et je répondis: 'd'Eure et Loir'. 'C'est un département', répondit avec une involontaire cruauté Monsieur votre Père.... Je restai pétrifié comme le petit garçon qui dans* Le Livre de mon ami *dit "Bonjour Monsieur" à la dame qu'il aimait"*, letter no. 354 to Max Daireaux, shortly after 19 June 1913, in Correspondance, ed. by Philip Kolb, 20 vols. (Paris:Plon, 1970–93), vol. XII, p. 622. The scene also finds its way into the *Recherche*, where the sense of embarrassment is associated with the social inferiority of the flustered person: '*à une personne qui lui demandait de quelle province étaient les Guermantes,* [Odette] *répondit: "de l'Aisne"*', RTP I 510. Aisne is a *département* in the province Hauts-de-France.

28. Anatole France, *Le Livre de mon ami*, chapter XI: 'La Fôret des myrtes', in *Œuvres complètes*, ed. by Marie-Claire Bancquart, 4 vols. (Paris: Gallimard, 1994), vol. I, pp. 514–20 (p. 517).
29. France, *Livre de mon ami*, pp. 516–517/trans. by James Lewis May as *My Friend's Book* (London: John Lane, Bodley Head, 1913), p. 164.
30. Goffman, *Interaction Ritual*, p. 100.
31. Caron disentangles this gender malaise beautifully, and in relation to Barthes, in *The Nearness of Others*, pp. 252–5.
32. Goffman, *Interaction Ritual*, p. 102.
33. I cite from Le Berre, *Truffaut*, p. 100.
34. See Chapter 2: Proxemics (Proust).
35. Simmel, 'Geselligkeit', p. 54/'The Sociology of Sociability', p. 256.
36. See also the analysis by Jonathan Everett Haynes, who observes that 'both [Antoine and Fabienne] are at risk', 'Truffaut-Hitchcock', in *Companion to François Truffaut*, pp. 265–82 (pp. 268–9).
37. Goffman, *Interaction Ritual*, p. 103.
38. My translation.
39. I refer to Luhmann's theory of the systemic uncertainty of the tactful communication here, as discussed in Chapter 2: Proxemics (Proust).
40. I discuss aspects of Sartre's argument in the Introduction and in Chapter 2 Proxemics (Proust).
41. Jean Cocteau, *Le Coq et l'arlequin: notes autour de la musique* (Paris: Éditions de la Sirène, 1918), p. 20.
42. My translation.
43. France's story ends with the lady's tactful acknowledgement of the young man's admiration fifty years after the embarrassing incident occurred. Balzac's narrative, in turn, concludes with the lady lamenting on her death bed the bliss of love she has never been able to enjoy.

44. See Chapter 1: Tact's History for more on this point.
45. Jacques Derrida, *Copy, Archive, Signature: A Conversation on Photography*, ed. and introduction by Gerhard Richter, trans. by Jeff Fort (Stanford: Stanford University Press, 2010), p. 24.
46. Martin Heidegger, *Parmenides*, introduction by Mary Louise Gill, trans. by Mary Louise Gill and Paul Ryan (Bloomington: Indiana University Press, 1992), p. 81.
47. Truffaut himself used the pneumatic tube to send messages to his actors; *Truffaut on Cinema*, p. 154.
48. See le Berre, *Truffaut*, p. 103.
49. In *Un Amour de Swann*, Proust associates a similar oscillation of sensuality and sensibility with the pneumatic post system when referring to the relationship between Swann and Odette: '*voici que comme un caoutchouc tendu qu'on lâche ou comme l'air dans une machine pneumatique qu'on entrouvre, l'idée de la revoir, des lointains où elle était maintenue, revenait d'un bond dans le champ du présent et des possibilités immédiates*' (and like a stretched rubber band that is let go or the air in a pneumatic machine that is opened, the idea of seeing her again would spring back from the far distance where it had been kept into the field of the present as an immediate possibility) (RTP I 301/SLT I 309). I thank Hannah Freed-Thall for directing me to this passage.
50. I refer here to Jacob Muth, who associates tact with the defiance of touch when stating that '*Takt ist der letzte Respekt vor der Unnahbarkeit des anderen*' (Tact is the ultimate respect before the inaccessibility of the other person; my translation), in *Pädagischer Takt: Monographie einer aktuellen Form erzieherischen und didaktischen Handelns* (Heidelberg: Quelle & Meyer, 1967), p. 20. Laura Marks in *The Skin of the Film* (Durham, NC: Duke University Press, 2000) and Jennifer Barker in *The Tactile Eye: Touch and the Cinematic Experience* (Oakland: University of California Press, 2009) have famously looked at the role of touch in film. Closer to my approach, however, than the modes of 'haptic visuality' they propose, is Laura McMahon's *Cinema and Contact: The Withdrawal of Touch in Nancy, Bresson, Duras, and Denis* (Oxford: Legenda, 2012). McMahon draws on Nancy's conception of touch as withdrawal to explore cinema 'as a medium of simultaneous contact and separation, proximity and distance', where touch 'does not function as a sign of intimacy, knowledge, and understanding but rather as a site of contact in separation which becomes fraught with the tension of that necessarily hesitant and intermittent relation', p 5. This idea resonates very well, I think, with the conception of tact I am trying to describe in this chapter, and I thank Shohini Chauduri for pointing this out to me.
51. Fabienne is, however, referred to again in the film's sequel, *Domicil Conjugal* (Bed and Board) (1970). Here we see Delphine Seyrig's mannerisms

caricatured on television by the comedian Claude Véga impersonating Fabienne, to the disconcertment of Antoine, and the merriment of Christine.

52. See Aristotle, *Nicomachean Ethics*, p. 33 and pp. 76–77.

53. See for example Montesquieu's 'Éloge de la sincérité', in. cited in Thomas, *Civility*, p. 435.

54. Jean-Jacques Rousseau, *Projet pour l'éducation de Monsieur de Sainte-Marie*, in *Œuvres complètes*, vol. IV, pp. 35–51 (p. 43).

55. See Chapter 2: Proxemics (Proust).

56. 'Truffaut à propos du métier de réalisateur', 10:24–11:04. My translation. Interestingly, Truffaut undermines his own point by rather tactlessly exposing Simone Signoret.

57. See Truffaut: '*je me suis rendu compte que même pour exprimer quelque chose de sincère, il fallait faire un détour par le mensonge*' (I quickly realized that even to express something sincere, it was necessary to make a detour through a lie), *Cinéma selon Truffaut*, p. 135/ *Truffaut on Cinema*, p. 182.

58. See Truffaut: '*Les constantes sont secrètes; par exemple, le personnage central chez moi ne doit jamais dire exactement ce qu'il pense, les choses ne doivent pas être directes. Je crois qu'il n'y a jamais eu un 'je vous aime' dans mes films. C'était inenvisageable pour moi*' (The continuities are secret; for example, the central character in my films must never say what he is thinking explicitly – things cannot be conveyed directly. I think there has never been a single 'I love you' in my films. That's something I can't envisage), *Cinéma selon Truffaut*, p. 231/ *Truffaut on Cinema*, p. 179.

59. *Truffaut on Cinema*, p. 209. This view also informs *L'enfant sauvage* (The Wild Child) (1970), the film Truffaut was preparing to make when shooting *Stolen Kisses*, and in which he defends the value of civilization against a romantically inspired, anti-societal form of escapism.

60. See Anne Gillain's interpretation in *Truffaut: The Lost Secret* (Bloomington: Indiana University Press, 2013), p. 119, and of a parallel scene in *Les 400 Coups* (*400 Blows*) (1959) where the child Antoine is sitting at his mother's dressing table, the reflection of his image split in three different mirrors, *Lost Secret*, p. 28.

61. I discuss this point in Chapter 2: Alienation (Plessner – Adorno).

62. We followed a similar movement in Hegel's conception of formation (*Bildung*) as alienation in Chapter 1: Tact's History.

63. Plessner, 'Zur Anthropologie des Schauspielers', in *Gesammelte Werke*, vol. VII, pp. 399–418 (p. 409). For a more detailed discussion of the 'inevitability of roles' in Plessner and Simmel that informed my own interpretation, see Jaeggi, *Entfremdung*, pp. 115–17.

64. See Baecque and Toubiana, *Truffaut*, p. 250.

65. My translation.

5 *Approchement* (Barthes)

1. From Roland Barthes, *How to Live Together* ed. by Claude Coste, trans. by Kate Briggs. Copyright © 2002 by Éditions du Seuil. English translation copyright © 2013 Columbia University Press. Reprinted by permission of Columbia University Press and Georges Borchardt, Inc., on behalf of the author's estate. HLT 132/CVE 179.

2. In his foreword to *Comment vivre ensemble* Éric Marty mentions the general sense of disappointment that, despite their immense popularity, marked the overall response to Barthes' lecture course; Marty, 'Avant-propos', CVE 7–14 (10–11). Similarly, Alain Robbe-Grillet reports in relation to Barthes' inaugural lecture at the Collège in 1977: '*À l'issue de (l)a leçon inaugurale au Collège de France une jeune fille inconnue a bondi sur moi avec véhémence, avec colère: 'Qu'admirez-vous là-dedans? D'un bout à l'autre il n'a rien dit!* (At the end of [Barthes'] inaugural lecture at the Collège de France an unknown young woman jumped on me and said, outraged: 'What do you admire in all this? From beginning to end he did not say anything!' My translation); 'Le Parti de Roland Barthes' (1981), cited in Lucy O'Meara, *Roland Barthes at the Collège de France* (Liverpool: Liverpool University Press, 2012), p. 27.

3. Bourdieu, *Distinction,* p. 7. Bourdieu was writing his magnum opus at the time Barthes was convening his lectures.

4. Bourdieu, *Distinction*, p. 2.

5. For example: the indicative as an amodal form, that is, neither conjunctive nor imperative; see: Claude Zilberberg, 'Relation et rationalité: Actualité de Brøndal', cited in Tiphaine Samoyault, *Roland Barthes* (Paris: Seuil, 2015), p. 318.

6. See Barthes' comments in 'Table ronde sur Proust', in Gilles Deleuze, *Deux Régimes de fous: textes et entretiens 1975–1995*, ed. by David Lapoujade (Paris: Minuit, 2003), pp. 29–55 (p. 35).

7. See Chapter 1: Tact's History.

8. For more information on biographical context see again Samoyault's *Roland Barthes*, which begins with an account of the death of the author.

9. References to historical detail or personal experience of the Second World War are an exception in Barthes' work. They may be found, for example, in the letters Barthes wrote while at the sanatorium St-Hilaire-du-Touvet in the 1940s, reprinted in: *Roland Barthes Album: Inédits, correspondances et varia*, ed. by Éric Marty (Paris: Seuil, 2015). For Barthes, fascism was mostly of interest in terms of the alleged fascism of language. For his controversial claim that '*langue est fasciste*', see Barthes, *Leçon*, OC V 429–50 (432).

10. Emphasis in original.

11. Barthes, *Leçon* (OC V 427–46 (446)), trans. by Richard Howard as *Inaugural Lecture*, in Susan Sontag (ed.), *A Roland Barthes Reader* (New York: Vintage, 1993), pp. 457–78 (p. 478).

12. The film I have in mind is *Le dernier métro* (1980).

13. Barthes, *Leçon*, OC V 440.

14. *Leçon*, OC V 441/*Lecture*, p. 472.

15. Plessner, 'Selbstdarstellung', p. 323. My translation. I address this point in Chapter 3: Plessner – Adorno (Alienation).

16. Barthes decided to leave Paris in 1969 for a teaching position in Morocco as the events of 1968 and their aftermath had left him feeling *'mal à l'aise'* as Claude Coste notes, cited in Baldwin, 'Rewriting Proust', *Esprit créateur*, 55:4 (2015), pp. 70–85 (p. 76).

17. For a more detailed discussion of Barthes and Adorno within this context, see O'Meara, 'Adorno, Barthes, and Aesthetic Reflection', pp. 185–9.

18. As Barthes observes in an interview: *'Toute philosophie qui essaye de se soustraire à ces impératifs de collectivité est extrêmement singulière, et, je dirais, a une mauvaise image de marque'* ('Propos sur la violence' (1978), OC V 549–553 (553)). See also the following statement: *'Il faut partir de ce vieux cheval de bataille: l'individualisme discrédité (cf. critique sartrienne de la démocratie bourgeoise: les individus comme des petits pois dans une boîte+critique marxiste +critique gauchiste: vraie conjuration contre l'individualisme!)'*, Barthes, PR 77.

19. Following Rosalind E. Krauss and Denis Hollier, Kate Briggs translates Barthes' *'délicatesse'* as 'tact'. Although it suits my own purposes, this decision is not without problems. It prioritizes criteria of sound and implication over a more careful consideration of the conceptual history of the term. (The word 'tact' also exists in French and so Barthes could have used it.) At the same time, however, Briggs' choice of translation corresponds to Barthes' own associative approach to the term, bringing into play a whole variety of words highlighting different aspects of the same idea: *'douceur'*, focusing on the notion of tenderness; *'discrétion'*, indicating a sense of secrecy; the neologism *'idiorrythmie'*, emphasizing the aspect of rhythm, and so on. For a brief reflection on her decision, and on the practice of translation more generally, see Briggs, *This Little Art* (London: Fitzcarraldo, 2017), p. 325. Note that Richard Howard, in his 2009 translation of Barthes' *Journal de deuil*, opts for 'delicacy' instead of 'tact'.

20. Note that the term is first introduced in *Sade, Fourier, Loyola* (1971), OC III 699–870 (849). We shall return to this passage.

21. I draw in this discussion of Barthes' engagement with compassion on aspects of my more detailed analysis in '"J'ai mal à l'autre": Barthes on Pity', *L'Esprit créateur*, 55:4 (2015), pp. 131–47 (pp. 134–7).

22. Schopenhauer, 'Zur Ethik', in *Parerga und Paralipomena II,* § 110 p. 242. For a variation of the same idea, see Schopenhauer, *Die beiden Grundprobleme der Ethik* in *Sämtliche Werke,* vol. III, p. 763.

23. Note that on one of his famous '*fiches*' (of 8 August 1979) Barthes distinguishes between '*un "bon égotisme" et un moins bon*', Barthes *Album*, p. lv. (In the same way we find he distinguishes between two different forms of tact.)

24. Barthes' above-mentioned section heading, '*J'ai mal à l'autre*' (OC V 87), first introduced in the book version, already encapsulates the egocentrism of this conclusion. Trans. by Richard Howard as *A Lover's Discourse: Fragments* (New York: Hill and Wang, 1978), pp. 57–8.

25. Schopenhauer, 'Zur Ethik', § 110 p. 242.

26. Barthes uses the word '*saine*' (healthy) here; OC V 88. Briggs' decision to translate Barthes' '*délicatesse*' as 'tact' emphasizes this particular facet of the term. 'Tact', she writes in *This Little Art*, further motivating her choice, is 'more robust (healthier?) than its cognate, "delicacy"', *This Little Art*, p. 325.

27. For a detailed discussion of '*idiorrhythmie*', a term I am unable to do justice to within the context of my own argument, see Macé's 'Barthes, rythmicité du vivre', *Esprit créateur*, 55:4 (Winter 2015), pp. 7–20.

28. In one of his '*fiches*' Barthes reflects on this substitution. On 27 July 1979 he notes, contemplating his 'double year of morning and vita nova' in response to his mother's death: '*quelle lumière (quelle Béatrice?)? – Maman (la valeur civile, la Délicatesse se substituant à la Pieta*'; *Album*, p. lii.

29. The figure that comes closest to compassion in *Le Neutre* is '*bienveillance*' (benevolence). The concept does not share the aspect of identification on which Barthes' earlier definition of compassion in *Le discours amoureux* relied but grows out of a particular combination of '*émoi et distance*', N 40–42 (42)/ TN 14–16 (15).

30. I borrow this term form Lucy O'Meara who offers a detailed discussion of the reception of Japanese thought in Barthes' lectures in *Roland Barthes at the Collège de France*, pp. 118–63.

31. Barthes distinguishes between '*la "politesse" superficielle et mondaine (de classe) de l'Occident*' (the superficial and worldly (class-related) politeness of the Occident), and the perfectly shaped oriental politeness that, as an '*exercice du vide*', takes on a spiritual quality precisely because it is utterly self-referential (CVE 173/HLT 126); *L'Empire des Signes*, OC III 401. (Briggs translates 'politesse' as 'good manners' here, a decision that slightly obscures the conceptual history of the term within which Barthes' use of the word is – however loosely – lodged.)

32. Barthes offers a more benevolent interpretation of politeness in relation to the '*studium*' in *La Chambre Claire*. '*Le studium*', he notes, '*est une sorte d'éducation (savoir et politesse) qui me permet de retrouver l'Operator*' (The

studium is a kind of education (knowledge, civility, politeness) that allows discovery of the operator' (CC 51/CL 27–28).

33. See also Barthes' entry of 17 July 1977 in *Délibération*, OC V 668–681 (674).

34. Barthes uses this formulation in a personal note of 11 March 1979, characterizing his late mother: '*FMB veut à tout prix me présenter Hélène de Wendel, comme femme (du monde) d'une délicatesse exceptionelle etc. Je n'en ai nulle envie, car: – certes je suis assoiffé de délicatesse chez les êtres, mais en même temps je sais que mam. n'avait aucun intérêt pour ce monde, ou ce genre de femmes. Sa délicatesse était absolument atopique (socialement): au-delà des classes: sans marque*' (FMB is very eager for me to meet Hélène de Wendel, as a woman (of the world) of exceptional delicacy, etc. I have no interest in doing so, because: – of course I am eager to encounter delicacy in people I am introduced to, but at the same time I know that *maman* had no interest in that world, or in that sort of women. Her delicacy was absolutely atopic (socially): exclusive of classes; without insignia) (JD 263/MD 251).

35. The original passage reads as follows: '*Das war aber nicht nur Verfressenheit sondern eine ganz ausgesprochene Höflichkeit gegen die Speisen, die ich nicht durch eine Ablehnung beleidigen wollte*'; Benjamin, 'Protokolle zu Drogenversuchen', in *Gesammelte Schriften*, vol. IV:1, pp. 558–617 (p. 583). For Fabienne's and Antoine's tact in this context, see Chapter 4: Individuation (Truffaut).

36. Alan Watts, *The Way of Zen* (New York: Vintage, 1957), pp. 181, 186.

37. Note the similarity of Barthes' formulation to Watts' description of *wu-wei*, as a 'special kind of stupidity ... not simply calmness of mind, but "non-graspiness" of mind', *The Way of Zen*, p. 19.

38. Okakura describes Japanese 'Teaism' in precisely these words, *The Book of Tea*, p. 12.

39. In *The Book of Tea* Okakura depicts 'teaism' as follows: 'Teaism is the art of concealing beauty that you may discover it, of suggesting what you dare not reveal. It is the noble secret at laughing at yourself, calmly yet thoroughly, and is thus humour itself, – *the smile of philosophy*'; p. 12, my emphasis. Okakura ends the book on that same motif: 'With a smile upon his face Rikiu passed forth into the unknown', *The Book of Tea*, p. 108. Plessner writes: 'Im Lächeln ... bewahrt er (der Mensch) seine Distanz zu sich und zur Welt ... . Lachend und weinend ist der Mensch das Opfer seines Geistes, lächelnd gibt er ihm Ausdruck' (Humans retain their distance to themselves and to the world by smiling. ... In laughing and weeping they fall victim to their spirit, in smiling, they give expression to it), 'Das Lächeln' (1950), in Schriften, vol. VII, pp. 419–34 (p. 432). My translation.

40. Barthes takes this quote from Rousseau's 'Cinquième Promenade', in *Les Rêveries du promeneur solitaire* (Paris: Garnier: n.d.), p. 96/'Fifth Walk', in

Reveries of the Solitary Walker, trans. by Charles E. Butterworth (New York: New York University Press, 1979), p. 62.

41. Barthes uses the word '*discrétion*' as another manifestation of tact (N 183).

42. See Chapter 1: Tact's History.

43. On Barthes' preference for '*paideia*' as digression over '*"méthode" comme art du marcher droit*', see also Claude Coste, *Barthes ou l'art du détour* (Paris: Hermann, 2016), p. 30.

44. Barthes adds this orally (CVE 34, n. 6/HLT 177, n. 11).

45. See Adorno (M 45/MM 41) and Barthes, *Leçon*, OC V 444.

46. *Leçon*, OC V 443/*Lecture*, p. 475.

47. Gadamer, 'Hermeneutics of Suspicion', p. 316. For earlier discussion see Chapter 1: Tact's History.

48. Barthes, *S/Z*, OC III 133. See also, for example, '*la sémiologie . . . n'est pas une herméneutique*', *Leçon*, OC V 443.

Bibliography

Adorno, Theodor W., 'Filmtransparente: Notizen zu Papas und Bubis Kino', in *Die Zeit*, no. 47 (18 November 1966), p. 24.

'Kleine Proust-Kommentare', in *Noten zur Literatur*, ed. by Rolf Tiedemann (Frankfurt: Suhrkamp, 1974), pp. 203–15.

Minima Moralia: Reflexionen aus dem beschädigten Leben, in *Gesammelte Schriften*, ed. by Rolf Tiedemann in collaboration with Gretel Adorno, Susan Buck-Morss, and Klaus Schultz, 20 vols. (Frankfurt: Suhrkamp, 2003), vol. iv.

Minima Moralia: Reflections from Damaged Life, trans. by E.F.N. Jephcott (London: Verso, 2005).

'On the Classicism of Goethe's *Iphigenie*', in *Notes to Literature*, ed. by Rolf Tiedemann, trans. by Shierry Weber Nicholsen, 2 vols. (New York: Columbia University Press, 2019), vol. ii, pp. 153–70.

'Short Commentaries on Proust', in *Notes to Literature*, ed. by Rolf Tiedemann, trans. by Shierry Weber Nicholsen, 2 vols. (New York: Columbia University Press, 1991), vol. i, pp. 174–84.

Versuch über Wagner (Frankfurt: Suhrkamp, 1981).

'Zum Klassizismus von Goethes Iphigenie', in *Noten zur Literatur*, ed. by Rolf Tiedemann. (Frankfurt: Suhrkamp, 1974), pp. 495–514.

Aristotle, *The Nicomachean Ethics*, trans. by David Ross, revised, introduction and notes by Lesley Brown (Oxford: Oxford University Press, 2009).

Baecque, Antoine de and Serge Toubiana, *François Truffaut* (Paris: Gallimard, 1996).

François Truffaut, trans. by Catherine Temerson (Oakland: University of California Press, 1999).

Baldwin, Thomas, 'Rewriting Proust', *Esprit créateur*, 55:4 (2015), pp. 70–85.

Barker, Jennifer, *The Tactile Eye: Touch and the Cinematic Experience* (Oakland: University of California Press, 2009).

Barthes, Roland, *A Lover's Discourse: Fragments*, trans. by Richard Howard (New York: Hill and Wang, 1978).

Camera Lucida: Reflections on Photography, trans. by Richard Howard (London: Vintage, 1993).

Comment vivre ensemble: Simulations romanesques de quelques espaces quotidiens: Notes de cours et de séminaires au Collège de France (1976–1977), ed. by Claude Coste (Paris: Seuil/Imec, 2002).

How to Live Together: Novellistic Simulations of Some Everyday Spaces: Notes for a Lecture Course and Seminar at the Collège de France (1976–1977), ed. by Claude Coste, trans. by Kate Briggs (New York: Columbia University Press, 2013).

Journal de deuil, ed. by Nathalie Léger (Paris: Seuil/Imec 2009).

La Chambre claire: Note sur la photographie (Paris: Gallimard/Seuil, 1980).

La Préparation du Roman I et II: Notes de cours et de séminaires au Collège de France 1978–79 et 1979–80, ed. by Natalie Léger (Paris: Seuil/Imec, 2003).

Le Discours amoureux: séminaire à l'École pratique des hautes études 1974–1976, ed. by Claude Coste (Paris: Seuil, 2007).

Le Neutre. Notes de cours au Collège de France (1977–78), ed. by Thomas Clerc (Paris: Seuil/Imec 2002).

Mourning Diary, ed. by Nathalie Léger, trans. and with an afterword by Richard Howard (New York: Hill and Wang, 2009).

Œuvres complètes, ed. by Éric Marty, 5 vols. (Paris: Seuil, 2002).

Roland Barthes Album: Inédits, correspondances et varia, ed. by Éric Marty with the help of Claude Coste (Paris: Seuil, 2015).

The Neutral: Lecture Course at the Collège de France (1977–78), ed. by Thomas Clerc, trans. by Rosalind E. Krauss and Denis Hollier (New York: Columbia University Press, 2005).

The Rustle of Language, trans. by Richard Howard (Berkeley: University of California Press, 1998).

Bauer, Martin, 'Das Ende der Entfremdung', *Zeitschrift für Ideengeschichte*, 1:1 (Spring 2007), pp. 7–29.

Benjamin, Walter, 'Das Kunstwerk im Zeitalter seiner technischen Reproduzierbarkeit', in *Gesammelte Schriften*, ed. by Rolf Tiedemann and Gerhard Schweppenhäuser, 7 vols. (Frankfurt: Suhrkamp, 1974), vol. 1.2, pp. 471–508.

'Karl Kraus', in *Gesammelte Schriften*, ed. by Rolf Tiedemann and Gerhard Schweppenhäuser, 7 vols. (Frankfurt: Suhrkamp, 2003), vol. II.1, pp. 334–67.

'Karl Kraus', in *Selected Writings*, ed. by Howard Eiland and Michael W. Jennings, trans. by E.F.N. Jephcott et al., 4 vols. (Cambridge, MA: Belknap, 2003), vol. II, pp. 194–8.

'Protokolle zu Drogenversuchen', in *Gesammelte Schriften*, ed. by Rolf Tiedemann and Gerhard Schweppenhäuser, 7 vols. (Frankfurt: Suhrkamp, 2003), vol. IV.1, pp. 558–617.

'The Work of Art in the Age of Its Technological Reproducibility', in *Selected Writings*, ed. by Howard Eiland and Michael W. Jennings, trans. by Edmund Jephcott et al., 4 vols. (Cambridge, MA: Belknap, 2003), vol. IV, pp. 251–83.

Bidou-Zachariasen, Catherine, *Proust sociologue: De la maison aristocratique au salon bourgeois* (Paris: Descartes & Cie, 1997).

Bloom, Paul, *Against Empathy: The Case for Rational Compassion* (New York: Vintage, 2016).

Bourdieu, Pierre, *Distinction: A Social Critique of Taste*, trans. by Richard Nice (Cambridge, MA: Harvard University Press, 1984).

Breithaupt, Fritz, *Die dunklen Seiten der Empathie* (Frankfurt: Suhrkamp, 2018).

Briggs, Kate, *This Little Art* (London: Fitzcarraldo, 2017).

Brumlik, Micha, 'Entfremdung', in *Archiv für Begriffsgeschichte* (Sonderheft) (Hamburg: Meiner, 2015), pp. 145–64.

Canby, Vincent, 'The Screen: Truffaut's Lyrical "Stolen Kisses" Bows', *New York Times* (4 March 1969), p. 4.

Caron, David, *The Nearness of Others: Searching for Tact and Contact in the Age of HIV* (Minneapolis: University of Minnesota Press, 2014).

Cassirer, Ernst, *The Philosophy of the Enlightenment*, trans. by Fritz C. A. Koelln et al. (Boston, MA: Beacon, 1955).

Certeau, Michel de, *The Practice of Everyday Life*, trans. by Steven Rendall (Berkeley: University of California Press, 1984).

Chaudier, Stéphane, 'Tact et contacts dans *La Recherche*', *Marcel Proust aujourd'hui*, 9 (2012), pp. 69–95.

Chauvet, Louis, 'Les Films par Louis Chauvet: *Baisers volés*', in *Le Figaro* (12 September 1968), p. 24.

Cocteau, Jean, *Le Coq et l'arlequin: notes autour de la musique* (Paris: Éditions de la Sirène, 1918).

Coplan, Amy, and Peter Goldie (eds), *Empathy: Philosophical and Psychological Perspectives* (Oxford: Oxford University Press, 2011)

Coste, Claude, *Barthes ou l'art du détour* (Paris: Hermann, 2016).

Cunningham, Valentine, *Reading after Theory* (Oxford: Blackwell, 2002).

Danneberg, Lutz, '"Ein Mathematiker, der nicht etwas Poet ist, wird nimmer ein vollkommener Mathematiker sein": Geschmack, Takt, ästhetisches Empfinden im kulturellen Behauptungsdiskurs der Mathematik und der Naturwissenschaften im 19., mit Blicken ins 20. Jahrhundert', in *Zahlen, Zeichen, und Figuren: Mathematische Inspirationen in Kunst und Literatur*, ed. by Andrea Albrecht, Gesa von Essen and Werner Frick (Berlin: de Gruyter, 2012), pp. 600–57.

Deleuze, Gilles, *Deux Régimes de fous: textes et entretiens 1975–1995*, ed. by David Lapoujade (Paris: Minuit, 2003).

——— *Proust et les Signes* (Paris: Presses Universitaires de France, 1972).

Derrida, Jacques, *Copy, Archive, Signature: A Conversation on Photography*, ed. and introduction by Gerhart Richter, trans. by Jeff Fort (Stanford: Stanford University Press, 2010).

——— *On Touching – Jean-Luc Nancy*, trans. by Christine Irizarry (Stanford: Stanford University Press, 2000).

Doubt, Keith, 'The Pedagogy of Tact in Theoretical Discourse', *Phenomenology + Pedagogy*, 8 (1990), pp. 103–17.

Dubois, Jacques, *Le Roman de Gilberte Swann. Proust sociologue paradoxal* (Paris: Seuil, 2018).

Dudley, Andrew and Anne Gillain (eds.), *A Companion to François Truffaut* (Malden, MA: Wiley-Blackwell, 2013).

Elias, Norbert, *Der Prozess der Zivilisation*, 2 vols. (Frankfurt: Suhrkamp, 1976).

Esposito, Roberto, *Immunitas: The Protection and Negation of Life*, trans. by Zakiya Hanafi (Cambridge: Polity, 2011).

Eßbach, Wolfgang, Joachim Fischer and Helmuth Lethen (eds.), *Plessners 'Grenzen der Gemeinschaft': Eine Debatte* (Frankfurt: Suhrkamp, 2002).

Felski, Rita, *The Limits of Critique* (Chicago: Chicago University Press, 2015).

Fischer, Joachim, 'Kritische Theorie der Gesellschaft vs. Philosophische Anthropologie der Moderne: Alternative Paradigmen aus dem 20. Jahrhundert', in *Mensch und Gesellschaft zwischen Natur und Geschichte: Zum Verhältnis von Philosophischer Anthropologie und Kritischer Theorie*, ed. by Thomas Ebke, Sebastian Edinger, Frank Müller, and Roman Yos (Berlin: de Gruyter, 2016), pp. 3–28.

'Nachwort', in Helmuth Plessner, *Grenzen der Gemeinschaft: Eine Kritik des sozialen Radikalismus* (Frankfurt: Suhrkamp, 2002), pp. 135–42.

'Plessner und die politische Philosophie der zwanziger Jahre', in *Politisches Denken. Jahrbuch 1992*, ed. by Volker Gerhardt, Henning Ottmann, and Martyn P. Thompson (Stuttgart: Metzler, 1993), pp. 53–77.

Foucault, Michel, *The History of Sexuality*, 2 vols., trans. by Robert Hurley (New York: Pantheon, 1978).

France, Anatole, *Le Livre de mon ami*, in *Œuvres complètes*, ed. by Marie-Claire Bancquart, 4 vols. (Paris: Gallimard, 1994), vol. 1, pp. 433–583.

My Friend's Book, trans. by James Lewis May (London: John Lane, Bodley Head, 1913).

Frei, Norbert, *1968 – Jugendrevolte und globaler Protest* (Munich: Deutscher Taschenbuchverlag, 2008).

Paris, 13 Mai 1968: Kulturprotest und Gesellschaftsreform (Munich: Deutscher Taschenbuchverlag, 1999).

Freud, Sigmund, *Beyond the Pleasure Principle* (New York: Liveright, 1961).

Gadamer, Hans-Georg, 'The Hermeneutics of Suspicion', in *Phenomenology and the Human Sciences*, ed. by J. N. Mohanty (The Hague: Nijhoff, 1985), pp. 313–23.

Truth and Method, trans. and revised by Joel Weinsheimer and Donald G. Marshall (London, New York: Continuum, 2004).

Wahrheit und Methode (Tübingen: Mohr, 1960).

Gamble, Cynthia, 'From Belle Époque to First World War: The Social Panorama', in *The Cambridge Companion to Proust*, ed. by Richard Bale (Cambridge: Cambridge University Press, 2001), pp. 7–24.

Gillain, Anne (ed.), *François Truffaut: The Lost Secret* (Bloomington, IN: Indiana University Press, 2013).

Le Cinéma selon François Truffaut (Paris: Flammarion, 1988).

Truffaut on Cinema, trans. by Alistair Fox (Bloomington, IN: Indiana University Press, 2017).

Goethe, Johann Wolfgang, *Die Wahlverwandtschaften* (Frankfurt: Insel, 1972).

Elective Affinities, trans. by David Constantine (Oxford: Oxford University Press, 1994).

Italian Journey, trans. by W. H. Auden and Elisabeth Mayer (London: Penguin, 1962).

Italienische Reise (Munich: Hanser, 1992).

Goffman, Erving, *Relations in Public: Microstudies of the Public Order* (Harmondsworth: Penguin, 1971).

Encounters: Two Studies in the Sociology of Interaction (Harmondsworth: Penguin, 1972).

The Interaction Ritual: Essays in Face-to-Face Behaviour with a new introduction by Joel Best (New Brunswick, N.J.: Aldine Transaction, 2005).

Gödde, Günther, and Jörg Zirfas, 'Die Kreativität des Takts', in *Takt und Taktlosigkeit: Über Ordnungen und Unordnungen in Kunst, Kultur und Therapie*, ed. by Günther Gödde and Jörg Zirfas (Bielefeld: transcript, 2012), pp. 9–30.

Gratiolet, K. (i.e., Karin Struppe), *Schliff und vornehme Lebensart* (Berlin: Holzinger, 2013).

Habermas, Jürgen, 'Interpretive Social Science vs. Hermeneuticism', in *Social Science as Moral Inquiry*, ed. by Norma Hann, Robert N. Bellah, Paul Rabinow and William M. Sullivan (New York: Columbia University Press, 1983), pp. 251–69.

Hall, Edward T., *The Hidden Dimension* (New York: Anchor Books, 1966).

Haucke, Kai, 'Plessners Kritik der radikalen Gemeinschaftsideologie und die Grenzen des deutschen Idealismus', in *Plessners 'Grenzen der Gemeinschaft'*, pp. 103–30.

Haustein, Katja, 'How to Be Alone with Others: Plessner, Adorno, and Barthes on Tact', *The Modern Language Review*, 114:1 (2019), pp. 1–21.

'"J'ai mal à l'autre": Barthes on Pity', in *What's So Great About Roland Barthes*, ed. by Thomas Baldwin, Katja Haustein, and Lucy O'Meara, special issue of *Esprit créateur*, 55:4 (2015), pp. 131–47.

Regarding Lost Time: Photography, Identity, and Affect in Proust, Benjamin, and Barthes (Oxford: Legenda, 2012).

Haynes, Jonathan Everett, 'Truffaut–Hitchcock', in *A Companion to François Truffaut*, ed. by Dudley Andrew and Anne Gillain (Malden, MA: Wiley-Blackwell, 2013), pp. 265–82.

Hegel, Georg Wilhelm Friedrich, *Phänomenologie des Geistes* (Stuttgart: Reclam, 2020).

Heidegger, Martin, *Parmenides*, trans. by Mary Louise Gill and Paul Ryan, introduction by Mary Louise Gill (Bloomington, IN: Indiana University Press, 1992).

Helmholtz, Hermann von, 'The Relation of the Natural Sciences to Science in General', in *Selected Writings*, ed. by Russell Kahl (Middletown, CT: Wesleyan University Press, 1971), pp. 122–43.

Über das Verhältniss der Naturwissenschaften zur Gesammtheit der Wissenschaften (Tübingen: Mohr, 1862).

Henry, Anne, 'Proust und die Krise des Subjekts: Die Funktion des philosophischen Models in *À la recherche du temps perdu*', in *Marcel Proust und die Philosophie*, ed. by Ursula Link-Heer and Volker Roloff (Frankfurt: Insel, 1997), pp. 29–44.

Heyd, David, 'Tact, Sense, Sensitivity and Virtue', *Inquiry*, 38:3 (1995), pp. 217–31.

Holmes, Diana and Robert Ingram, *François Truffaut* (Manchester: Manchester University Press, 1998).

Hughes, Edward J., *Proust, Class, and Nation* (Oxford: Oxford University Press, 2011).

Irmscher Hans Dietrich, 'Aus Herders Nachlaß', *Euphorion*, 54 (1960), pp. 281–94.

Jaeggi, Rahel, *Alienation*, ed. by Frederick Neuhouser, trans. by Frederick Neuhouser and Alan E. Smith (New York: Columbia University Press, 2016).

Entfremdung: Zur Aktualität eines sozialphilosophischen Problems (Frankfurt: Suhrkamp, 2016).

Jaucourt, Chevalier de, 'Tact, le', in *L'Encyclopédie* (1765), vol. xv, pp. 819b–22b, https://bit.ly/3wWBZQv.

Jhering, Rudolph von, *Der Zweck im Recht*, ed. by Christian Helfer, 2 vols. (Hildesheim: Olms, 1970).

Kant, Immanuel, *Anthropology from a Pragmatic Point of View*, trans. and ed. by Robert B. Louden, introduction by Manfred Kuehn (Cambridge: Cambridge University Press, 2006).

Critique of the Power of Judgement, ed. by Paul Guyer, trans. by Paul Guyer and Eric Matthews (Cambridge: Cambridge University Press, 2000).

'Idea for a Universal History with a Cosmopolitan Purpose', in *Political Writings*, ed. by Hans Reiss, trans. by H.B. Nisbet (Cambridge: Cambridge University Press, 1991), pp. 41–53.

'Idee zu einer allgemeinen Geschichte in weltbürgerlicher Absicht', in *Werkausgabe*, ed. by Wilhelm Weischedel, 12 vols. (Frankfurt: Suhrkamp, 1977), vol. XI, pp. 31–50.

Kritik der Urteilskraft, in *Werkausgabe* ed. by Wilhelm Weischedel, 12 vols. (Frankfurt: Suhrkamp, 1977), vol. X.

'On a Recently prominent Tone of superiority in Philosophy', in Immanuel Kant, *Theoretical Philosophy after 1781*, ed. and trans. by Henry Allison and Peter Heath, trans. by Gary Hatfield and Michael Friedman (Cambridge: Cambridge University Press, 2002), pp. 430–45.

Schriften zur Anthropologie, Geschichtsphilosophie, Politik und Pädagogik I, *Werkausgabe*, ed. by Wilhelm Weischedel, 12 vols. (Frankfurt: Suhrkamp, 1977), vol. XI.

Schriften zur Anthropologie, Geschichtsphilosophie, Politik und Pädagogik II, in *Werkausgabe*, ed. by Wilhelm Weischedel, 12 vols. (Frankfurt: Suhrkamp, 1977), vol. XII.

'Von einem neuerdings erhobenen vornehmen Ton in der Philosophie', in *Kants Werke: Akademie-Textausgabe*, vol. VIII: *Abhandlungen nach 1781*, ed. by the Königlich Preußische Akademie der Wissenschaften (Berlin: de Gruyter, 1968), pp. 387–406.

Kohut, Heinz, 'Introspection, Empathy, and the Semicircle of Mental Health', in *The Search for the Self: Selected Writings of Heinz Kohut: 1978–81*, ed. by P. H. Orstein (Madison, CT: International Universities Press, 1981), pp. 537–67.

Kolesch, Doris, *Das Schreiben des Subjekts: Zur Inszenierung ästhetischer Subjektivität bei Baudelaire, Barthes und Adorno* (Vienna: Passagen, 1996).

Koschorke, Albrecht, *Körperströme und Schriftverkehr: Mediologie des 18. Jahrhunderts* (Munich: Fink, 1999).

Koselleck, Reinhart, 'On the Need for Theory in the Discipline of History', in *The Practice of Conceptual History: Timing History, Spacing Concepts* (Stanford: Stanford University Press, 2002), pp. 1–19.

La Rochefoucauld, François de, *Maximes: suivies des Réflexions diverses, du Portrait de La Rochefoucauld par lui-même, et des Remarques de Christine de Suède sur les Maximes*, ed. by Jacques Truchet (Paris: Garnier, 1967).

Le Berre, Carole, *François Truffaut at Work*, trans. by Bill Krohn (London: Phaidon, 2005).

Leopold, David, 'Alienation', in *The Stanford Encyclopedia of Philosophy* (Fall 2018 Edition), ed. by Edward N. Zalta, https://plato.stanford.edu/archives/fall2018/entries/alienation/

Lethen, Helmuth, 'Anleitung zur Schlaflosigkeit: Über den Formzwang in der Politischen Anthropologie von Helmuth Plessner und Arnold Gehlen', in *Kunst, Macht und Institution: Studien zur philosophischen Anthropologie*, ed. by Joachim Fischer and Hans Joas (Frankfurt: Campus, 2003), pp. 89–103.

Verhaltensweisen der Kälte: Lebensversuche zwischen den Kriegen (Frankfurt: Suhrkamp, 1994).

Lethen, Helmuth, and Caroline Sommerfeld-Lethen: 'Schein zivilisiert', in *Höflichkeit: Aktualität und Genese von Umgangsformen*, ed. by Brigitte Felderer and Thomas Macho (Munich: Fink, 2002), pp. 155–73.

Luhmann, Niklas, *A Sociological Theory of Law*, ed. by Martin Albrow, trans. by Elizabeth King and Martin Albrow (London: Routledge & Kegan Paul, 1985).

'Soziologie der Moral', in *Theorietechnik und Moral*, ed. by Niklas Luhmann and Stephan H. Pfürtner (Frankfurt: Suhrkamp, 1978), pp. 8–116.

'Takt und Zensur im Erziehungssystem', in *Schriften zur Pädagogik*, ed. and introduction by Dieter Lenzen (Frankfurt: Suhrkamp, 2004), pp. 245–59.

Lukács, Georg, *Die Theorie des Romans: Ein geschichtsphilosophischer Versuch über die Formen der großen Epik* (Stuttgart: Luchterhand, 1971).

The Theory of the Novel: A Historico-Philosophical Essay on the Forms of Great Epic Literature, trans. by Anna Bostock (London: Merlin Press, 1978).

Lühe, Astrid von der, 'Zart, Zärtlich', in *Historisches Wörterbuch der Philosophie*, ed. by Joachim Ritter, Karlfried Gründer, and Gottfried Gabriel, 12 vols (Basel: Schwabe, 2004), vol. XII, cols. 1149–55.

Macé, Marielle, 'Barthes, Rythmicité du vivre', *L'Esprit créateur*, 55:4 (Winter 2015), pp. 7–20.

Façons de lire, manières d'être (Paris: Gallimard 2011).

'Ways of Reading, Modes of Being', *New Literary History: The French Issue: New Perspectives on Reading from France*, 44:2 (Spring 2013), pp. 213–29.

Marks, Laura, *The Skin of the Film* (Durham, NC: Duke University Press, 2000).

Martin, Adrian, 'The Untimely Moment and the Correct Distance', in *Companion to Truffaut*, ed. by Andrew Dudley and Anne Gillain (Malden, MA: Wiley-Blackwell, 2013), pp. 205–17.

McMahon, Laura, *Cinema and Contact: The Withdrawal of Touch in Nancy, Bresson, Duras and Denis* (Oxford: Legenda, 2012).

Menninghaus, Winfried, *Disgust: Theory and History of a Strong Sensation* (Albany, NY: State University of New York Press, 2003).

Mul, Jos de (ed.), *Plessner's Philosophical Anthropology: Perspectives and Prospects* (Amsterdam: Amsterdam University Press, 2014).

Murakami, Haruki, *Men without Women*, trans. by Philip Gabriel and Ted Goossen (London: Harvill Secker, 2017).

Muth, Jacob, *Pädagogischer Takt: Monographie einer aktuellen Form erzieherischen und didaktischen Handelns* (Heidelberg: Quelle & Meyer, 1967).

Mülder-Bach, Inka, 'Kommunizierende Monaden: Herders literarisches Universum' (23 January 2004), *Goethezeitportal*, bit.ly/3mjyYHO.

Nietzsche, Friedrich, *The Anti-Christ, Ecce Homo, Twilight of the Idols and Other Writings*, ed. by Aaron Ridley and Judith Norman, trans. by Judith Norman (Cambridge: Cambridge University Press, 2005).

Okakura, Kakuzō, *The Book of Tea* (London: Penguin, 2016).

O'Meara, Lucy, '"Not a Question but a Wound": Adorno, Barthes, and Aesthetic Reflection', *Comparative Literature* 65:2 (2013), pp. 182–99.

Roland Barthes at the Collège de France (Liverpool: Liverpool University Press, 2012).

Peary, Danny, *Guide for the Film Fanatic* (New York: Simon and Schuster, 1986).

Plessner, Helmuth, 'Das Lächeln', in *Gesammelte Schriften*, ed. by Günter Dux, Odo Marquard, and Elisabeth Ströker, 10 vols. (Frankfurt: Suhrkamp, 2003), vol. VII, pp. 419–34.

'Das Problem der Öffentlichkeit und die Idee der Entfremdung', in Gesammelte Schriften, ed. by Günter Dux, Odo Marquard, and Elisabeth Ströker, 10 vols. (Frankfurt: Suhrkamp, 2003), vol. X, pp. 212–26.

Die verspätete Nation: Über die politische Verführbarkeit bürgerlichen Geistes (Frankfurt: Suhrkamp, 1994).

Grenzen der Gemeinschaft: Eine Kritik des sozialen Radikalismus (Frankfurt: Suhrkamp, 2002).

'Selbstdarstellung', in Gesammelte Schriften, ed. by Günter Dux, Odo Marquard, and Elisabeth Ströker, 10 vols. (Frankfurt: Suhrkamp, 2003), vol. X, pp. 302–41..

'Soziale Rolle und menschliche Natur', in *Gesammelte Schriften*, ed. by Günter Dux, Odo Marquard and Elisabeth Ströker, 10 vols. (Frankfurt: Suhrkamp, 2002), vol. X, pp. 227–40.

The Limits of Community: A Critique of Social Radicalism, trans. by Andrew Wallace (Amherst, NY: Humanity Books, 1999).

Übergänge: Politik, Anthropologie, Philosophie, ed. by Salvatore Giammusso and Hans-Ulrich Lessing (Munich: Fink, 2001).

'Zur Anthropologie des Schauspielers', in Gesammelte Schriften, ed. by Günter Dux, Odo Marquard, and Elisabeth Ströker, 10 vols. (Frankfurt: Suhrkamp, 2003), vol. VII, pp. 399–418.

Proust, Marcel, *À la recherche du temps perdu*, ed. by Jean-Yves Tadié, 4 vols. (Paris: Gallimard, 1987–9).

Contre Sainte-Beuve, ed. by Pierre Clarac and Yves Sandre (Paris: Gallimard, 1972).

Correspondance, ed. by Philip Kolb, 20 vols. (Paris: Plon, 1970–93).

In Search of Lost Time, ed. by Christopher Prendergast, trans. by Carol Clark, Peter Collier Lydia Davies, James Grieve, Ian Patterson, John Sturrock, and Mark Treharne, 6 vols. (London: Penguin, 2002–3).

Les Soixante-quinze feuillets et autre manuscrits inédits, ed. by Nathalie Mauriac Dyer, preface by Jean-Yves Tadié (Paris: Gallimard, 2021).

On Reading Ruskin, ed. and trans. by Jean Autret, William Burford, and Philip Wolfe (London: Yale University Press, 1987).

Préface, traduction et notes à La Bible d'Amiens *de John Ruskin*, ed. by Yves-Michel Ergal (Paris: Bartillat, 2007).

Raulff, Ulrich and Andreas Bernard (eds.), *Theodor W. Adorno: 'Minima Moralia' neu gelesen* (Frankfurt: Suhrkamp, 2003).

Ricœur, Paul, 'Book I: Problematic: The Placing of Freud', in *Freud and Philosophy: An Essay on Interpretation*' (New Haven: Yale University Press, 1970), pp. 3–58.

Ronzheimer, Elisa, '"Der Takt der Hand": Adornos Taktbegriff und die Kritik des Klassizismus', in *Takt und Taktilität*, ed. by Andrea Erwig, Sandra Fluhrer, Jakob Gehlen, and Elisa Ronzheimer, special issue of *Sprache und Literatur*, 50:2 (Dec. 2021), pp. 204–25.

'Eine Frage des Takts: Zur Übereinstimmung in Goethes *Unterhaltungen Deutscher Ausgewanderten*', in *Stimmungen und Vielstimmigkeit der Aufklärung*, ed. by Silvan Moosmüller, Boris Previšić, and Laure Spaltenstein (Göttingen: Wallstein, 2017), pp. 277–91.

Rousseau, Jean-Jacques, *Discourse on the Origin and Foundations of Inequality Among Men*, in *The Collected Writings of Rousseau*, ed. by Roger D. Masters and Christopher Kelly, trans. by Judith Bush et al., 13 vols. (Hanover, NH: University Press of New England for Dartmouth College, 1992), vol. III, pp. 1–95.

Discours sur l'origine et les fondements de l'inégalité parmi les hommes, in *Œuvres complètes*, ed. by Bernard Gagnebin and Marcel Raymond 5 vols. (Paris: Gallimard, 1959–95), vol. III, pp. 131–223.

Essai sur l'origine des langues, in *Œuvres complètes*, 5 vols. ed. by Bernard Gagnebin and Marcel Raymond (Paris: Gallimard, 1959–1995), vol. V, pp. 371–429.

Essay on the Origin of Languages, in *On Philosophy, Morality, and Religion*, ed. by Christopher Kelly, trans. by John T. Scott (Hanover, NH: University Press of New England for Dartmouth College, 2007), pp. 102–46.

Projet pour l'éducation de Monsieur de Sainte-Marie, in *Œuvres complètes*, ed. by Bernard Gagnebin and Marcel Raymond (Paris: Gallimard, 1959–1995), vol. IV, pp. 35–51.

Ruprecht, Lucia, *Gestural Imaginaries: Dance and Cultural Theory in the Early Twentieth Century* (Oxford: Oxford University Press, 2019).

Ruskin, John, and Marcel Proust, *Sésame et les Lys: Précédé de Sur la lecture*, trans., notes and essay by Marcel Proust, ed. by Antoine Compagnon (Brussels: Éditions Complexe, 1987).

Russell, David, *Tact: Aesthetic Liberalism and the Essay Form in Nineteenth-Century Britain* (Princeton: Princeton University Press, 2018).

Samoyault, Tiphaine, *Roland Barthes* (Paris: Seuil, 2015).

Sartre, Jean-Paul, *Anti-Semite and Jew: An Exploration of the Etiology of Hate*, trans. by George J. Becker (New York: Schocken, 1995).

Scheler, Max, *Der Formalismus in der Ethik und die materielle Werteethik – neuer Versuch der Grundlegung eines ethischen Personalismus* (Bern: Francke, 1954).

Schiller, Friedrich, *Kallias oder Über die Schönheit: Briefe an Gottfried Körner*, in *Schillers Werke in vier Bänden*, ed. by Herbert Kraft (Frankfurt: Insel, 1966), vol. IV.

On the Aesthetic Education of Man, in a Series of Letters, ed. and trans. by Elizabeth M. Wilkinson and L. A. Willoughby (Oxford: Clarendon Press, 1967).

Schneider, Christian, 'Deutschland I: Der exemplarische Intellektuelle der Bundesrepublik', in *Adorno Handbuch: Leben – Werk – Wirkung*, ed. by Richard Klein, Johann Kreuzer, and Stefan Müller-Doohm (Stuttgart: Metzler, 2011), pp. 431–34.

Schneider, Manfred, 'Das Ereignis der Zeit: Proust und die Theorie des Erhabenen', in *Proust und die Philosophie*, ed. by Ursula Link-Heer and Volker Roloff (Frankfurt: Insel, 1997), pp. 121–37.

Schopenhauer, Arthur, *Parerga und Paralipomena: Kleine philosophische Schriften II*, in *Sämtliche Werke*, ed. by Wolfgang Frh. von Löhneysen, 5 vols. (Frankfurt: Suhrkamp, 1994), vol. V.

Sennett, Richard, *The Fall of Public Man* (Cambridge: Cambridge University Press, 1977).

Together: The Rituals, Pleasures and Politics of Cooperation (New Haven: Yale University Press, 2013).

Simmel, Georg, 'Die Geselligkeit', in *Grundfragen der Soziologie: Individuum und Gesellschaft* (Berlin: de Gruyter, 1970), pp. 48–67.

'Der Raum und die räumlichen Ordnungen der Gesellschaft: Exkurs über die soziale Begrenzung', in *Soziologie: Untersuchungen über die Formen der Vergesellschaftung* (Berlin: Duncker & Humblot, 1908), pp. 467–70, http s://socio.ch/sim/soziologie/soz_9_ex1.htm.

'The Sociology of Sociability', trans. by Everett C. Hughes, *American Journal of Sociology*, 55:3 (Nov. 1949), pp. 254–61.

Sontag, Susan (ed.), *A Roland Barthes Reader* (New York: Vintage, 1993).

Sprinker, Michael, *History and Ideology in Proust* (London: Verso, 1998).

Stan, Corina, *The Art of Distances: Ethical Thinking in Twentieth-Century Literature* (Evanston, IL: Northwestern University Press, 2018).

Sünkel, Wolfgang, 'Takt', in *Historisches Wörterbuch der Philosophie*, ed. by Joachim Ritter, Karlfried Gründer, and Gottfried Gabriel, 12 vols. (Basel: Schwabe, 1971–2007), vol. X, cols 882–5.

Szondi, Peter, *Hölderlin-Studien: Mit einem Traktat über philologische Erkenntnis* (Frankfurt: Suhrkamp, 1970).

Thomas, Keith, *In Pursuit of Civility: Manners and Civilisation in Early Modern England* (New Haven: Yale University Press, 2018).

Torra-Mattenklott, Caroline, 'Blindheit und Takt in Goethes *Wahlverwandtschaften*', *German Life and Letters* 70:4 (Oct. 2017), pp. 491–505.

Truffaut, François, *Baisers volés* (Munich: Concorde Home Entertainment, 2005).

Correspondance, ed. by Gilles Jacob and Claude de Givray, preface by Jean-Luc Godard (Rennes: Hatier, 1988).

'François Truffaut à propos du métier de réalisateur' (4 May 1967), Institut national de l'audiovisuel, bit.ly/4o2od8.

Les Aventures d'Antoine Doinel (Paris: Mercure de France, 1970).

Letters, ed. by Gilles Jacob and Claude de Givray, trans. by Gilbert Adair, foreword by Jean-Luc Godard (London: Faber, 1989).

Unold, Johannes, *Grundlegung für eine moderne praktisch-ethische Lebensanschauung* (Leipzig: Hirzel, 1896).

Watt, Adam, 'État présent: Marcel Proust', *French Studies*, vol. 72:3 (2018), pp. 412–24.

Watts, Alan, *The Way of Zen* (New York: Vintage, 1957).

Wiser, Antonin, 'Le Tact, expérience de la littérature ou Proust lu par Adorno', *Philosophie*, 113:2 (2012), pp. 79–93.

Wittgenstein, Ludwig, *Philosophical Investigations: The German Text with a Revised Translation* by Gertrude Elizabeth Margaret Anscombe (Malden, MA: Wiley-Blackwell, 2001).

Wollheim, Richard, *Art and Its Objects* (Cambridge: Cambridge University Press, 1980).

Ziegler, Theobald, *Das Gefühl: Eine psychologische Untersuchung* (Stuttgart: Göschen, 1893).

Žižek, Slavoj, 'Good Manners in the Age of Wikileaks', *London Review of Books*, 33:2 (20 January 2011), pp. 9–11.

Index

Printed in the USA
CPSIA information can be obtained
at www.ICGtesting.com
LVHW021523111123
763669LV00006B/158